PEOPLE OF
THE ICE WHALE

PEOPLE OF
THE ICE WHALE

Eskimos, White Men, and the Whale

David Boeri

E. P. DUTTON, INC. | NEW YORK

I have changed the names of several Gambell whaling captains
and a woman in Barrow. Benjamin, Isaac, Solomon,
and Sarah are all pseudonyms.

The illustrations on pages 83, 120, 124, and 125, the first illustration on page
165, and the illustrations on pages 177 and 216 are from
The Marine Mammals of the Northwestern Coast of North America,
by Charles W. Scammon (originally published in 1874; reprinted
by Dover Publications, Inc., New York, 1968). The second illustration on page
165 is from
Sea Guide to Whales of the World by Lyall Watson,
illustrated by Tom Ritchie (New York: E. P. Dutton, 1981).
The drawing of the bowhead whale on pages 5 and 103, and
the three maps on pages xvi, 13, and 238 are by Judy Lyons.

Copyright © 1983 by David Boeri

Published in the United States by
E. P. Dutton, Inc., 2 Park Avenue, New York, N.Y. 10016

Library of Congress Cataloging in Publication Data
Boeri, David.
People of the ice whale.
Includes bibliographical references and index.
1. Eskimos—Alaska—Fishing. 2. Bowhead whale.
3. Indians of North America—Alaska—Fishing. 4. Whaling—Alaska.
5. Wildlife conservation—Alaska.
I. Title.
E99.E7B677   1983   305.8'97'097987   83-14072
ISBN: 0-525-24206-6

Published simultaneously in Canada
by Fitzhenry & Whiteside Limited, Toronto

Designed by Nancy Etheredge

COBE

10 9 8 7 6 5 4 3 2 1

First Edition

To my mother and father,
to Sook and Silook, and to Islay

Contents

Author's Note

"Eskimo" is an Indian name—it means "eaters of raw flesh"—that European explorers applied to a culturally, genetically, and linguistically distinct group of Native people who inhabit Greenland; northern Canada; northern, western, and southern Alaska; and the tip of Siberia. Understandably, the Eskimo people prefer to be identified by the names they have given themselves, which vary from one region to another. In eastern Canada and Greenland, for instance, Eskimos call themselves *Inuit*, while in western Canada they use the name *Inuvialuit*, and in northern Alaska, *Inupiat*. The people of these three regions all speak the same language, known in northern Alaska as *Inupiaq*.

In western and southern Alaska, the islands of the Bering Sea, and Siberia, Eskimos call themselves *Yuit*. They speak a different language called *Yupik*, which has four major dialects, including the Siberian Yupik spoken by the people of Saint Lawrence Island. Though Yupik is closely related to Inupiaq, the two languages are mutually unintelligible, just as several dialects of Yupik are.

Unfortunately, there is no term other than *Eskimo* that collectively refers to the Inupiaq-speaking Inupiat of northern Alaska and the Yupik-language groups in the rest of the state. So, in writing about the people of Saint Lawrence Island, Barrow, and other Alaskan whaling villages, I call them Eskimos to avoid hopeless confusion and cumbersome terminology. I apologize in advance to anyone who is offended by the term; certainly I do not use it derogatorily.

For Native words, I have tried to use spellings that are either standard or generally agreed upon by the speakers themselves. Unfortunately, however, there is often no consensus among Natives or non-Natives about the correct spellings; since Inupiaq and Yupik were unwritten languages until recent times (when they were translated by missionaries and other Westerners) and because both have sounds that are quite alien to Indo-European languages, at least several and sometimes many different spellings have often been used for the same word. The original name for the village of Gambell, for instance, is variously spelled *Sevuokuk, Chibukak, Sivuqaq, Sivokak, Sēēvuookôk,* and *Seevookak*.

In choosing to spell Native words the way I have, I relied upon conventions where there were any, advice from my hosts when it was forthcoming, and my desire to approximate the sounds, as I heard them. The Yupik word for walrus skin and the attached layer of blubber, for instance, is commonly spelled *manguna,* but it is pronounced more like *mahn-goo-na;* I spell it *mahngoona.* For the sake of simplicity and ease of reading, I have avoided phonetic transcriptions and used English orthography. The Inupiaq word for *whale,* for instance, is commonly spelled *aġviq.* The *ġ* sound has no English equivalent; it is pronounced far back in the throat as if gargling without water. I spell the word *agviq* and transcribe its pronunciation as *ahg-vik.* Pronunciations of common Yupik and Inupiaq words are indexed in the Glossary.

Acknowledgments

From the time I left my home in Petersburg, Alaska, to travel to Saint Lawrence Island five years ago, I have encountered the most humbling generosity and kindness. To my friends and family and to the Eskimos I lived and hunted with in northern Alaska I wish to express my heartfelt gratitude.

I am forever indebted to Silook and Sukaruwaaq (Paul and Charlene) Apangalook of the village of Gambell on Saint Lawrence Island. Their love, trust, and goodwill opened up the doors of a world that might have stayed closed to me otherwise. Dear old Lloyd Oovi, who is dead now, and Samuel Irrigoo, who still lives, welcomed me into their homes and gave willingly of their memory and spirit. My memory and love of them burn brightly. So too does my appreciation for the kindnesses extended by Johnny Silook, Clarence Irrigoo, Edna Apatiki, and Leonard Apangalook, the whaling captain who first welcomed me aboard his skin boat.

In Barrow, Ralph Aveoganna bestowed on me overwhelming hospitality, goodwill, and acceptance. He and Johnny Ogeaktuk, his equally kind crewman, provided me a privileged entrance into Barrow's hunt for bowheads and an understanding of traditional values that evoke my greatest admiration. I am also grateful to Ralph's family and to Jon Buchholdt, David Brower, Dale Stotts, the North Slope Borough, and especially to Shehla Anjum.

Along my way to and from the Arctic and toward the completion of my book, Rick Paquette and Carole Lynn Ives, Wes and Andrea King, Scott Pollock and Jay Brevik in Seattle, John and Robin Roat Martin in Juneau, Terry Otness and Andy Mathisen in Petersburg, Janet Fries in Anchorage, and Ben Baldwin and Liz Doucette in Kittery Point, Maine, showed themselves to be wonderful hosts and friends.

Over the course of writing, I have greatly valued the scientific, social, and philosophical insights provided by Jim Cubbage. He has proven a most knowledgeable and affable researcher of whales, white men, and Eskimos. For their comments and suggestions, I also wish to thank J. C. Louis, Howard Dubner, Dr. John Bockstoce (Curator of Ethnology at the Old Dartmouth Historical Society and Whaling Museum), Ken Balcomb of the Whale Museum in Friday Harbor, Washington, and Rick Paquette. My sister, Judy Lyons, graciously contributed her artistic talents in preparing illustrations and maps. And for their day-to-day hospitality and assistance I am indebted to Philip Meriam and to Tina (Molesevich) Stewart and the rest of the staff of Wilmington Memorial Library in Wilmington, Massachusetts, where I did much of my writing in comfort and quiet and wore out a chair in the process. To Paul De Angelis, my shrewd, persistent yet patient editor, goes special thanks for contributions that go beyond measure. My sincerest thanks go as well to Tory Pryor, my agent, for her encouragement and cheer.

Finally, I want to express my deepest gratitude and affection to my parents, whose contributions to this book have been greatest of all, to my sisters, Judy and Karen, to Helen and Bill Leonard, and to my wife, Islay, whose cheerfulness, encouragement, and sage advice steered me to a saner conclusion. To them I owe more than I can ever say.

ACKNOWLEDGMENTS

Prologue

Every spring, for as long as their legends recall, the Eskimos of northwestern Alaska have hunted the bowhead, a magnificent polar whale. In spring's thaw, whales as long as sixty feet and weighing as much as seventy tons follow the melting pack ice northward, traveling through narrow channels in the ice, close to shore, past Saint Lawrence Island, through the Bering Strait into the Chukchi Sea, northeastward to Point Barrow, then east into the Beaufort Sea and the Canadian Arctic. After them chase the hunters of Alaskan Eskimo villages whose sustenance and identity have been forever linked to the bowhead, a species whose future is as uncertain as their own. The first village the whales pass is Gambell. The last one is Barrow.

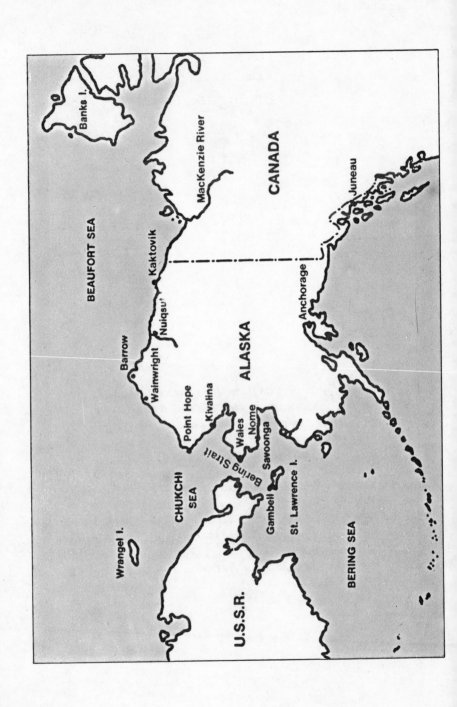

GAMBELL

Part One: The Hunt

1. "A Whale Has Come Upon Us"

Siku. The ice. It came to them in the fall and left them in the spring. Always moving, constantly changing, it was like their lives, and it was life itself because the ice was their hunting grounds.

Siku was one word among many that the sons of Apangaluq used to describe the world into which they ventured. For each stage of ice from its formation to its dissolution they had a word, about sixty in all, each describing a distinct phenomenon the hunters must identify if they were to succeed and to survive. Apangaluq and his sons hunted on ancient pack ice that came from the polar basin. They hunted on shore-fast ice, *duvaq*, that grew seaward from land, and when springtime sheared away duvaq's grasp of land, they hunted among drifting floes of ice called *ii-ghwil-nguq*.

This was the time of ii-ghwil-nguq, for the frozen mantle of the Bering Sea had cracked, shifted, split, and finally torn apart. The ocean appeared, in narrow channels that widened into ponds that grew into lakes amidst the melting pack. All was in flux. As the pack moved northward like a glacier in retreat, its edges

5

disintegrated into a treacherous, shifting rubble of old ice, slush ice (*genu*) and new ice (*sallek*) forming from the slush. At no other time were the hunting grounds as dangerous as they were now. They opened and shut at the whim of currents and wind, of tides and swells, so that from one hour to the next a boat could be crushed in their jaws or men could be cut adrift and swallowed as the ice they stood on was ripped away from land. Under this broken yet tireless field of ice swam the biggest prey of all, and along siku's edge sailed the hunters who hoped to capture it.

Earlier in the day, Piitkaq, who was Apangaluq's oldest son and captain of the crew, had come to wake his brothers. They dressed quickly and passed through the darkness of their snow-banked sheds into bright, white daylight. Spring had come indeed. The days were growing fatter and the sun rose in an arc that was no longer obstructed by Seevookak, the mountain that loomed like a sentinel behind their village. "Old-timers say that mean it getting warmer, whales coming, coming," said old Oovi, who had risen as enthusiastically as a child at Christmas. A beatific smile on his round fat face reached up to the bold crown of a laughing Buddha head in anticipation of the rich, oily hazelnut taste of *mungtuk*.* Once outside, Piitkaq and his brothers climbed to the rooftop of their father's home. All along the skyline of the old village, men and boys were scanning the horizon in search of bowheads. They saw steampipe explosions of vapor several miles away and could sometimes hear a distant, percussive rush of air, like the sound of a locomotive leaving the station. "Did you hear? Did you see that one?" they asked each other. Excited by the presence of whales, they searched for a path that would take them through the grinding ice that ran like a river along the shore, blocking them from the hunting grounds.

When the tide changed a few hours later, they found an opening and the villagers surged forward. Piitkaq, his three brothers, and his two cousins lifted their walrus-skin boat off its wood and whalebone rack, loaded it with gear, and slid it along its ivory keel down the sloping, snowpacked beach. With their crews holding onto the rails and running along to keep up, a fleet of skin boats scampered off like a pack of crocodiles heading for the river. At water's edge, the crews raised the masts, launched

---

Mungtuk is the Yupik-language version of the more well-known Inupiaq word *muktuk*.

their *angyaqs* from a ledge of shore-fast ice, and eighteen sails unfurled in the April breeze. Parading past blue-tinged icebergs as big as houses, the fleet pushed southward through a narrow passage of open water that lay between the beach and a barrier of offshore ice. When Piitkaq found a seaward-leading channel a few miles later, his crew headed into a kinetic field of ice, a half-dozen men in an open twenty-eight-foot boat.

They sailed westward toward Siberia. They could see the towering peaks of its mountains, gleaming white pyramids that stretched along the horizon. In the foothills of those mountains lay their ancient ancestors' homeland. Its shores were just thirty-eight miles away from their own village of Gambell, a spit of gravel on the northwest cape of Saint Lawrence Island. It was to this stormy, windswept, and treeless remnant of the Bering land bridge that their people had sailed in the same kind of angyaqs centuries ago, sometime after the last ice age ended and melting ice sheets drowned the overland path to North America.

For most of the day, their voyage had been as uneventful as any spent by whale watchers in the Lower Forty-Eight. They scanned the sea for hours and smoked great amounts of tobacco while waiting for *Aghvook* to come close. They saw but were uninterested in fat black forms lying on the ice, for those were seals and walrus basking in the sun. The Eskimos would stalk them another day. On this day, indeed for as long as Sea and Ice and Sky allowed, they stalked the great polar whale.

Occasionally, its giant head broke through the surface, snorting a dark vent of steam into the air. The hunters were electrified by the sight of it; their hearts pumped harder and their blood warmed. But Aghvook was always too far off, on the other side of the ice, and their sudden warmth dissipated like the breath of the whale.

They were lured into drowsiness once again by a sun-cast glare, a luffing of sail, and the lulling sound of slush sliding along the skin hull. Turning into a stiffening breeze, they could feel it grip the muscles of their cheeks and burn their noses and ears. Yet stoically, they pulled up the fur hoods of their parkas, instinctively took note of the change in weather, and continued on a course they hoped would converge with the whale's.

After negotiating the zone of broken ice near shore, they entered a great lake of open water only to encounter a seemingly impenetrable zone of pack ice farther seaward, about four miles from land. In search of a solution to the maze of bergs, floes, and slabs that kept them from their prey, Gambell's angyaqs scattered. With the aim of going around rather than through this field of boulders, Piitkaq sailed along the edge to its farthest extent, away from the other angyaqs. Atop the thwart of the boat's wooden frame stood his brother Silook, holding on to the mast and staring impassively at the icescape to help navigate.

Piitkaq sat in the stern. It was his proper place as captain, a role he had been granted as the eldest of Apangaluq's sons when his father decided to transfer command the year before. Apangaluq had gone with him that first season, as he would have gone the second, to share the knowledge that had allowed him to take six whales in his own time as boat captain. But now Apangaluq was very sick, and his thirty-nine-year-old son was alone in the stern. Not that Piitkaq was unprepared or unseasoned for the role. In the tradition of Gambell's whaling fraternity, he had advanced through the ranks, from young apprentice sitting next to his father, forward, by advancing steps in position and duty, until he reached the bow. There he had become the boat's striker, the man who harpoons the whale and takes first shot at seals and walrus. It was only in the final step, as captain, that he returned to the stern.

Late in the afternoon, with one hand on the tiller and the other on the sail sheet, Piitkaq brought the angyaq up against a small slab of ice. His youngest brother, Angyaghmii, helped Silook strike the gaff-rigged sail while Yaghaq, the brother who would become boat-striker after Piitkaq, climbed over the bow, drove a tall pole into the ice, and secured the boat. Stepping cautiously onto the ice floe, the men stretched cramped legs, made hot water, and ate food they had packed in a sealskin bag that morning. Under lowering skies, they stared intently out onto a world of cold and gray.

"*Pugleghiinkut!* Pugleghiinkut!" Piitkaq had seen a whale seventy yards off to starboard. As the dome of its head broke surface, the rush of spent air shot upward from its nostrils in a V-shaped bolt. Right behind the nostrils, the whale's profile dipped into a hollow, then rose up into the hump of its smooth black back. Aghvook went under in a long wavelike arc. It was coming their way.

They crouched so the whale wouldn't see them and hurried into the angyaq, taking care that the whale would not hear them

GAMBELL: THE HUNT

either. Yaghaq pulled up the pole, pushed the boat off the ice, and climbed over the rail in one fluid motion. Piitkaq silently ordered them to raise the sail. Silook and Angyaghmii were already lifting the boom into place as Yaghaq reached for the long, wooden shaft of his finely crafted harpoon. Amidships, another crewman grabbed one of the floats to throw overboard at the right moment. It was the inflated hide of a spotted seal, headless but with its flippers intact and its neck opening, where a head once rested, corked up and sewn together.

"Puhhh! Puhhh!" Surfacing a second time, the whale exhaled with the force of a dozen horses. They saw its left eye above the rippling water just before it sank, thirty yards off and still coming. Yaghaq braced himself at the rail. He balanced the tapering shaft in his right hand and cocked his arm, ready to plunge the deadly blade into the base of Aghvook's skull when it passed underneath.

Awaiting the moment, they froze in place, staring over the rail into dark green water. "Old men said, when whale coming, put all thoughts out of mind."

"Coming, coming, just strike it!" A shadow darted toward the bow. An eddy sprang up. The whale was below them.

But it was too deep. The boom had struck the boat's frame while the crewmen tried to raise the sail. Alarmed by the resonant clunk of wood, the whale dove deep beneath them and under the nearby ice. The angyaq bobbed in its wake.

Waiting for the whale to return, the crew kept silent for several minutes more, until it was evident that the whale was gone. Then Piitkaq spoke. In a tommy-gun explosion of glottals, percussives, and compressed spasms of sound, the crew went over what had happened. Though disappointed by the lost opportunity, they were even more exhilarated at Aghvook's having come so close, for it was still early in the season and more whales were coming.

Understanding little more than that, I waited impatiently for Silook to translate the Yupik into English, which he did for me as we poured hot coffee from Thermos bottles and munched pilot bread, Spam, and granola bars. With a formal simplicity that conveyed dignity to the English he spoke, Silook remarked, "Whales are very hard to catch. Very hard. That's why there is so much excitement."

2. *Laluremka* ("White Man")

Reaching Nome on my way to Gambell in April of 1978, I looked for the first time over a plain of ice that extended the land onto the sea. To the west of Front Street ran what looked like tundra, finely sculpted in brown ridges and drifts, stretching unbroken into an all-encompassing dull white light where the icescape converged with its reflection in the sky. Two hundred miles outward lay my destination, one of the remotest villages in America, a place that was closer to Siberia than to the mainland of Alaska.

Turning in the opposite direction, I took in a view of dingy downtown Nome, from streets of mud and slush to wooden shacks and dreary buildings. On the jet from Anchorage, I'd sat among an Arctic Adventure Tour group from the Lower Forty-Eight, and I saw them again outside the Nugget Inn, dressed in the tour company's Windbreaker parkas and oversized, insulated rubber "bunny" boots.

I was contemptuous of it all. I had imagined my trip as an adventure into the outback and among the primitive, but here in Nome I was seeing the simulation of storybook Native life in what seemed like an Eskimo theme park. I was glad that Gambell was so far away.

A middle-aged housewife from Florida helped me realize how small the world has become. Upon hearing her complain she hadn't seen enough wildlife in Anchorage (population 175,000) or on the highways surrounding it, I replied quite coolly that *I* wasn't on tour: I was en route to distant Saint Lawrence Island. I was surprised that she knew where it was and indignant to discover she'd been there. Yes, she had visited Savoonga, the only other village on the island, during the walrus carnival the year before.

"It was wonderful." And as for the people, "Why, they're just like Americans," she marveled. I was less disturbed by her statement than by the possibility that, on some level, she was right. Of course they were Americans, but were they also just like us? Just like her?

I was downtown waiting for the weather to improve somewhere between Nome and Gambell for a flight with a schedule recognized more in its breach than its observance. Though I was eager to be off, I liked the idea of being stranded long enough to make a Florida housewife's arrival in Gambell seem the most remote possibility.

A twin-engine six-seater left Nome the next day, rising above a mantle of ice blistered by wind and thrust upward into pressure ridges wherever opposing forces had collided. A hundred miles out of Nome, I saw a herd of walrus sleeping on an ice floe; at the sound of our engines, twenty animals lunged into the sea, signaling our crossing into an outer realm of the frontier. Still westward we flew, by instruments alone, through squalls of snow and over ice fields that seemed indecipherable from land and sky. But suddenly, a lonely patch of colored box-shaped houses snapped into focus. "Savoonga," the pilot shouted as I strained to take it in. Savoonga was one of two villages on an island the size of Delaware. Its 450 people made up half the population. The other half lived in the last village between here and Siberia. In a few moments, the tundra was empty once more.

Farther west, on the horizon, lay a pool of orange-yellow light where the sun had cut through a cold steam bath of clouds and snow. Silhouetted against the spotlit glimmer was Seevookak, which rose ramplike from the south, then fell sharply to the sea. On its other side, on a narrow crescent beach of gravel, lay Gambell, one of the oldest villages in North America.

As we passed over it, a fleet of snowmobiles and fat, three-wheeled motorcycles were scurrying for the runway like tiger beetles over sand. The plane circled once, landed on the other end of the asphalt strip, and taxied toward a semicircle of hooded villagers assembled like cavalrymen astride their motorized mounts.

I was giddy upon my arrival. Having reached the destination I had so long desired, I smiled and quietly repeated Fermi's historic message to Roosevelt: "The Italian navigator has landed." I opened the door and stepped out onto the runway.

Several men from the crowd of curious and staring people approached me, smiling, and asked if I worked for the government. I assured them I didn't. Still smiling, one of them asked politely, "Why are you here then?" The question would be asked again and again over the next three years.

I had come to Gambell at whaling time in the hope I could join the hunters. Though I thought it might be difficult to do that, I was confident I could gain enough acceptance among the villagers to be invited along. I could not have chosen a less favorable time to come.

In 1978, the hunt for bowhead whales would be different than ever before. The hunters would take fewer whales than they wanted, not because of the ice or the fog or the waves, and not because they wouldn't see many. They would take fewer because, for the first time in their history, Eskimos had been told that they could not kill as many bowheads as they said they needed.

For untold centuries, nature alone had regulated their hunt. But fearing that Eskimos might destroy the world's last remaining herd of bowheads (Balaena mysticetus), the International Whaling Commission (IWC) and the federal government had intervened to assert their own jurisdiction. The year before, in June 1977, the IWC had unanimously voted to ban the hunt altogether, and although it later changed its mind and decided to allow a special hunt in the spring of 1978, the IWC planned to consider imposing the ban again at its next meeting scheduled for that summer. In the meantime, it decided, the hunt would be regulated by a strict quota, and as a result, the federal government had sent a small but obtrusive army of enforcement agents, scientific researchers, and administrators into remote villages where, with one or two exceptions, the only other white people

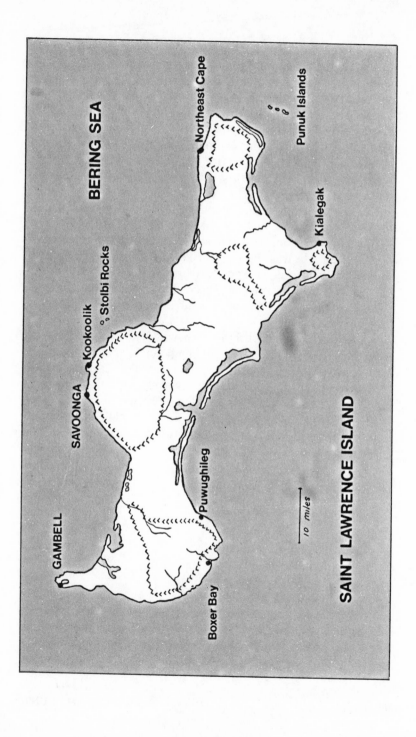

BERING SEA

GAMBELL

SAVOONGA

Kookoolik

Stolbi Rocks

Puwughileg

Boxer Bay

10 miles

Northeast Cape

Punuk Islands

Kialegak

SAINT LAWRENCE ISLAND

were a few teachers, missionaries, and far-flung entrepreneurs.

I stood on the runway looking for a man I couldn't recognize in a staring crowd that didn't recognize me either. After far too vigorously denying any association with the government or a hard-charging Associated Press reporter who'd flown in on the same plane, I asked for Paul Apangalook. Before coming here, I'd sent letters to the mayor and a couple of "city councilors." Paul was the only one to write back, and his encouragement made me hopeful I might stay with him. Paul was the Christian name by which Silook was known to white people.

I began to meet the people around me. We shook hands, they smiled warmly, and my anxieties melted. Someone introduced me to Preston Apangalook. In Yupik language, his name was Yaghaq. He was the boat striker for his brother Leonard, otherwise known as Piitkaq, and Leonard was captain of the crew. Long ago, a missionary gave their father the Christian name of John, thereby making a family surname out of his Native name Apangaluq.

Though Preston's brother Paul wasn't at the airport, I was soon on my way to his home, traveling atop a box of fruit on the back of a snowmobile, with a pack strapped to my back, my valise up front, and my arms around the large stomach of a native ex-Army cook named Winnie James. Too concerned about falling off as the "snowgo" sped over drifts and flats, I noticed little, but enough to feel grateful for the opportunity to have arrived in a place like Gambell.

3. Home Through the Ice

Some time after the whale escaped us, Silook turned with a smile and said, "That warmed you up, didn't it?" He was right. I'd forgotten about the cold, even though my feet were on the painful side of numb and my hands had become closed fists. After I had lived with the villagers a few days, I think I began to experience the insulating effects of eating blubber and oil. I was still cold on hunting trips, but at least I never seemed to feel as cold as I did that first day in the angyaq. Despite several layers of inner and outer clothing that made me waddle like the squattest, most bowlegged of Eskimo whaling captains, it was probably the coldest day of my life. I never admitted it to my crewmates, though. After all, the Associated Press reporter was sitting beside me.

He said he had come along to get an "action story." (Did newspaper reporters really talk like that?) I was indignant at the man's audacity. It was as if he were covering a beat in his native New York City. As a hedge against the cold, he came with only a light parka, ski pants, and a pair of hiking boots, a poor substitute for white man's bunny boots or Native skin *kamiks*. He expected to get an "action story" in a day, and presumed he could simply fly in and out of the storm-sieged island on schedule. He even asked to go out with the hunters. In contrast, I had tried to be low-key and sensitive, aiming at proving myself worthy of an invitation first—a process that, in retrospect, would have taken me a lifetime.

On my first night in Gambell, I was at Leonard's home with Silook when the reporter came to ask. I clenched my teeth as Leonard matter-of-factly said he could come along. Perhaps surprised by my reticence, Leonard turned to me a few moments later and asked if I didn't want to go along, too. Not wishing to be impolite, I nodded my head vigorously.

It was as simple as that for my AP companion. The next day, a whale came up under our boat, and a day or two later he flew out with his action story: the luck only a New Yorker might mistake as being a matter of course.

On second thought, it may have been as simple, but it wasn't easy. He was miserably cold, and although he had a camera, he never got his action shots when the whale came upon us. Oh, he snapped the pictures all right, but his fingers were so numb he hadn't been able to thread the film through the take-up spool.

I was hardly sympathetic to begin with, and all day long he'd been in my way. How could I compose storybook scenes of Eskimo hunters when a white man was sitting beside them? It was like trying to capture exotic Hawaii by shooting the condominiums. He had brought up the issue first when, still standing on shore, he asked me to step out of his picture. I understood all too well that in quest of the legendary hunt the two of us would have to crop our views. I took a lot of close-ups that day and had a hard time restraining my glee at his discomfort. I even tried to appear warm. I got my comeuppance two years later when my cameras and I fell off the edge of the ice while walking backward to get a more encompassing view of the hunters.

The Apangalooks were hardly unaware of our expectations. In fact, they seemed to have a lot of fun with us that day. When whales surfaced in the distance, Silook told AP he was getting "whale shivers," an extemporaneous invention that was duly recorded. The quote would later appear in his nationally circulated wire story. It was clear that Silook and his brothers were a lot more sophisticated about dealing with white men than we were with them.

In the late afternoon of the hunting trip, which had begun at dawn, I asked Preston, "What time do you go home?"

"In time to see *All in the Family*," he answered, as his fellow crewmen broke into convulsive giggling. The impish smile on his face remains with me like the grin of a Cheshire cat. His answer revealed so much: an understanding of my expectations, a good-natured rebuke of my stereotypes, and an acknowledgment of the obvious change that had taken place in his village.

We did go home early that day, because the current had changed, pushing the pack of ice from the north around the cape and against the village's western shore. We could see a shimmering band of black between the ice and an empty slate-gray sky. That was the old village, a row of houses upside down and undulating in the distortion of light between cold air and the relatively warm, open water. But home would remain no more than a mirage if we didn't run for shore soon, so the crewmen struck the sail, lifted a thirty-five-horsepower Evinrude engine into the motor well, and headed into the maze of ice to find their way back. Still at the bow, Preston stood with a pole to push small cakes of ice out of the boat's path, while the others used paddles to break patches of newly formed ice that occasionally brought the boat to a jerking halt. Under falling snow we ran southward, parallel to a jam of larger ice that blocked a direct path to the beach. When Leonard saw an opening several miles later, we sped inside and traveled northward back to the shores of the village.

Waiting for us there were wives, men too old to hunt, and children too young. They stood by clusters of snowgoes—their word for snowmobiles—at the spots where each crew had launched its boat, to help when the angyaqs came ashore. Leonard's wife and young son were there for us. They threw a line, and we jumped ashore and lifted the engine and fuel cans out of the angyaq. Chanting an Eskimo version of "heave-ho," a chain gang of crewmen and their families strained on the long nylon line to haul the boat out of the water and up the face of the ice bank where someone had chiseled a chute. "*Ohhh-Hook!*" A half-dozen people climbed atop the bank to pull on the line while another half-dozen of us grabbed the strips of walrus hide that lashed the boat's skin hull to its frame. *"Ohhh-Hook!"* Yanking and tugging with tensed muscles, we brought the angyaq over the ridge of ice.

One crewman came down with a snowgo and tied a hitch to the angyaq. His machine groaned forward, picking up speed until it was racing up the sloping beach. We hung onto the boat's gunnels while our feet tried to keep up, and though they failed, we were warm all over with the exhilaration of the communal effort.

When we reached the boat racks, out came the mast, the boom and canvas sail, the harpoon, the sealskin float, and the walrus-hide line. Out, too, came the large red polyethylene fishing float, the rifles, the walkie-talkie, and the boxed compass. We turned the angyaq upside down and lifted it up on to the racks so its walrus-skin hull would dry in the sun and the wind. Before carrying the equipment home, we lingered on the beach to talk with the other crews.

"Almost got a whale," Leonard said cheerfully as he began to explain why he hadn't. With remarkable grace, he took responsibility for the mistake of his crew, who had scared off the whale when they bumped the boom against the mast. "We should have just let the boat drift instead of raising the sail," he said with a half-sad smile. He was philosophical about the loss: perhaps it was better that his crew hadn't caught it, he said, for it was a small bowhead, and the village would be allowed only one whale that spring. Better to kill a big one. Still, he wondered how he would explain to his father the missed opportunity.

Far from passing judgment, which would have been impolite, the other villagers shared his cheerfulness. The real disappointment was that they couldn't hunt any longer that day. "No one likes to be the first one to go back to shore," a pudgy-faced man named Clement Ungott told me. "After seeing whales, no one wants to go home."

Silook was pleased by my sense of wonder and excitement at the day's events. As we walked amid the coming-and-going traffic of sleds, snowgoes, and villagers, he explained, "Everything livens up when we sight whales in the spring. It means sharing and being merry. It's a good feeling for our people. It's been our feeling for centuries."

Silook lived in the old village, which ran along the crest of

GAMBELL: THE HUNT

the beach in three ragged rows of frame houses a couple hundred yards from the sea. His home was a one-and-a-half-story structure with a pitched, wood-shingled roof and asphalt siding. By mid-April, it was nearly packed to the roofline with drifting snow. We walked down a passageway he'd cut through a snowbank, took a big step down past the front and only entrance, and came into a cold, windowless outer room or shed, common in these old houses. A few ducks hung from its walls, some animal hides were rolled up in a corner, and a couple of walrus heads propped up on their long ivory tusks sat on the floor amid a clutter of tools and whaling equipment. Against the opposite wall, an old freezer was rumbling as we brushed the snow off our clothes and boots and entered the warm, inner house where Silook's young daughter and his wife, Sukaruwaaq, were awaiting us.

4. He Who Asks Questions

A reporter is a guy who looks up in the sky and asks you if the sun is shining.

—SONNY LISTON

"Who built the angyaq? What kind of skins do you use? When do you put them on? How many does it take? Where do you get the wood? Who splits the hides? How often do you replace them?"

Who, what, when, where, and how? I asked a lot of questions. I always have. I don't know why. It's my business to ask questions, but I'm in the business because newspaper editors were the only people ever pleased by my propensity for asking. Eskimos were among those who were least pleased.

I sometimes thought I could become one of them. Silook was training me to hunt; his wife, nicknamed "Sook," began pointing out the village's single women, and Silook's mother Lilly was eager to match me up. "You should stay," they told me, and indeed, sometimes, in the early and euphoric days of my spring visits, I thought I *should* stay. I liked hunting. I felt immersed in good feelings and affection, and I even flattered myself with the delusion I wanted to learn Yupik, as if wanting to was sufficient in itself.

As much as I loved Silook and Sook, I could never have stayed because there were too many things that separated me from the islanders. But at the time, only one barrier seemed to matter. I thought I could become one of them if only I didn't have this terrible habit of asking questions.

At first, the villagers even seemed entertained by the flight of my rainbow-colored questions. That white men should come north to ask questions, or to trade, always reinforced the Eskimos' belief that they were at the center of the world. In their own language they called themselves "Real People" or "The People," or "The Men Preeminently," and by the same logic they expected we'd want to know more about them than they cared to know about us. Since in fact we did, our curiosity pleasantly fulfilled their expectations, even if they were suspicious about what we would do with the answers.

Because we flattered Eskimos by asking, our first few questions were answered patiently. But as they began to stream forth like a chain of bubbles through a wand, the questions lost their appeal. The Eskimos either swatted them away or retreated for cover.

So many of the answers were self-evident. Anyone with eyes could see for himself who built the angyaqs and when they did it and with what kind of skins and how often they replaced them and where they got the wood. Anyone could see for himself if he was patient enough.

Eskimos learned things differently than we did. They learned much more by watching and listening than by asking questions. For several years after he first went boating, Silook had no more than one duty: he bailed out the water that seeped through the angyaq's skin hull. The rest of the time he watched his father steer the boat and handle the sail; he watched his brothers as their angyaq came upon whales or walrus; and after they had killed their prey, he watched to see how it was butchered. Then, one day, someone gave him a knife and he began butchering. His father gave him a rifle and he began stalking animals. From bailing out the angyaq, he moved forward to experience another role. He learned that way, just as boys in Barrow learned by tending stoves and melting snow at whale camp. All those questions I had about the angyaq would have been answered in time, if I stayed long enough to see for myself.

Then again, had I stayed long enough, those questions and others would no longer have been important.

I had been warned before coming about asking too many questions. Impressed by a sermon on the virtues of just listening, I resolved to change my ways. I cut the number of questions in half. In Gambell that still put me well over par.

How many questions did I ask? Enough to warrant a nickname. For all my listening and self-control, Silook and Sook gave me the name Aapghuughaaq, which means "one who asks questions." It was the only name by which most villagers ever knew me. "Aapghuughaaq" was both appropriate and flattering, I thought. "One who asks questions" conjured up visions of a Zen warrior walking a path toward enlightenment. The villagers thought it was appropriate, too, but for a different reason. To them it had the parenthetical meaning "one who asks *too many* questions." How they laughed when they heard it. I was a walking question mark.

Despite its different shades of interpretation, my name appealed to me. Having any name at all in Yupik seemed flattering, and if I could make light of my quest, all the better. Silook and Sook accepted me and even encouraged me to ask when I wanted, but outside their home I was in a no-man's-land. Although I tried to tread carefully, there were times when I and my questions were met with the chill of an Arctic blast. With the judicious yet polite choice of a few words, or with utter silence, Eskimos could freeze me in my tracks.

It wasn't always clear when that was about to happen. Eskimos rarely said good-bye to each other, so the conversations had no punctuation marks to signal when they were done. They merely turned around and walked away, with an abruptness that disconcerted white men, who wondered what they might have done wrong. Together the hunters might stand for hours, hardly exchanging a word, as if no one else existed, so intent that they seemed transported into another time. How was I to interpret their silence when I was beside them? Only after the fact could I ever hope to find out.

There was C—— hanging up strips of walrus meat and hide to dry at his meat shed near the beach. He was alone, the only other person out in the chill morning fog, and I approached him as if I'd come upon a deer at the edge of the forest. I moved cautiously because he took no notice of me, hesitantly because I was uncertain about his reaction. I walked a few steps and stopped, walked a few steps and stopped, so as not to frighten him off. I had already felt the tension of my presence here, my questions, my desire to take pictures, yet I was impelled toward him by curiosity and a murkier need for reinforcement. I wondered how close I could come before he bounded back into the woods. Could I get close enough to take his picture? Close enough to touch?

I walked slowly past snowdrifts and rusty barrels of smoldering trash and feces and clumps of bleached-out bones that littered the backyard of a village weary with age. Resentful of my fear and disgusted with my stealth, I crossed the mist-shrouded battlefield of my own creation. I was stalking Eskimos in a game park. He was just a man, and I walked toward him in fear of being ridiculed and rejected, but intent on coming up to him, nevertheless.

I nodded hello to him underneath a stand of weathered poles draped with walrus flippers and dark red meat glistening with yellowed blubber. He said nothing but continued working with his knife. I'm sure I had a question on my mind, but I wasn't going to ask it right then. Just watching today: no questions, no pictures.

A half-hour went by, and neither one of us had said anything. Maybe I was making progress. I figured if I could stand around long enough without ever asking anything, maybe the villagers would feel more comfortable around me; and if they felt more comfortable around me, maybe they'd be friendlier.

Maybe they'd even answer my questions.

So, going on to forty-five minutes of silence, I was pleased with myself. Nothing had gone wrong yet. I'd waited that long once before to hear the completion of a sentence that had been suspended in midstream for who knows what reason. Sometimes you had to wait them out, the Eskimos.

We're coming past forty-five minutes now, and I'm rocking back and forth slightly, looking grave when C—— looks grave, smiling softly when C—— seems humored. At long last he looks up at me. I can see the words welling up. I smile acceptingly, anxiously. In a matter-of-fact tone, he says, "You're standing in my light." As I step aside, he silently returns to his work.

Listening had its virtues, but sometimes I still didn't understand. After that first spring, I told myself it would be easier to ask when I returned because they would be more familiar with me the next spring. They were, but it wasn't. In defense of asking questions, let me modestly point out that listening to the hunters speak Yupik or Inupiaq wasn't always instructive. So I told myself that second spring it would be easier to ask if I could speak some of their language when I returned the third spring. It still wasn't.

At the end of my third spring at Gambell, I was talking with some villagers who were plainly eager to know more about the whale my crew at Barrow had captured. At long last I was in the triumphant position of being questioned. But soon I got carried away with myself. Surrendering my advantage, I began asking questions of my own, as if I could expect them to reciprocate with answers. I shouldn't have, for with an eye to the others, one of the villagers commented, perhaps affectionately but with great amusement, "There you go Aapghuughaaqing us again." Oh, how they laughed.

5. Village Rhythms

Sook, or Charlene as she was called in English, was a pretty woman in her mid-twenties, tall and big-boned, with a soft round face and dark hair that she parted in the middle and pulled back with a barrette. When Silook and I returned from the hunt, she was wearing jeans and a plaid shirt, and sat cross-legged on the linoleum floor in front of a small boulder of thawing, dark red walrus meat. With a rocking motion of her wooden-handled, crescent-shaped knife, an *uluk*, she was cutting off chunks of hide and meat to boil later on. She already had the hot food ready as she always did when Silook returned from a hunting trip.

We hung wet clothes on a line above an old kerosene heater in the living room and sat down at the table to eat. I later suspected that this was a courtesy to their white guest, because they generally ate while sitting on the floor. Although she was shy at first, Sook graciously sought to make me comfortable in her home. She was so concerned that I might not like their food that she offered to cook a separate, white man's meal, which I strongly declined because eating their food was to have been part of the adventure and challenge I had imagined. On that first day with Sook and Silook, I experienced the courtesy and sharing for which Eskimos have always been praised. After Silook prayed in thanks for God's gift of the animals he hunted, we ate boiled *mahngoona*, soft chewy chunks of hide, blubber, and meat Sook cut into small pieces that we took with our fingers from a common plastic tray.

This was the home Silook and Sook gave me in a gesture of goodwill. For the next two springs I lived with them there, sleeping on the kitchen floor. On mornings when we didn't go hunting—which seemed the only good reason for Eskimos to awaken so early—I would sit alone at the table, staring out at Seevookak and the eerie rush of snow that ran down its slopes like a river and swept through the village. Alternately, I turned to the interior landscape of these sleeping hosts who had invited me in.

I looked around with a curiosity that sometimes made me feel like a thief in the night. I wondered about objects and the people I saw in pictures on the wall. John, the father, was there, a short, smiling man with a weathered face, dressed in an anorak and holding a baleen boat carving as if he were about to present it to the white man standing beside him, a military commander who appeared to have been the real subject of the photographer's interest and the source of the greeting underneath. Silook was there on the shelves, too, along with several other young men in separate pictures, formally posed and dressed in military uniform, while nearby, above the electric organ, a teenage girl was posed just as formally for what might have been an upcoming graduation. And farther up the cluttered wall, an image of Christ and the Sacred Heart of Jesus looked over the kitchen.

On days when the wind was a hawk and the disintegrating pack of offshore ice turned as impenetrable as a junkyard of broken glass and twisted steel, we were confined indoors. Life, which was pretty slow in Gambell, became slower still. Sleeping long and late, Silook might venture outside only to fetch water with plastic jerry jugs or to dump their near-to-full plastic-lined "honey bucket" that served as a toilet. Sometimes he'd go to the store for food. He said he really didn't have to go outside to see if the weather was changing; he could tell by the rattle of the flue on his furnace whether the wind had died or changed direction.

Besides those chores, Silook might spend the rest of his day carving ivory and packing ammunition or just sitting peacefully at the table while Sook did her housework. Typically, that meant sewing, washing dishes in a sink with straight-through plumbing, or washing clothes and putting them through the wringer of an old-fashioned machine. When we were hungry, she'd take frozen meat from the shed, cut it up, and cook it over the gas stove, or on the Coleman camping stove when they ran out of propane or money or both.

She did some of her chores while watching television. The state had just that year begun to beam it in by satellite to a communications dish that sat in the center of town. Like other villagers, she was engrossed by it, even if the picture on their black-and-white portable was often plagued by a blizzard of snow.

When the television was turned off, the radio might be on instead. There were two stations in Nome, both run by missionaries, that broadcast a mix of music, inspirational messages, worship, and village "hot line." The hot line was a vital network between Bush villages with only one overbooked and often malfunctioning pay phone apiece. "To Emma in Shaktoolik from Caleb," a typical announcement might read, "Father is in the hospital. Come quickly." Or, "To Franklin in Nome from Abraham in Savoonga: please send those parts for my Skiddoo three-fifty on the next flight." Villagers listened in on AC-DC radios, whose ability to run on batteries proved invaluable whenever the village's electrical generator broke down, which was often.

Besides watching TV and listening to the radio, Sook shared another pastime with young housewives in the Lower Forty-Eight. She loved reading Harlequin Romances, although the ability to read put her, and the friends with whom she exchanged books, in a minority. She could even read and write the newly established written form of Yupik. She was an intelligent and able woman, well qualified for teaching English in the adult basic-education program that some of the villagers attended. She would have made a fine schoolteacher too if she had ever had an opportunity to get a higher education.

The third member of their family was Nekipi, a pretty three-year-old who slept in the same bed with Sook and Silook. Like all Eskimo children, she imposed her reign on the household. She ruled with smiles, tears, a dreadful pout, and tantrums if all else failed. Any anger her parents might have felt quickly dissipated when their pretty little girl toddled over with wet eyes and said, "I'm sa-*ray*-ho [sorry]." Like little girls elsewhere, Nekipi had a rocking horse, a plastic tricycle, dolls, and a front-row seat for *Sesame Street*.

Life in the village had its rhythm, one that flowed with the seasons and followed the animals. In late springtime, Silook pushed off with his crewmates to hunt walrus and *mukluk*, the bearded seal. Off the northern shore, they shot migrating ducks and crested auklets, and at the foot of Seevookak they jigged for tomcods. In summertime, he climbed the seaside cliffs near Southwest Cape to collect murre eggs, or he and his family might fish for salmon in Koozata lagoon along the southern coast. Sook loved summertime because it was the season for going inland to camp among the mountains and the tundra. She had been named after a cliff on the south side of the island, where her clan, the Puwughileqs, had lived long ago. There in the Puwughileq mountains, in a summertime ritual as old as the clan itself, Sook and her daughter Nekipi picked berries and *nunivak*, the greens they ate fresh in summer and sour in winter.

As fall approached, it was time to go after geese and young auklets and cormorants. Spotted seals became more common. They too were a sign of the changing season, for they were fatter now and floated on the surface after Silook shot them. Until the ice came, he hunted them from an open boat. Then, as the sea closed up and the days grew shorter, he stalked them and walrus and mukluk on foot, from shore that grew onto the sea. When winter set in, he hunted seals that came up through breathing holes in the frozen ocean.

Sometimes, after the days began to grow longer, he and Sook chopped holes in the ice to jig with sparkplug sinkers baited with tomcod heads. She was quite good at this, as she was with her own 22. In fact, she was a better fisherman than Silook, and I remember her laughing as she brought home a string of sculpins and a bagful of crabs quick-frozen when they emerged from the water.

Springtime approached with the fall of snow, which old Oovi said was "God's way of putting down a mattress for walrus and seals to have babies on." It was a sign of warming and thawing and the time of a hunt that epitomized the challenges and rewards of native life in which Silook had immersed himself. At the time I met him, Silook was tallying some of those rewards on a balance sheet of life's fortunes.

6. Silook

At first I called him Paul because, like Charlene and almost everyone else in the village, he had a Christian name as well as a Yupik one, and he introduced himself to white people with the former. But after a while I began calling him Silook.

He was short and muscular. Like Sook, he was in his mid-twenties, and he had a prizefighter's jaw. A bang of black hair hung straight-edged over his forehead, and a strong chin completed the geometry of a face shaped like a blunt-tipped pentagon. What made him, and most of the islanders, look more Asiatic than Alaskan were the folds of his upper eyelids. Covering the corners of his eyes, they gave them a more slanted appearance. He looked like a Mongolian middleweight.

He was a thoughtful man, laconic, and like most of the hunters, he spoke in a measured, quiet, and dignified tone seldom disturbed by emotion. He was articulate, but that didn't mean he stepped outside himself to offer an account of his life. Silook and the people I lived among were less engaged with their individual pasts than I, less encumbered with self-definition. They did not draw straight lines between points of time. They thought of themselves as hunters, but a man wasn't defined by what he did—they were *all* hunters—and a man wasn't defined by his personal history either. The present held their attention, unless they began to talk about hunting trips and exploits like capturing the bowhead; then the past seemed to fuse with the present. Tomorrow was a fanciful world.

I remember how often Silook talked about special hunting trips and things we would do together the next day. Sometimes we did them, but much of the time we didn't. It wasn't because he was procrastinating. Procrastination is intentional, and he didn't mean to postpone those trips. He may even have meant to take them.

Silook saw how I squirmed with idle energy to do something or go somewhere, anywhere. I suspect he talked about doing those things to please me. It wouldn't be surprising; both he and Sook were gracious and generous hosts. They knew that being cheerful was the healthiest state of mind in the Arctic, and it must have pleased them to see my pout replaced by an excited smile as I anticipated tomorrow.

But I also suspect that for Silook, announcing and imagining those trips were often tantamount to taking them. Like the other villagers I knew, once he expressed an intention, he could return to the present with neither expectations nor plans to fulfill it. His travels were internal. Mine, on the other hand, though no less imaginary, were acted out on the surface.

If Silook talked imaginatively about tomorrow, he and all the Eskimos talked with an utter lack of exaggeration about yesterday. I was amazed by the discrepancy between their accounts of conditions and the conditions themselves. Among the hunters there was a shared understanding of each other's private triumphs and dangers; yet to an outsider's ears, their sparse accounts never indicated the frequency or intensity of either. Listening to their stories, I'd get hungry for adjectives—graphic accounts to fill my fantasy.

"We saw the whale come up and signaled the others with a flag. We were watching it a long time. Looks to me like it was resting. When we were about four hundred feet away, it went down, it turned sideways. It came closer and showed us its side. We struck it when it was six feet away. We hollered: 'We have struck a whale!' "

Compared to an account like that, police blotters seem thrilling.

I hadn't yet begun to appreciate the mute testimony of other evidence. Purple patches of frostbitten skin peeling from a hunter's face told a better story than adjectives describing hardships encountered on the trail.

While on a hunting trip with Silook one day, I had a glimpse of the routine dangers Eskimos faced while hunting. We were traveling under the evening sun when Silook spotted a seal basking on the ice about sixty yards from shore. (Two years later, I can't remember what kind it was, but Silook can, though he may have shot a hundred seals since then.) Every thirty seconds or so, the seal raised its head, looked around for danger, and fell back to sleep again. While it relaxed, Silook brought his scope up, drew a bead on its head, and squeezed the trigger. The bullet stopped it where it lay—which was important on spring ice, because a seal would use its last breath of life to wriggle into the water.

After killing the seal, we carefully made our way over broken ice that had drifted together along the shore. Silook was concerned that the changing tide might push the ice jam offshore, so he told me to watch behind us while he retrieved the dead seal. Because he was also concerned that the ice between us and the seal was too thin, he took out his seal hook, an eggplant-shaped wooden block with three large hooks embedded in its sides, and threw it bolo-fashion onto the far side of the seal ten yards away. He pulled on the attached twine line to drag the hooks over the seal to snag it so he could pull the animal over the thin ice. I was so fascinated I didn't notice we were drifting away from shore.

Silook turned, saw what was happening, and told me simply, "Hurry." We ran toward land, jumping from ice floe to ice floe. On the way I broke through the ice, but Silook pulled me up. I was wet and shaken.

When we returned home Silook never spoke about the incident.

In some ways he was different from most of the villagers. Perhaps it was because of the greater contact he had had with white people. When he was a boy, visitors to the island often stayed with his family, and they continued to come to the same house to visit Silook now that he had grown up and his parents had moved out. Unlike most of the others in Gambell, Silook had gone to high school on the mainland.

But who was he? Although we talked easily about hunting and subsistence, current events and sports, and especially the whale, it took me three seasons to learn about Silook's past. On the last day of the last season I lived with him, while I was waiting for a plane to arrive to take me away, I learned more than I had during the preceding three years. Here is some of the shell I pieced together.

Silook was the second youngest of six children born to John Apangalook and Lilly Koonooka. John was one of the Kookoolik-miet, a descendant of those who had survived the great famine at Kookoolik. While captain of a hunting crew, he had captured six whales, and he was also acclaimed as a dancer and a storyteller. His wife, the descendant of a family from Siberia, was the daughter of a famous whaler—as shown by two rows of whale's tails tattooed on her right forearm.

Silook grew up in the same wooden house where he now lived in the old village. Its five rooms were cramped by white men's standards, although Eskimos were accustomed to smaller living spaces and shared quarters; even today, mothers and fathers may sleep on the same mattress with three or four of their children. Like other boys in springtime, Silook would climb up into the attic to look for whales through a window that faced seaward; or he'd look for them from the rooftop, which he reached by scaling up a snowbank. At the end of the day, he'd watch from the beach for his father's return in the angyaq.

Like most Eskimo boys, he began hunting when he was eleven, and within a year or two, John handed him his first rifle, an old lever-action 2-19. Advancing a rank in apprenticeship, Silook moved to a spot in the stern, where his father taught him gun discipline: how to handle a rifle, where to aim, and when to shoot. "I'd shoot from right beside him," Silook recalled. "I got real good with that rifle." He had learned quite a lot through experience by the time he finished the eighth grade.

There was no high school in Gambell, or any other Bush village in the 1960s, so schooling ended for Eskimo children after they graduated from the local grade school run by the Bureau of

Indian Affairs (BIA). It ended, that is, unless they were bright and able and willing to leave the island. Leonard had gone Outside, but Silook's older sisters hadn't, and John had pulled Preston out of school because he needed him for hunting. Reluctantly, his father let Silook go.

There was a BIA-run high school in Nome, but it was full. The next closest school, and the only other one in the state, was near Sitka, thirteen hundred miles away. It, too, was full, which meant Silook would have to attend school in the Lower Forty-Eight. There was a Native high school in Oregon, but it didn't have any vacancies either, so in the fall of 1967, Silook—or Paul as he called himself among whites—left Saint Lawrence Island on a long journey to Oklahoma, the nearest state with a BIA school and a vacant desk.

"I was anxious to get there to see what it was like. I remember very clearly when I first got off the plane in Seattle. Air was real warm. I was out of breath like a dog in a real warm place. It was big and hazy, and I was excited."

From Seattle, he and his boyhood friend rode on the bus down to Oklahoma. "We took in the country. We saw farms and cattle and horses, like we'd seen in schoolbooks." But their excitement was tarnished by a disappointment that proved white people had no monopoly on fantasy and stereotype. "We were looking for tepees," Silook giggled. "I wondered when we'd see the buffalo and Indians."

He laughed when he told me about it, but going to school in Oklahoma was a profound shock. It meant homesickness, fights with Indian boys, and a life with no ocean. He missed training in winter hunting and spring whaling. In class, he was pulled away from Eskimo ways. But Silook/Paul was not easily torn away from Native instincts. The urge to hunt led him to explore the outdoors and though a lightning storm, something unknown in Gambell, sent him and his classmates running for cover at first, an innate curiosity about the weather led them back outside to snap pictures of lightning bolts to send back home. In the woods, he caught frogs and small prey.

His first impulse had been to write home for a ticket out, but Silook/Paul adjusted to his new surroundings. He made honor roll, and though he was no doubt happy to return home at the end of his freshman year to hunt walrus and bearded seals and to climb cliffs for bird eggs, he was also eager to begin his sophomore year.

On the eve of Silook's departure for a second year in Oklahoma, however, his father, worried that his son would be too far away, decided not to let him go. But instead of dropping out, Silook got permission to take advantage of a last-minute vacancy at Mount Edgecumbe, the BIA school near Sitka in southeastern Alaska. Once there, in a former Army barracks in a rainforest even more alien to Saint Lawrence Island than Oklahoma was, Silook realized how much better the other school had been. Yet he stuck it out for three years to get his diploma.

Despite its limitations, Mount Edgecumbe had fostered "Paul's" ambitions: wanting a career, he applied to and was accepted into a vocational training program with the Federal Aviation Administration. The training program would be held in northern California.

That summer, after graduating from high school, Silook/ Paul felt deeply the clash of two cultures. Schooling implanted the notion of personal autonomy, namely that an individual had the right to choose his own career. "It was a good deal the FAA offered me," he said nine years later. "I felt like my years of schooling had to pay off somewhere, and at the time, I was looking forward to leaving the island. It was a real good deal."

Silook's father thought otherwise. He had just returned from a trip to the Lower Forty-Eight, one of the few trips he ever made there, and he had not liked what he had seen in San Francisco. It did not matter that the training school was far from the city. He decided that Silook was not going. And in deciding this, he was asserting his traditional authority. While "Paul" had been encouraged toward independence, Silook had been taught to obey his father, his elders, and his boat captain.

Silook obeyed—indeed, there seems not the slightest indication that he considered anything less. Yet he ended up in California anyway, because he lost his student deferment by not entering the FAA program, and the National Guard sent him south for basic training. When he returned to the island, to a village that still had no roads, no cars, no telephones, and no television, Silook was much more aware of what he lacked and what it could not provide: a career and the prospects of having one. After four years Outside and a high school diploma, Paul's formal education in white studies had ended.

A few years after he came back to Saint Lawrence, Silook and Sook married, although getting married was not simple. By custom, he was required to enter into a year's service—carrying water, hauling fuel, and performing other chores for his in-laws, while his family had to provide hers with gifts of guns and rope. (When asked about the custom a few years later, Silook laughingly declared, "*I* did it, and when my daughter gets old enough, I'm sure going to be on the other end.") Conscripted into custom, married, and committed to fatherhood, Silook was a man with little choice but to stay on Saint Lawrence, whether he wanted to or not.

As far as I can connect the dots of what he told me, this is what I know about Silook's life before he came back to Gambell. I am not suggesting that his return was tragic—certainly, he never considered it that—nor that his life was unfulfilled. He was not haunted by the specter of what could have been, and I never heard him express any bitterness over the opportunities he had lost by coming home. Six years after he returned, he talked wistfully at times to his white friends about going to college, about getting a degree in public administration, or maybe starting his own business, but he no longer thought, as he may have earlier, of abandoning the island or his life as a hunter. He was becoming increasingly absorbed in both.

However limited it might be in its opportunities and its outlook, life in Gambell gave Silook a sense of purpose and freedom. At times life was as simple as old men and women chopping holes in the ice, and young boys throwing twine bird nets to catch food. On the mainland, "Paul's" life had been complicated and scheduled, down to the time he ate and slept. In the village, he was free of that. He could eat when he was hungry and sleep when he was tired, neither of which was predictable in the Eskimos I knew. On the mainland, the economy rewarded specialized skills that were not self-sustaining. On the island, Silook was independent of structure, and as he watched his wife and their daughter eat the food he had brought home, he could feel self-reliant, too.

Hunting posed a physical challenge that Silook took on with determination and met with self-contained joy when he was successful. But Silook may have enjoyed its intellectual challenge even more keenly. Successful hunting involved far more than endurance and marksmanship. It also required great knowledge of the movements of animals, of where to be and when to strike. A marksman might fire a killing shot at a distant walrus in open water, but to what avail if the dead animal sank before the hunters could reach it? A smart hunter waited until he was closer, and when he shot, he aimed for the body because he knew a wounded animal would stay on the surface long enough for him to harpoon it. A hunter might motor off to the coast of Siberia and catch several walrus, but to what avail if the fog closed in on his return home? Even with a compass it was easy to miss the island altogether and end up far out to sea instead. Successful hunting required great knowledge of the currents and tides and the signs that augured bad weather. It was an education in solving puzzles as challenging as a chess match, and Silook responded with the same relish with which he played chess.

The highest achievement of an Eskimo hunter was to provide his household and his family with all the meat they needed. It was an achievement that was especially significant in Gambell, for perhaps no other village in North America was more dependent upon hunting for its food. In the local store, there were white men's staples, like coffee, tea, sugar, and flour; they long ago became Eskimos' staples, too. There were also canned goods and even frozen meats, such as beef and chicken. But even if the villagers had wanted to eat a steady diet of white men's food, they could not have afforded to. Groceries from the mainland were exorbitantly expensive; in short and undependable supply; and on the whole they couldn't match Native foods for nutrition, energy, and taste. Families shopped at the store after they sold ivory or collected assistance checks or when someone found a job. Some families could shop there more often than others. But they never stopped hunting. Though families might be inconvenienced when the store ran out of food, they were likely to go hungry when the village ran out of seal and walrus and whale. Hunting was still the source of life. To sustain life so directly was a hunter's greatest reward.

7. Palace of the King Polar Bears

Silook! Silook!

Early in the morning, Leonard entered his brother's house and called out to him in a low voice. It was time for the whale hunt. Once his right-hand man had responded, Leonard left and Silook rose, yawning and rubbing his eyes. He pumped and primed the Coleman stove to make coffee and pancakes, and after we ate, he climbed into sealskin boots, insulated canvas overalls, and a fur-side-in parka covered with an Army-issue camouflage outershell. We passed through the shed and out into Arctic spring.

The temperature was twenty degrees and a fifteen-knot breeze was blowing out of the north when we left Silook's house on Monday morning, the day after that first whale had escaped us. The sky was somber gray. The land had no trees, no pinnacles of rock, no tall buildings. Only Mount Seevookak rose up as if to challenge the dominant sky. On those infrequent days when the sun shone brightly, Seevookak surged upward and outward like a giant launching ramp perched at the edge of land. But when the sun was obscured by clouds, Seevookak's reflection was mirrored in the sky, and like a breaching whale, the mountain fell back to Earth to be swallowed up, along with everything else, by the gray.

In a world that reflected back on us and closed in on me, the sight of villagers standing on rooftops was always dramatic. Atop an entire row of houses in the old village, boys and men climbed in springtime to look for whales passing offshore. Raising their binoculars and pointing to Aghvook's vaporous blows, they waited for a lead to open up through the blockade of moving ice. Others watched from inside, out westward-facing attic windows from which they occasionally poked their heads to scan a wider arc. On knolls and ridges, wherever the relief rose just a few feet, the Eskimos found a vantage point to look for whales. All over the Arctic, they seemed to reach upwards in springtime. I once asked my captain in Barrow what he thought of the Lower Forty-Eight. "I didn't like it," he responded. "There were too many trees there. I couldn't see far. Here, I can just climb on an ice ridge."

Silook and I lay prone on the steep, pitched roof and scanned the sea. It was actually a sea now, because overnight the wind had pushed the broken ice far offshore and in its place was "big water." I was surprised the icescape could change so quickly. Earlier in the morning, after Silook's uncle Roger had sighted a pair of bowheads two miles offshore, his crew had launched their angyaq. A couple of other boats put out to sea a little later, but most of the captains were concerned about an impending storm and stayed ashore. The same wind that pushed the ice away grew harder, blowing snow off the slopes of Seevookak like sands over the Sahara. Blinding swirls reduced visibility to less than a hundred yards and squalls lashed the open boats with freezing spray. When the weather worsened, the angyaqs found themselves sailing into a zone of ice floes and slush. They turned back, but had a bad time of it. Even though every crew has a compass, no one can travel a straight line through the ice, and by the time Roger's crew came ashore, they were wet and cold. They had seen no whales.

While waiting for the weather to change, the villagers turned their attention to a new rite of spring, for April had become more than the time of whaling. It was also the time for the village league basketball championships. They were advancing to the quarter-finals the week I arrived, and as on a Friday night in the suburbs, the high school lot was busy with motor vehicles. Driving up with Sook sitting behind him holding on to his waist, and little Nekipi in front sitting between his arms, Silook parked their snowgo among the pack. Around them were snowmobiles of every color and design; fire-engine red, three-wheeled motorcycles with fat, studded tires; and six-wheeled, insectlike amphibians, the closest thing they had to a sedan out here.

Until the gymnasium and three satellite classrooms were built the year before, Gambell had never had a high school, let alone basketball. Now, Silook played guard for a team in the men's league, Sook was a starting forward in the women's league, and her sister Laura was the star player for the high school.

Inside, the stands were nearly filled with attentive fans sitting with their friends and families, and still more were filing in. There were squirming kids dressed in store-bought ski parkas with homemade face ruffs of coyote, wolf, and dog fur; teenagers in jeans; "ooh"ing mothers knitting or rounding up their kids; analytical fathers, some dressed in sneakers and bright-colored basketball uniforms; and amused grandparents. Old Oovi was there—he hardly ever missed a game. Following the action up court and down, his face alternated between rapt, wide-eyed attention and that wonderful Buddha laugh. Nearby sat his sister Thelma, whose smile highlighted pretty tattooed lines radiating downward from her lower lip in four pairs and a single threesome. Down the bench from her, in the high school cheering section, some of her grandchildren were jumping and stomping, waving and chanting for the boys' team, which was playing in the men's league now that its school season was over.

Whether they were playing another high school or one of Gambell's men's teams, the boys were the crowd's favorites. They owned the place, as could be seen from a big painted sign on the wall: WELCOME TO THE PALACE OF THE KING POLAR BEARS. The boys always drew a crowd. During the high school season, the gym was packed for their biggest game of the year against the team's toughest—and only—opponent, the Savoonga High Siberian Huskies. Ever since Savoonga was established by reindeer herders from Gambell, the two villages had been friendly but intense rivals, and the high school series continued the tradition.

If the home games were striking, the road trips were spectacular. After all, there weren't any roads, so instead of a school bus, a squadron of snowgoes carried the fur- and snow-suited players, cheerleaders, and most of the other villagers forty miles across the snow-lashed hills and tundra (thereby giving new meaning to the importance of pregame warm-ups). In rival territory, Gambell's cheerleaders danced the Eskimo Bump and shouted for support from vocal fans who wore T-shirts emblazoned with the Yupik slogan, POLAR BEAR POWER.

Because the game of basketball had just been introduced to the island, many of the players hadn't developed shooting or ball-handling skills, but that didn't seem to bother anyone. They played good-naturedly, with very little aggressiveness. When an overenthusiastic defender knocked down the man dribbling the ball, for instance, everyone laughed, including the man who had been knocked down. Nor did anyone object when, after whistling the action to a stop, the referee called a jump ball instead of a foul, as someone helped the dribbler to his feet. The rules of the game hadn't been mastered either. I'd never seen basketball played with so little arguing among players. When a white kid who could play better than the others refused to pass the ball, or when he shot from too far out, none of his teammates complained. No one got mad because other players made mistakes either.

Watching the players on the men's teams, I could pretty well guess who had lived off the island. High scorers like Bruce and Barry had learned fundamentals while attending BIA high schools. They passed agilely, went to the basket with confidence, and shot accurately, while those who had stayed on the island were several steps behind.

Even without off-island training, the newer players were improving, in part because of new teaching aids. They could watch "Red on Roundball" on the *CBS Game of the Week* every Sunday now. Television and basketball had arrived at the same time.

On Silook's team, the Blue Streaks, there was a center named Johnny Silook (a surname for one village family as well as the Eskimo name for my crewmate) who dominated the men's league. He was tall, lean, young, and cocky; an irrepressible personality who exuded good-time cheer. Johnny dominated life under the backboard and off the court as well, magnetizing both the villagers and young white visitors, to whom he was drawn as they were drawn to him. No one who met him ever doubted that Johnny could succeed in either world. He was less cautious than most villagers, perhaps because he felt less threatened by whites. He undercut white men with laughter and refused to take them seriously. Under the guise of teaching me names for ice conditions, for instance, Johnny trained me instead to pronounce Yupik words for selected body parts and functions and, like a proud teacher, had me repeat them in front of his hysterical wife and friends. He loved to party and always had buoyant spirits. He reminded me of some Jamaicans I knew. Jokingly, I called him Johnny Too Bad, and he called me Slokok, or Walrus Flipper, and went into his lumbering walrus act every time he saw me coming. His tastes ran from *Hee-Haw* to the Seattle Supersonics, whom he called the home team, and he loved to prepare whale meat by frying it up with Hamburger Helper. He talked about selling enough ivory to come down to Seattle to "boogie" with me, yet he had no intention of ever moving off the island.

Like Silook, Johnny would not say much about his past, but I thought he might have picked up the game of basketball in Chicago, where he had lived for a time as a child. About those days, all he would say, with his funny, wise-guy smirk, was, "I'd rather live on walrus than on the streets of Chicago." He was indeed supporting himself and his family by hunting walrus and seals.

In the game that night, Johnny led the Blue Streaks to an easy though unpopular victory over the boys' team. Afterward, he walked off the floor with a jaunty air of superiority. The boys were in good spirits too. After all, they would surely get better at the game. And as one of them told me while we filed out into the cold, "We're playing again tomorrow night if we don't go hunting."

By early Wednesday morning, the wind had died and instead of snow and rain, a curtain of fog hung over the sea. Anxious to find bowheads, two crews sailed into it and out of sight. When the sun burned through several hours later, we too put out, sailing in a light wind across five miles of open water to the edge of offshore ice where whales were within range. The radio popped with reports of crews closing in on bowheads. I watched spellbound as whales that seemed as big as battleships broke through the surface, vented air like bellows, then rose and fell in a long smooth arc. Aghvook's head took up a third of its body, and, in the words of one nineteenth-century Yankee captain, its mouth was "as large as a room, and capable of containing a merchant-ship's jollyboat, full of men. . . ." Streamlined and reinforced with cartilage, the whale's huge head could ram through the sea's frozen mantle. In addition, Aghvook had centuries ago lost the dorsal fin that might hinder its movement among the ice, where it spent most of its life. As one elder concluded, "Whale, he like 'em ice."

Like guards on patrol, we spent long, uneventful hours searching for our prey. Time seemed to pass slowly until "Puhhh!"—the sound of a bellows or the sight of a blow. And then our crew began to plot and plan. If the whale dove, it might not surface again for thirty minutes; it might be far away the next time we saw it; or we might never see it again. But as scattered and unpredictable as they might be, the sightings created an expectancy that hung like sea smoke. Wednesday morning and early afternoon were filled with excitement, because some crews saw over twenty whales. Some boats even came close enough to strike.

The action seemed compressed into a few mintues, though it must have taken place over the course of an hour. Several forty- to fifty-foot bowheads, one of them a mother accompanied by a twenty-foot calf, swam close to our boat. Darting up and down like whitecaps alongside them came ten- to twenty-foot-long, cream-colored toothed whales called belugas. Belugas were easier to capture—they could be killed with a rifle shot—but shooting them would scare off the bowhead, so the hunters let them pass.

I got "whale chills" when they swam underneath our angyaq and off our port side. Then, in awe, I gasped, "Over there!" and pointed, which I never should have done, to the great hulk of Aghvook rising up in our wake.

"Keep mum!" the captain ordered. He pulled the tiller to starboard and let out sail to head down after it, but it outran us easily. Like the other bowheads, it was moving north-northwest, between the edge of offshore ice and a line of the villagers' angyaqs. Looking behind us and to the south, we saw someone raise a black flag to signal that they had come upon a whale. The radio went silent as we watched an angyaq approach the lounging animal. We held our breath when the striker raised his six-foot-long harpoon. He was poised to strike, but the wind died and the angyaq stalled before he could get any closer. Quietly sinking out of sight, the whale disappeared.

I'd seen Eskimo whaling harpoons in museums before coming here. They were connected to a set of sealskin floats by a long walrus-hide line. When the striker threw one of those harpoons, it drove into the whale and the swiveling ivory harpoon head rotated downward at a right angle when the line pulled taut. This made the harpoon much harder to pull out, thus securing the line and the floats to the whale.

Today's weapon, called the darting gun, worked the same way. But its harpoon was a steel rod three feet long and mounted atop a gun barrel like a bayonet. The barrel itself was at the end of a long wooden pole that was thrown just like the old harpoon. With the darting gun, today's Eskimos could harpoon the whale and at the same time shoot it with a black-powder bomb fifteen inches long and three-quarters of an inch in diameter. Deep inside the whale, the bomb would explode three to seven seconds later while Aghvook raced underwater toward its great protector, the ice. If the hunters were both blessed and proficient, the injury and the buoyant, dragging floats would stop the whale from getting there first; then, hungry for air, Aghvook would grudgingly yield to the floats' upward urgings: to the surface, and to the waiting hunters.

Farther south, a whale lifted its crescent-shaped flukes so that their turned-up tips pointed to the sky. It dove shallowly near another angyaq and, intending to intercept it when it surfaced, the captain followed a trail of slick water caused by the flukes' underwater turbulence. He sailed too fast, however, for his crewmen saw the white flash of Aghvook's chin twenty feet below them as they traveled over it and out of range. Another boat tried to intercept the whale by making a slower pass, but the hunters still crossed its path too soon, and the whale, swimming on its back, stayed down to avoid the danger.

A few minutes later, a voice burst out from the walkie-talkie. *"Aghvengukuut!"* ("We have struck a whale!") Moments later we heard the cry again, this time echoing, fanning out across the water. "Aghvengukuut!" I still remember the long triumphant ring of that last syllable. But even as we heard the distant shouts, the excitement faded, because the bomb hadn't exploded and the harpoon had pulled out of the whale. Downwind of a stiffening breeze, we caught the sweet smell of blubber spilled from the wound onto the water, while somewhere below us the whale escaped with a bomb inside its body. I wondered why no one chased after it, but without floats the whale could not be found unless it surfaced nearby. All that was now left was a small slick of oil that dampened the sea as it began to grow choppy.

We were bouncing about in our skin boat when the message came from shore over the walkie-talkie: we should come in, the voice said. Pacific ocean swells were slamming against the western shore, shattering the shore-fast ice and heaving house-size icebergs up against the beach where we had launched our boats.

Striking the sail, lowering the mast, and mounting the engine into a motor well cut through the skin hull, the crews raced for home. Poised like masts, the boat strikers stood in the bow to direct their captains around dangerous reefs of ice, as waves broke against the bow and icy spray soaked the outer fur of their sealskin parkas.

Just around the cape, the villagers had chopped a chute through the relatively safer, steep-sloped north beach. When we arrived, a long chain gang of villagers was pulling the angyaqs up one by one on the surge of heaving swells. Somehow, our angyaq and two others fell into a trough that sucked the sea down to the tumbling gravel. Behind us, an iceberg suddenly rose up on the crest of a wave. Teetering, it rolled toward us as we leaped for our lives. But luckily, the berg staggered backward, and we were able to get ourselves and our angyaqs up onto the beach without being crushed.

Each day I was learning that, like our lives, siku, the ice, was always changing, often dangerous, and much more complicated than I'd ever expected.

8. Grandfathers of Gambell, Grandsons of the Stone Age

Awaiting the hunters' return were two old men who knew better than anyone else the dangers of being trapped offshore. Samuel Irrigoo, age eighty-eight, and Lloyd Oovi, age eighty-two, sat on a sled, binoculars in hand, and scanned the sea intently from the beach. Both were dressed in white cotton snow shirts pulled over parkas and fur-trimmed hoods that fit snugly around their faces. Irrigoo's face was lean and furrowed, and his eyes were magnified by a pair of glasses as thick as storm windows. He couldn't see or hear or walk as well as Oovi, but he could be heard from farther away. In a near-shout, he liked to boast, "I saw Oovi when he was a baby." Saying that, he would break into convulsive laughter that shook his shoulders. His cockiness was easily forgiven, for Irrigoo was the oldest villager or, as he phrased it, "I am the last man."

Oovi was a bigger, if also younger, man. Though he had the voice of a bear, he spoke softly like a storyteller, in the deep, sometimes whispering tones of a wave climbing the gravel shore. Whether among a crowd or alone on the beach, he radiated dignity and a cheerful presumption of goodwill in others. He greeted visitors and villagers alike with a marvelous smile that enveloped his round face, drew the eyelids together, and brought back memories of grandfathers at Christmas.

They would sit for hours, Irrigoo and Oovi, looking outward, occasionally interrupting the silence with which they were so comfortable to comment about the effect of currents and wind, the moon and the tides. Every so often someone would come by with news or with a walkie-talkie so they could hear for themselves the talk of captains far from land. "North and south currents real strong," Irrigoo would inform his audience as he gestured to the pack of ice cakes and bergs moving steadily along the shore. "One must learn the currents and the cake ice. It's hard, just like learning arithmetic, but when those ice cakes close behind us, we have to stay among the ice for the night."

His use of the present tense seemed to transpose Irrigoo into the past as if he were a hunter again. Yet Irrigoo and Oovi didn't seem to divide their identities into a past and present; they had been and always would be hunters. "In the springtime I never sleep," Oovi said. "It's like I am whaling again."

When they were young, both of them had spent cold and hungry nights amid the offshore ice. They had been the lucky ones, however, because they had found their way back.

There were a number of ways, all of them simple, in which the unlucky ones were lost. The shore-fast ice might snap off behind them while they were hunting on foot; loose pack ice might surround their boat; or they might become lost in the fog or blinding snow and travel in the wrong direction, out to sea. The fate that befell them was drowning or freezing or, for the truly unlucky, starving on an ice floe drifting to oblivion. Those who escaped were blessed by a fickle but propitious movement of the ice.

In those days, death on the ice was a common occurrence. The dangers were greater then, not because ice conditions were more severe, but because the Eskimos weren't as well equipped as they are today. So small was the chance of rescuing anyone and so great the regularity with which the ice claimed its victims that Eskimos reacted in an often fatalistic manner when villagers were cut adrift or trapped offshore. How dramatic it must have been for Oovi and Irrigoo, when they were old men, to watch a Coast Guard helicopter rescue a crew of Gambell hunters from the ice. Grandsons of the Stone Age, they were witnessing the ascendance of the jet age.

Irrigoo and Oovi were among the last of a generation born in the nineteenth century, the grandchildren of those who had met the first whaling ships a half-century earlier. They grew up in a world already reshaped by white men, for the coming of Western tools and goods had ushered Saint Lawrence Island out of the Stone Age into an era of firearms and calico, gunpowder and sugar, iron and flour. The population of whales and walrus had already been plundered by the commercial fleet, and before Oovi was born, the first missionary had arrived to "make boot talk" and civilize "barbarous people."

Despite the abrupt and overwhelming intrusion of Western material culture, young Irrigoo and Oovi had been guided into a pattern of life substantially the same as their grandfathers', and now, long after that pattern had changed, the two old men on the beach seemed the last living connection to Eskimo antiquity. Their memory, their manners, and even their bodies bore witness to a distant culture. On their joints were two small dots that had been tattooed many years earlier, after each man had struck his first bowhead.

The remains of the past to which Oovi and Irrigoo were connected lay close to the surface of Gambell, although I did not see the extent of them until the snow melted late in the spring. On the gravel spit that extends from the base of Mount Seevookak lay four low mounds littered with thousands upon thousands of bleached-out bones from walrus, whales, and seals. These were the sites where the people of now extinct cultures lived some two thousand years ago. Underneath the mounds were buried semisubterranean sod homes called *ningloos*, the construction of which identified those who lived in them as a people of the whale, for the walls were built with whale ribs, walrus skulls, and driftwood. The floors were made out of mammals' shoulder blades, and the sod roofs were held up by jawbone beams.

Oovi and Irrigoo's fathers had grown up in the same sort of ningloos, but like the rest of the villagers they had abandoned them in favor of loaf-shaped houses that were built aboveground. The new dwellings had walrus-skin roofs and floors; and inside, like a house within a house, was an inner room made out of walrus and reindeer skins, where the families cooked, slept, and worked in wintertime. "They were nice and warm, not like today's houses," Irrigoo said of the dwellings he and Oovi grew up in. Pointing to the light switch in his new prefabricated home, he alluded to the modern world's abject dependence on the constancy of electrical power. "When the lights go out, it gets cold." (About the white men's–style houses, an old mainlander was even more unhappy. "Before the missionaries came," he lamented, "we lived underground in sod houses and laid our dead out on the tundra. Now we live aboveground and bury the dead, and I haven't been warm since.")[1]

Not only were houses built with sea mammals, they were heated and lit by them as well. Women filled long, shallow clay bowls with oil rendered from seal, walrus, and whale blubber, and they tended low flames from the wicks of moss they had collected on the tundra. In the soft, warm light of the seal-oil lamps, Irrigoo and Oovi had watched as hunters fed wooden idols by rubbing fat on them in hope the animal-shaped figures would bring good fortune.

When Irrigoo and Oovi were still young, the universe was full of spirits and souls at whose mercy the Eskimos lived each day. Judging by the amazing array of taboos that governed an Eskimo from waking to sleeping, the chances of offending these spirits were many. Yet the occasions for honoring them were just as common. Elaborate rituals had evolved to conciliate the spirits and souls whose beneficence Eskimos so desperately needed if they were going to survive.

When a hunter killed a seal, for instance, he would melt ice in his mouth and give it a drink of fresh water to placate its thirst—which he knew must be great because seals live in salt water. After its meat had been eaten, the seal's skull and bones were returned to the sea to further appease its soul so that it would return again as a seal to give itself up to the hunters once more.

Before Aghvook approached them in springtime, whalers worshipped the Moon, because it was he who ruled over the animals, especially the whale, around whom the greatest ceremonies revolved. Oovi's father made his sacrificial offering to the April moon. His crew cut up meat from whale and young walrus they had killed the previous spring and left it in a certain place to "give it back to God, to the Moon," Oovi recalled.

It was to honor the spirit of Aghvook that the islanders performed so many rituals and respected so many taboos. When a crew came upon a whale, for instance, reverence dictated that the harpooner strike the animal only once with his weapon. Then, if they captured it, the men sang ceremonial songs while they paddled homeward using oars decorated with whales' tails painted on with lamp soot and eye fluid from a previous whale catch. Once ashore, the hunters prayed and chanted secret songs in their homes for several days in thanksgiving for the honor and for the tons of food, heat, and building materials that had been bestowed upon them.

Cutting little pieces of meat from the whale, Irrigoo's people would string them together to wear around their throats. Returning home, they would hang the meat to dry and, later, put the necklaces into their charm bags along with such things as dried whale eyes, pieces of the fluke, parts of the sex organs, and rocks that might be shaped like Aghvook. So sacred were the charms that nobody else might open a hunter's bag. So sacred was Aghvook that even the bag's owner might open it only after killing the whale or if someone in his family were sick.

It was after striking their first whales that both Irrigoo and Oovi had been tattooed with a long thread and needle and a mixture of urine, soot, and whale oil. "Oh, it hurt!" Oovi grinned when he thought back on it. Unlike Irrigoo, he had been given a second set of tattoos, in the corners of his mouth and chin, to commemorate his surviving an incredible event in which a whale fell on top of his boat.

He had been out at the point of Mount Seevookak one summer day when it happened. A whale surfaced close to a boat containing him and a couple of others. "I turn and watch for where it comes up again," whispered Oovi—he was reenacting the event with his voice and hands. "Coming, coming. Ooh, big thing. Oh, it covered the sun when it jumped out of the water. Sky got dark and the whale came over us. When it tumbled back, its flukes tore the boat in three pieces. We went into the water. I tried to swim. Another boat came to the rescue, but one man died. Smashed in half. The whale was gone. Later that day, my sister tattooed me. I don't know why my father tell her to do it."

It was in front of the seal-oil lamps that Irrigoo and Oovi were instructed in the ways of their people, if not always in the reasons why. As the oblong ring of flames cast dancing shadows on walrus and reindeer walls of their skin houses, they listened to the elders talk about the ice, the animals, and "the men" who had lived *I-you-me-rooh-lak*, "long, long ago."

You know that little camp the other side of Tapphook? One of our people from there knew of the white men's coming long before they came here. Long, long ago, he made an igloo that looked like a two-masted schooner. He cut up a spotted sealskin, then toothed 'em up, toothed 'em up to make it soft, and formed the masts and made a leather flag. Our people had never seen such a thing before the white men come here.

When he hoist up that leather flag, he sang this song:

Eye-stow EE-eye-o
Oy-*kan*-a EE-a-low
Bowhead.

Another one, maybe when he lowered that flag:

AA-AA-coooy AA-AA-coy
An-kan-ning kan-ning new *kat*-zi kan-ning
Va-va-cat-tin tem-pa-kal-y
Va-cas va-cat-tin tem-pa-kal-y, ta-cooy coy.

Irrigoo sang it for me when we were alone. The melody rose and fell softly like a walk across the tundra. He finished with childlike laughter, and I asked him what the lyrics meant.

"I don't know," he said. "Maybe that man did. I don't know none of them. Must be Chinese." His shoulders jumped up and down before he stopped laughing to add, "That's a *true* story. Not a fairy tale."

Inside the skin houses where Irrigoo had heard such stories as a boy, the seal-oil lamps and crowded bodies made the air so warm that the Eskimos wore loincloths or nothing at all. There was a strong practicality to many Eskimo ways that most missionaries and teachers never accepted. In each home, for instance, families kept a urine tub whose collected contents were used as soap for tanning hides and for bathing, because uric acid

GAMBELL: THE VILLAGE

breaks down the animal fats that smeared clothes, skin, and hair. "Effective grease cutters" is how modern admen might have described urine, but to missionaries like Vene Gambell, after whom the village of Sevookak was renamed, the odors of both his namesake's homes and their inhabitants were "unspeakable." (With the advent of real soap, however, the urine tubs were relegated to the status of chamber pots.) "When I was your age I used to wash in urine," Irrigoo informed me. He paused to reflect. "I don't care for that way now," he added, a statement that set him and an assembly of grandchildren to fitful giggling.

Intent on civilizing the likes of young Irrigoo and Oovi, the missionaries instituted conventions that gave Gambell's people the form if not the substance of Christianity. At birth, Irrigoo and Oovi had one name apiece. But the missionaries named them Samuel and Lloyd and made their Eskimo names surnames, a practice that may have flattered the Natives, who liked giving and getting names, but caused endless confusion for the white men who came here. It was the missionaries, too, who decided how old Irrigoo and Oovi were. "They just picked a day, any day, and tell us, 'That's your birthday,' " Irrigoo said, laughing.

Although they had proper names and birthdays, young Irrigoo and Oovi hardly passed for the Hardy boys. Their hair was cut like a friar's—bald on the crown—and as boys, they wore sealskin pants, boots, and socks. Their parkas were made with reindeer skins or bird skins of auklets, cormorants, murres, puffins, and ducks. In the wintertime, they wore inner clothes also made from reindeer skins obtained from Siberian tribesmen, who had been the islanders' sole trading partners until the arrival of *Laluremka*, the white men.

For perhaps as long as Saint Lawrence was an island, an island with neither caribou nor reindeer, Siberians had supplied it with deerskins; for as long as a thousand years, Siberians had supplied small amounts of iron; and even before the islanders ever met Europeans, Siberians were trafficking in tobacco.

From Asia had also come waves of emigrants to coexist or conquer. Within the reach of oral history, Oovi's mother's clan, the Aymaaramkas, had come from Siberia, as had Lilly Apanga-look's forefathers. Well into the twentieth century, families were still arriving. With the Siberians of the Chukchi peninsula the islanders shared both an ancestry and a language that were foreign to Alaska's mainland Eskimos. Indeed, the people of Saint Lawrence had had little contact with the eastern continent until this century. By blood and economy, their ties were to Siberia. Even their wars, of which there was a long history, had been with Siberians. And in times of peace, they sailed their skin boats westward every spring, to trade, visit, and hold games after whale and walrus hunting were over.

"Nearly every year when I was young," said Irrigoo, "I went to Siberia. Good people. Hospitality people. You see that end of the Siberian mountains? On the other side of that place I went to wrestle. They never beat me. I beat them all." Laughing, he repeated the last line.

Looking westward many years later, Oovi could still see the Siberian mountains, silhouetted on clear spring sunsets by a brilliant crimson curtain. But Irrigoo had grown poor-sighted and both had grown old since last traveling there. Today Siberia is a world apart. Wrestling matches, trade, and travel ended during the last world war when the Soviets closed the borders, thereby culminating a hundred-year-long shift of the island's orientation from Asia to America. Though Saint Lawrence was an island in between, the economic and cultural bridge traveled only eastward now.

It was from the coast of those Siberian mountains that the European explorers had first come to Saint Lawrence. In search of the geographical relationship between Siberia and America, Vitus Bering sighted the island in a bank of fog and rain in the summer of 1728, on the feast of Saint Lawrence. How bitterly ironic, I thought on so many bone-chilling hunting trips with the Eskimos, that their island was named for a martyr the Romans had roasted over a slow-burning fire.

Although Bering observed "a few huts," his crew found no one ashore, perhaps because the Natives chose not to be seen. (Stories are told of people hiding in the mountains after sighting "a great angyaq with sails.") Bering's ship sailed onward in what proved an unsuccessful mission to find an eastern continent, and almost a century passed—during which other explorers like Cook sighted the island—before Europeans apparently made their first contact with the islanders. Even if they had not yet seen them, the islanders must have known about Laluremka already, from the Siberian traders who brought them such exotic goods as tobacco and metals that had come far from the west, from Russia. In an account of his voyage, Russian explorer Otto von Kotzebue described the encounter and the culture he found.

> We were met by a [skin boat], with ten islanders, who approached us without fear, calling aloud to us, and . . . holding fox-skins in the air, with which they eagerly beckoned us. . . . After some salutations . . . their first word was Tobacco!
>
> We observed several European utensils of iron and copper. Every islander is armed with a knife [two feet long] . . . adorned with large blue and white glass beads. . . .
>
> They do not appear ever to have seen any European, to judge by the amazement with which they beheld us. Nothing attracted their attention so much as my telescope; and when I showed them its properties, and they really saw quite distant objects close before their eyes, they were seized with the most extravagant joy.[2]

Dramatic though it may have been, there was little in Kotzebue's encounter to arouse European economic interest. Poor in commercially valuable furs, the island remained isolated until the middle of the nineteenth century, when another resource, the world's last unhunted stock of bowheads, was discovered by American whalemen amidst the ice-strewn waters of the Bering Strait.

Because the bowhead swam slowly, was easily pursued in open water, and tended to float after being killed, it made a ready catch for Yankee whalemen. They valued it for two anatomical features: its thick coat of blubber and the two rows of tall, fringed mouthplates—called baleen—that hang from its upper jaw. The blubber of one whale might fill a hundred barrels with lighting oil and the jawbone could yield fifteen hundred or more pounds of fiberglasslike baleen that was proving increasingly valuable as a raw material in the manufacture of carriage wheels and springs, upholstery, umbrellas, and especially women's undergarments. When the trend in women's fashions turned to tight waists and hourglass figures in the latter half of the nineteenth century, its use in corset stays and skirt hoops drove the price of baleen skyward, to the point where an average bowhead fetched over $10,000, enough to pay for the expense of a ship's entire whaling season. Excited by reports of large catches in the Bering Strait, a wave of whaling ships sailed northward after 1848, and for the next sixty years the waters of the western Arctic would sustain America's most profitable whaling industry.

Between 1848 and 1885, over three thousand voyages were made. Many of them brought the ships into regular contact with Irrigoo and Oovi's parents and grandparents. Sailing to the Arctic from Hawaii in springtime, the whaling ships worked their way through the ice pack north of the Aleutian Islands, following leads of open water that generally channeled them toward the western coast of Saint Lawrence or mainland Siberia, on the opposite shore. While waiting for an open passage to the Bering Strait, they hunted whales at the edge of the retreating ice front, and when the whales migrated farther into the ice—where ships couldn't follow until June or July—they spent their time hunting walrus and trading with the Natives for valuable baleen, walrus ivory, and fur clothing.

Whaling ships were greeted eagerly whenever they arrived. It was toward the schooners, anchored offshore or still under sail, that a flotilla of skin boats would stream, their Native paddlers anxious to trade for Winchester rifles, whaling guns, shotguns, fixed ammunition, primers, powder and shot, tobacco, pipes, hard bread, beads, matches, molasses, and whiskey. The firearms and matches were revolutionary. So was the whiskey, for the Natives had never distilled their own form of alcohol.

In recent years, we have come to view all past dealings with Native Americans as unfair, but it is interesting that Irrigoo remembered just how advantageous the trading sessions with whalemen had proved for his people. For the Eskimos' pragmatic adoption of white men's tools and goods made hunting, and life in general, easier and safer. Certainly the Eskimos must have thought as much, since they were the ones who initiated almost all the trading sessions with white men.

Along with the technological genius of Western civilization, however, came the effects of its commercial application. Thousands of whales were slaughtered, at first for both blubber and baleen. Then, after the market for whale oil fell, even the blubber was discarded and the headless carcass cut adrift once the whale's upper jawbone was hacked out with axes. That they were destroying tons of meat, organs, and blubber that would otherwise be used so resourcefully by Eskimo hunters did not seem to bother most Yankee whalemen.

With fewer and fewer whales to hunt at the edge of the ice pack in springtime, the waiting ships turned their attention to herds of lumbering walrus for their blubber and ivory tusks. From 1860 to 1880, ships' riflemen may have gunned down 200,000 walrus, a staggering number from a herd that harpoon-carrying Eskimos were becoming increasingly dependent upon for food in the wake of the whale herd's decimation.[3]

Destruction of the Eskimos' sea mammals was matched by another kind of turmoil that was engendered not by bread and guns, but by whiskey, disease, and a plague of bad ice. Eskimos "drank excessively from the first sip of liquor," writes historian Dorothy Jean Ray; they chose to use it as both a stimulant and a temporary escape from behavioral restrictions within Native society.[4] The results were often disastrous. Yet despite the refusal of many captains to traffic in it, large quantities were traded by the rest of the fleet.

The bouts of drunkenness always ended after the whale-men sailed away for the year and the supply of whiskey ran out. Disease and famine did not go away as readily, however, and they proved devastating. By 1880, they had decimated the island's population, according to that year's report of Alaska's first census-taker. Speaking of events in his own lifetime, Oovi said, "All winter we didn't get nothing, but whenever ships came in springtime, the men bring fever, flu, measles, other things." During the whaling era, "other things" included syphilis, which was spread by Yankee whalemen who exploited Eskimo attitudes toward sex and often used trade goods and money to induce Native husbands to lend them their wives.

The Eskimos never counted or recorded the deaths that might have dramatized events for later historians. It was white missionaries and anthropologists who compiled the statistics that documented for outsiders, far too late, what had happened. When an outbreak of flu hit Gambell in 1916, for instance, white men reported that it killed 10 percent of the population. But an outbreak of measles a generation earlier, when no white men were there to count, may have been far deadlier, to judge from a report of gold prospectors turned away from the village, who then traveled to Siberia to find half a village killed off by the same disease.

Worse than disease was famine. It followed in the wake of the whaling ships, with equal effect on both sides of the Bering and Chukchi seas. Twelve years before Irrigoo was born, famine had wiped out seven of the eight villages on Saint Lawrence Island in what became known as the Great Starvation.

As children, Oovi and Irrigoo knew occasional days of hunger, times when summer tents made of walrus skin were boiled for food. Hunger came with extraordinarily high and persistent winds from the north or the south, winds that either blocked the hunting grounds with ice or pushed them too far out to sea. When the seas were open and whipped with wind, the hunters could not launch their boats. When the ice was piled against the shore, they could not reach the main ice pack. And being unable to find or reach sea mammals or even fish, most of the islanders starved to death in the two winters between 1878 and the spring of 1880, a time when bad winds seemed unrelenting.

Some survivors and later villagers said the famine was caused by no more than bad winds and ice. If they were right, then weather conditions must have been unprecedented that year, for the island has no evidence of earlier famines like this one. To the contrary, earlier islanders enjoyed a luxuriant supply of fresh meat, to judge from rubbish heaps piled nearly thirty feet high with walrus and whale bones at some old village sites. A famine that could kill off two-thirds of the population seems such an aberration as to suggest that more than just bad weather was to blame. Indeed, the evidence points in other directions as well.

In the late summer and fall of 1878, Yankee ships traded barrels and barrels of whiskey along the coast of Saint Lawrence. According to some Eskimos who talked with white men who came to investigate afterward, islanders drank to the point of oblivion. They gave no thought to hunting, and by the time they recovered, it was too late: bad winds were upon them, and in their frenzy for whiskey, many Eskimos had traded away the very nets with which they might have caught enough seals to tide them over until hunting conditions improved.

Widespread drunkenness in the fall undoubtedly aggravated the disaster that came in the winter. But afterward, many white men sensationalized its role and made it the only cause, which it was not. Crusading missionaries, for example, saw the disaster as an object lesson in the evils of liquor, and at least one popular writer described it as an example of how Eskimos "were cheated and misused and debauched with whiskey."

Even whaling captains found in the disaster a confirmation of their own prejudice. Shrugging off responsibility they or other captains bore for trading the whiskey, some of them blamed the disaster on Eskimos' improvidence. One captain criticized that improvidence as reaching "the point of often failing, through . . . sheer laziness, to provide sufficient food for their winter consumption." But the islanders' drunkenness or alleged improvidence hardly absolved commercial whalers of depopulating the herds that served as their source of food. Had the industry not killed so many whales and walrus, the hungry Eskimos might have found more food during the Great Starvation. Instead, the extraordinary years of bad ice coincided with the end of a twenty-year-long slaughter of walrus and thirty years of whaling.

Plagued by bad ice, short on food, and weakened by drunkenness, the islanders must have been even more susceptible to the outbreak of diseases they apparently contracted from white men that same year of 1878 (according to several ships' logs). But in the end, establishing the relative importance of this and all other possible causes is no more than conjecture among white men. The only clear thing about the sequence of events leading up to the famine is its result. At Kialegak, on the island's southeast cape, there were no survivors to tell what happened: just skeletons that still lie about like parts of a rock garden in the grass that they and countless other bones have kept green on an otherwise drab and dun-colored tundra. At Kookoolik, 250 skeletons were found where the villagers had been laid, first on the burial grounds, then atop rubbish heaps, then outside ningloos as the survivors weakened, inside the sod houses where they were piled like logs, and finally, under furs on the sleeping platforms where death overtook those who had attended the other victims.

For food the people of Kookoolik had boiled not only the skin roofs of their houses but skin dog harnesses and skin rope as well. There were no dogs left, so the only way to get food was to walk across the mountains to Gambell and pull the meat back on a little sled. After a while the visitors stopped coming. Returning home from the coast near Kookoolik, two Gambell hunters found out why. Irrigoo explained: "The people of Kookoolik all lay down dead."

Perhaps accelerated by the sharing of meat with Kookoolik, famine overtook Gambell as well. A man came from a village in the east with his dogs, only to find that people were hungry here, too. They ate his dogs. Giant breakers and gales made hunting impossible, and the ice did not come until late in the winter.

When animals were killed, the hunters were too weak to carry full loads of meat back home. Some died from exposure and exhaustion, and in the desperate attempt to get food, others fell through thin ice and froze to death while retrieving walrus. Still more providers were swept away.

In the village, they too boiled skin roofs and "gut" raincoats made of dried walrus and seal intestines. "I heard of one woman who fed her husband with her breasts when there was no more food," Irrigoo recalled. Even after enough walruses were caught and butchered to sustain life, people still died . . . from gorging themselves on food their shrunken stomachs could not assimilate.

Gradually, animals appeared in greater abundance on safer ice, closer to shore, where they were killed by crews made up of women and boys, for so many men had died. And in the spring, the famine ended when a large bowhead whale was harpooned and brought to shore with its tons of meat, skin, and blubber. This single event may best exemplify what Aghvook meant to the Eskimos.

Only three hundred islanders were left when Irrigoo was born in 1890; there had been as many as twenty-five hundred when the white men came a half-century earlier. Kookoolik and Kiagelak were desolated; the southwest cape would soon be abandoned; and Seevookak, later to be renamed Gambell, was the only major settlement that remained. Neither Irrigoo's family nor Oovi's were true Seevookakmet, "people of Seevookak." Irrigoo's father was from Nungoopugahk, to the east of the mountain; and Oovi's father was from Puwughileq, near the island's southwest cape. Like almost all the famine's survivors, they had come to Seevookak.

Growing up there, Irrigoo and Oovi saw the last of the whaling fleet. The diligence with which it pursued the whale had led the industry to the historical fate of all commercial whalers. Out of a population that once may have numbered thirty-thousand bowheads, probably no more than three-thousand remained.[5] Most ships could not catch enough to make a profit. Indeed, the scarcity of whales drove the price of baleen so high that a cheap substitute—steel spring—was developed and the market for whales collapsed altogether. Foiled by their own proficiency and overzealous hunting, the whalers abandoned the Arctic by 1914, leaving behind them a new technology for killing that might enable the Eskimos to finish off the slaughter the Yankees had begun.

From the sailing ships' first arrival it was probably inevitable that Eskimo culture would be transformed, but the offshore commercial whalemen didn't cause that transformation. Although they traded with the islanders aboard ship, they seldom went ashore, and stayed only when shipwrecked. When the whalemen left for good, the islanders were still engaged in an ancient way of life. Even though Eskimos had adopted guns, the pattern of hunting remained the same, and their religious rituals endured for a long time after.

What cut far deeper than the whaling industry ever could were Western institutions that came ashore to stay. Christianity and white men's education, trading posts, and the economic system they represented changed values, customs, and people's relationship to the world around them. Among the villagers of Gambell, Irrigoo was the only one left who had been alive when the second era began. It started with the ringing of a church mission's school bell, first rung by V. C. Gambell, that brought the whole village running.

I came to Gambell eighty-three years later, expecting to find a village that had last existed in Irrigoo's youth. Of that village, however, there remained little more than Samuel Irrigoo, Lloyd Oovi, and the hunt for whales. And like others who came here, I wondered if Aghvook too would die, like the two old men who looked out eagerly for whales and boats on the ocean where their people had hunted for as long as there had been Eskimos.

9. Nanook II and the Incredible Hulk

There were moments on and around Saint Lawrence Island when life was simple. These were the moments when I soared with joy for the life I had been missing. Moments that I found stalking seals with Silook or catching fish with Sook. Moments spent sitting with Oovi and Irrigoo, or alone atop the pinnacled cliffs of Seevookak. I looked out onto a vast ocean of ice with a gaze that transcended time and transported me back to I-you-me-roh-lak, the starting point of the heroic tales the old storytellers related about those who had come before. Moments of communion, sharing food from platters filled with the hunters' kill.

Pulling clam meat from the stomach of a walrus that had been alive just minutes before, I relished their sweet taste, but even more than the taste I relished the smiling approval of those who had shown me how. "Hey, Slokok," grinned Johnny. "You like them pretty good." One day, while on their way home from an unsuccessful hunt for whales, the hunters had turned their attention to walrus. Johnny had shot this one in open water, then harpooned it as it lunged up with its tusks, and now, before a captive audience of forty hunters standing atop a bloodstained ice floe, he launched into the walking-walrus routine for which he'd named me. Turning my way, his father, Roger, who had had a book published about the islanders, announced to everyone's delight: "My next book will be named 'The Clam That Was Eaten Twice,' " These were moments when the hunters' hearts sang out like their ancestors' had before them:

> This land of ours
> has become habitable
> because we came here
> and learned how to hunt.[6]

... And how to share.

But there were also moments of great complexity. Moments increasing in number and degree that taxed and challenged and troubled the villagers and made the village seem weary not with age but with anxiety.

"We must become modernized," Silook would say as we sat at the kitchen table drinking instant coffee and eating pilot bread and jam. I wondered why, and I had lots of time to wonder, because outside the wind howled and floe ice choked our path to the hunting grounds. So we sat beside a window that looked out onto a snowdrift obscuring everything but the profile of Seevookak.

I asked why, as many other white men had. Why must they become modernized? We didn't want them to change, at least not beyond the point where we could still consider them Native. Whether we came as tourists, anthropologists, adventurers, liberals, or romantics, we had the same vested interest: we all grieved that they were becoming like us. In Native culture we found or invested meaning and mystery that seemd so lacking in our own.

But what did it mean to be Eskimo? We had a static idea of a culture frozen in time. Since the turn of the century we'd been calling them the last of the few, a dying race, a vanishing people. Yet if anything, their numbers were increasing. How could a dying race be multiplying?

Of course, most of us had an ideal type of Eskimo in mind: Nanook of the North.

A few robes of polar bear and a caribou skin, a lamp and a
pot made of stone. Their few primitive tools and hunting
aids. These are all they have and all they need . . .[7]

As the screen credits of this film from 1922 told us, "Nanook of
the North was not staged—it was lived." There was no question
of that. There was only a question of how long ago Nanook had
ceased to reflect the life of Eskimos.

From legend mixed with dusty chronicles we had an idea
of what an Eskimo should be like, and we sought to define him in
terms of our expectations. We invented words to describe his
way of life, or the life we imagined, because for years, Natives
had been as remote as any people could be from the nation's
focus. They weren't just living on the edge of society; they were
living on the edge of the edge. *Subsistence* conjured up images of
a self-sufficient way of life with little need for money. *Subsistence*
was our own word and it formed expectations, then contradictions that were of our own making. We wanted Eskimos to follow
a type, but, to those who came looking for Nanook II, today's
villagers were disappointingly sophisticated. Nanook didn't wear
Eddie Bauer down jackets. He didn't eat TV dinners and watch
the *Six-Million-Dollar Man*. He didn't heat his home with oil and
light it with electricity, and when it came to bills, he didn't have
any. But Son of Nanook did.

Jim Brooks lived in the outside world now, but he had
known the Eskimos well. Back in the late 1940s he lived among
them up in Wales, a village along the Bering Strait, while
working for the Weather Bureau. A crackerjack Bush pilot, he
had risked his own life to save others' by flying missions of mercy
through Arctic gales. The Eskimos were his friends, and long
after he had gone they remembered him as a hero.

Jim Brooks was a well-known man in Alaska. He had gone
on to become Commissioner of Fish and Game, and now he was
the regional head of fisheries management for the National
Marine Fisheries Service. That meant he was presiding over the
enforcement of bowhead whaling quotas. On my way back to
southeast Alaska one year, I stopped in Juneau to see him.

He was a fine man with a dignity of bearing suggestive of
the old Natives I had met. Though he had lived through great
adventure, he spoke of it mildly, without exaggeration. But as we
conversed, it became clear he was absorbed in memories. Look-

ing out the window, he reminisced about his days in the Arctic. When he returned to me and to the present, he asked if the villagers still wore duck-skin parkas and gut coats.

Suddenly, it dawned on me that his idea of Native life was still fixed in the 1950s. The duck-skin parkas and gut coats were museum pieces now. Jim Brooks was in charge of regulating a people who dressed and often acted far differently than he remembered. That spring he had advised his enforcement agents to raise the Stars and Stripes at their ice camp because three decades earlier, he remembered, Eskimos had always rallied round the flag. He seemed not to know about the depth of resentment and hostility among Eskimos nowadays, many of whom would just as readily burn an American flag.

Changes had come, big changes, and the disappearance of gut coats and duck-skin parkas was only a small symptom. While most of the outside world wasn't looking, Eskimos had been incorporating Western goods into their lives at an accelerating pace. It should have surprised no one, because the process was historical, often pragmatic, and seemingly inevitable.

At the turn of the century, the symbol of material change had been the Eskimos' adoption of guns. In the 1960s, it was snowmobiles. Until the late 1950s, dogs and boats were the Eskimos' only mode of travel. Dogs took the Natives to camps and to hunting grounds on the tundra, and on Saint Lawrence Island, dogs even went along in the skin boats after pulling them out over the ice to the edge of open water. "I could go anyplace with my dogs," Oovi used to say. "Nothing bothered them." But dogs were good for more than power. When coming upon rough ice, for instance, sled drivers let the lead dogs take over because they knew the best way through; and in a storm, they could bring the hunters home. Dogs smelled danger. They smelled other animals, too. And because they meant good hunting, a man back then might measure his wealth in good dogs, just as Nanook of the North had. His expenses, still considerable, were the time and effort it took to hunt for and feed them meat, fish, blubber, and "dog soup." Only the corn and oats that went into making dog soup cost him money, or an equivalent of that in trade with white men. But a man wasn't likely to evaluate the merits of dog travel when there were no alternatives, and until the 1950s there weren't any.

"It was more exciting going out to camp with the dogs,"

my captain in Barrow recalled one day. Ralph and his father once traveled the tundra with fifteen dogs, an impressive number. At the time he bought his first snowgo he owned seven Greenland huskies, whom he still bragged about twenty years later. But sentimentality for dogs became a luxury of the future when that ten-horsepower Mustang came along.

"I could sit on it and just go," Ralph smiled. "I didn't have to harness the dogs. I didn't have to feed them—that was a lot of work."

Of course, snowgoes had to be fed too and they couldn't eat blubber: they burned gas, which required money. They couldn't smell their way home through a storm either, and they also broke down. When a dog got sick, you could run your sled on the other six, but when a snowgo broke down you were in trouble. The winter before I arrived in Gambell, two people froze to death after their machines failed outside the village. Searchers found one of them, who had been out trapping, with his foxes still strapped to his back. His snowgo's carburetor had jammed.

But death on the trail wasn't new; it was just more complicated now. Eskimos knew most of the disadvantages, and lament as we might about the good old days, they knew the advantages of today better than any of us. Snowgoes traveled farther faster, which meant they could hunt over wider distances. And as soon as Eskimos found the money to buy them, they chose snowgoes in a big way. "I told someone to take my gun and take the dogs to the dump and shoot them," Ralph said. "I didn't need them anymore. I had my Mustang." Horsepower had replaced dog power.

In 1960, Gambell's dogs outnumbered its people two to one. By the late 1970s, there wasn't a dog team to be found anymore, except on the mainland, where white men and a handful of Eskimos raised them for racing at sporting events like the Iditarod and the Kuskokwin 300. Silook and Sook beamed with joy after buying their first family snowgo the spring I arrived. They too were traveling farther faster, and they weren't doing it by looking backward.

Why must Eskimos become modernized? "Because we've come too far to turn back now," Silook answered, which was true, of course. "We dig up the tools of our ancestors and we don't know how to use them." But to ascribe the change to sheer

GAMBELL: THE VILLAGE

necessity conveys the impression of a people bidding reluctant farewell to paradise, when in fact they never wanted to stay there. The first snowgoes were followed by bigger and better snowgoes with electric starters and greater horsepower. Then came all-terrain-vehicles ("ATVs," the Eskimos called them), which traveled over lakes and tundra in any season, and all-terrain-cycles (Honda "ATCs"). There were aluminum boats, with bigger motors now, to travel farther faster than the angyaqs ever could in late spring when the walrus came north. And there was television, too.

When first beamed into the Bush in the mid-seventies, it had been an instant hit, a dazzling fantasy for people who were cooped up, weathered in, contracting cabin fever by springtime. I've written of beautiful moments of simplicity, but I've not yet written of the long bouts of crushing boredom while we waited for whales to come and for the ice to open. I grew tired of sleep and I had to force myself, against all inclination, to visit or talk. I was a prisoner of the Arctic, squirming on the verge of Arctic hysteria, a sudden emotional frenzy that sometimes seized and convulsed old-time Eskimos the way it might a bunch of Holy Rollers. For me and for many of the villagers, television and basketball were a welcome diversion from boredom.

Though TV wasn't communal like dancing or visiting the men's gathering houses (closed by early missionaries), it was absorbing recreation in villages that had more leisure time than ever before. Such traditions as storytelling and dancing were no longer enough. People who traveled to the mainland, listened to Western music, paged through magazines, and went to white men's schools wanted more entertainment. Television filled the bill as a wonder-filled escape and a look Outside. So they sat together before it, amused, absorbed, and with undivided attention. It didn't matter that there was only one channel to watch. Oftentimes, it didn't even matter that the volume was turned down, for nuances of plot or dialogue might be lost on those who couldn't understand English or had never left the Arctic. The picture was the thing.

Eskimos had plugged into the global village, and I didn't need a survey to see how popular or pervasive the new medium was. Whether in Gambell, Nome, or Barrow, little kids would accost me with pointed fingers and say, "You're David Banner."

Not only did they think I looked like actor Bill Bixby, who plays the role of David Banner in *The Incredible Hulk*, they actually thought I *was* David Banner, because to them and other villagers there was a thin, sometimes nonexistent line between TV fantasy and truth.

There were valuable programs to be found on television, such as courses in arithmetic and English. TV had a tremendous potential for helping Natives make a less troublesome transition to the world they were entering. It could teach them about managing money, making budgets, getting loans, and becoming commercial fishermen, for example. Through satellite communications, they were already being linked into live public hearings held hundreds of miles away for an audience that was now statewide; in some places, villagers could even testify and ask questions as if they were in the same room as the hearing in Juneau. State and national news, statewide hearings, extension courses, and prime time: television made today's Eskimos more aware than any Eskimos had ever been before of the mainland world around which they now revolved. They were quick to see its advantages.

Standing on the crest of Gambell's western shore in the early-morning hours, a small group of intent yet expressionless hunters looked outward to determine if the wind would die and the ice open up. Occasionally they would point as if tracing a path through the maze. White men kept respectfully silent during these sessions as if we were among monks in a cathedral, an impression that was enhanced by the big sky, the silent expanse of sea and ice, and the huddled men quietly speaking a mysterious language of ice like ecclesiastics praying in Latin.

After a while, Silook's uncle Roger spoke in English for the benefit of the white men beside him. "There is going to be a storm today," he announced. We wondered how he knew this. Was it a shift of wind or a change in the sea? What marvelous things had he learned as a hunter that made his prediction so self-assured? One of us asked him for an explanation. Roger replied: "I saw the satellite weather map on the television last night."

Along with its practical advantages and possibilities, however, came grave liabilities that sometimes made me think of television as a disease to which Eskimos had no immunity. Kids watched too much of it, which meant that they were spending less time learning how to hunt. Oovi and other older villagers blamed it for a breakdown in authority, complaining that TV was destroying courtesy and respect for elders, two virtues that parents once instilled in young people. Television seemed even to have touched off a craze of handguns, which some young hunters wore strapped to their sides like TV cops and cowboys. The heroes of prime time hardly fit into traditional role models. Even worse, perhaps, was the sense of impoverishment that TV created when villagers discovered what white men had and they did not. In the village, almost all television was tantamount to a commercial. Eskimos' reactions to TV were dramatic, sometimes even alarming, as when an old woman said that after watching it, "We realize just how cruel the white men really are." For her and for who knows how many others, there was no difference between *Hawaii Five-O* and the NBC *Nightly News.*

I remember Solomon, a victorious hunter of bowheads, for being a rascal of a businessman, but I remember him too for a moment of tender innocence that made him seem so vulnerable. He was watching an episode of *Star Trek* on his big color console one day, when suddenly his face clouded over with concern. There before his eyes a whole planet was being eaten up by some vile enemy of the starship *Enterprise.* Alarmed and confused, Solomon turned, his finger pointing to the picture, and asked, "Real?"

"No, Solomon, it's just a story," we white men assured him. And beaming back at us with a smile of relief, a smile that showed all of two teeth positioned kitty-corner to each other, Solomon replied, "Ah. I like stories," and turned back intently to the picture.

Six months after TV was beamed into the Bush, a state survey of several villages found that the Eskimos' favorite shows were *The Six-Million-Dollar Man, Charlie's Angels,* and *Hawaii Five-O.* The survey caused a lot of white people to express their disapproval of television in Native villages. I felt more ambivalent. What seemed to be worrying us white people was that Eskimos were watching the same junk we were. Blood, sex, and guts apparently had universal appeal; and according to the survey, Eskimos wanted more. (The most asked-for programs were *Policewoman, SWAT,* and *Starsky and Hutch.*) I wondered whether we would have felt better if the villagers had been watching *Masterpiece Theater* instead. Though I shared other white people's concern about the harmful effects of television, I wasn't going to advocate pulling the plug on the transmitter. In the name of protecting Eskimos, white people could junk the communications dish in the village, but it was too late to isolate traditional culture. And it seemed wrong to deny the villagers the opportunity to have what white people had and they wanted.

We in the West live in a world that doesn't have islands anymore, even though some of us would have liked to build moats around places like Saint Lawrence. Reporters, writers, and others who came here wanted Irrigoo and Oovi to be wistful, because they embodied our romantic vision of a Native past. We sought the elders out to tell us that changes made life less Native and hence inferior to what it used to be. We often heard only what we wanted to, but to the surprise of those who listened, the elders didn't quite fulfill our expectations.

Oh, there were the usual reminiscences of people looking back: that life and men had been tougher in the old days. "I walked all the way around the island when I was a boy," Irrigoo boasted. "But now, no one walks anywhere: they take a Honda to go next door." He cackled scornfully. Oovi laughed more gently. He had kept a team of dogs until the mid-1970s, using them to go trapping until he quit altogether. "I could go anywhere." That laughing Buddha smile appeared. "I always passed snow machines with worn-out parts." Oovi thought that was awfully funny, but neither he nor Irrigoo had any illusions about life without Western machines and medicine.

Oovi had lost three children to TB and other illnesses in an era when the island was too remote to allow villagers to get help in distant hospitals. "White doctors help us now," Oovi said, and if one needed evidence, there were the old men's glasses, the local health clinic, and the patients headed for the Native hospital in Anchorage.

Though they laughed at machines breaking down, Oovi and Irrigoo were the first to recognize their advantages. They were the ones, after all, who built lumber houses, switched to kerosene lamps, bought oil-burning stoves, and mounted motors to their skin boats, but these were things that seemed to escape the notice of white men who came to them today wanting them to grow wistful about old ways. Of course, Eskimos never saw the adoption of Western objects as philosophically inconsistent with being Native. Obsessed as we were with materialism, we often equated who they were with what they owned, as if the simple adoption of our machines and goods turned them into half-breeds or, worse yet, white men. The elders were more able than we, however, to separate their lives from their objects.

In Barrow, I once asked a ninety-year-old man to name the biggest change he had seen in his lifetime. He lived in a home heated by natural gas, he had a pacemaker in his chest, and a fast-food truck was delivering hamburgers and french fries next door. He answered without hesitation. He said it was warmer now: the ice was thinner than when he was a boy.

10. Ivory Talks and Nobody Walks

Leonard Apangalook saw himself as a modern man, and it was in a modern role of making money that he would have been most recognizable to white men. If you wanted to buy a new outboard engine in Gambell, Leonard was the man to see. He was the manager of the Native store, a position he had held for ten years, which meant two things: one, he was one of the few villagers with steady employment; and, two, he sold a lot of engines. In fact, he had sold so many Evinrudes in 1976 that he won a trip to Hawaii for being a top Alaskan dealer.

He was a shy man, soft-spoken and boyish-looking, with a gentle self-conscious smile that came to his face as he told about the fun he had on that trip. With a sense of playfulness or perhaps just irony that he, an Eskimo, had won a trip to Hawaii along with a group of engine dealers from middle America, Leonard arrived in Waikiki with his wife and a polished two-foot-long walrus bone. It was a cylindrical, slightly curved, and graceful bone, called an *oosik*. Eskimos once used oosiks as tools, but nowadays they sold them to white tourists as ornaments. In fact, an oosik is the supporting bone for the penis of a male walrus.

But not many Evinrude dealers from Des Moines know that, so Leonard had a lot of fun. Eskimos do not think oosiks pornographic, just a piece of real life and a source of good-natured joking with white men, especially those who want to talk about igloos or rub noses. In Waikiki, Leonard passed it to admiring salesmen and their wives, letting them fondle the thing and wonder where it came from, for it was really quite beautiful. When they found out what it was, they could not get rid of it fast enough.

Leonard's trip seemed incongruous with life in this Artic village. But it wasn't his only travel outside. Buying trips regularly took him to cities like Portland and Seattle, where he would have passed for any other businessman from Alaska. Although such travels are invisible to white men who come here looking at outboards and snowgoes, they speak more poignantly than objects about the changing ways of life.

Leonard saw himself as a modern man, and although other villagers thought of themselves in the same way, he was one of the few who could have lived in mainstream America, I think, had he wanted to. Being modern, according to Leonard's way of thinking, was not incompatible with living in Gambell or being a hunter. After all, it was because of his modern role that he was able to pay $5,000 for the new aluminum skiff and outboard Evinrude that were essential for hunting.

His brothers Mike and Silook were more representative of Gambell's villagers. Neither had full-time jobs, and Mike, the more typical, had no job whatsoever. He had gone to technical training school in south-central Alaska to learn auto repair but came back to look after his mother, Lilly, when his father got sick and was sent to the hospital in Anchorage. John's condition worsened and he died later the same year, leaving Lilly to the care of his children. By choice of fate and family obligation, Mike, the only unmarried child, stayed on the island to live with his mother. Half trained for a career nonexistent in a village without roads or cars, Mike returned to hunting just as Silook had when he came back. He and Silook weren't nearly as prosperous or as well traveled as Leonard, but all three of them resembled white men in at least one way: they needed more and more money.

From the time Eskimo hunters first acquired guns, they had become dependent upon white men. Their ability to buy ammunition, new guns to replace the old ones, and whatever else they desired from white men would always be limited by the medium of exchange and the value white men placed on what Natives could offer. For the first few decades of contact with American whalemen, for example, the Eskimos' resources had had little commercial value, so the Natives owned few guns. After the demand for baleen soared, however, they acquired guns and whatever else they desired by trading baleen, skin clothes, and their own labor. Then, when outside markets lost interest, the Natives' purchasing power shriveled up again; they could afford little until white men returned after World War I, this time in eager pursuit of fox furs.

It must have amazed Eskimos that the outside world would desire the skins of an animal they had always disdained as inferior, hence worthless. Yet while it lasted, America's passion for fox furs made affluent men out of young Irrigoo and Oovi. Richer by far than any of their ancestors had ever been, they were able to purchase wooden boats, motors, guns—and ammunition and fuel, necessities that had been created by the first set of purchases.

The medium of exchange with white men had changed since the whaling era, however. Unlike earlier Eskimos, Irrigoo and Oovi made transactions in cash, not barter. In the Roaring Twenties, Oovi and his three brothers had made $3,000 to $4,000 a year selling blue and white fox pelts. "Lots of money," Irrigoo would say now, resting his hands atop a cane while convulsing with loud, self-satisfied laughter.

They had been wealthy men all right, but the money they got from selling skins went right back to the traders or to the store for an equivalent value in supplies brought by the ships. A wooden Yankee whaling boat, the painted numbers intact on its bow, still sat in front of Irrigoo's house a half-century after he bought it, along with an old brass whaling gun, "from Captain Pedersen." He remembered the details well. The money he paid was the money Pedersen paid him for his fox skins. Though transactions were in cash, money was merely an accounting system for old-fashioned barter. It stayed in Eskimo hands only briefly, then was gone again.

With the money they got, Eskimos could buy much more than what they needed for better hunting. Irrigoo and Oovi bought kitchen ranges, pots and pans, and lumber to build houses like white men's, which one visitor called "the height of a man's ambitions." Accumulating money made no sense, for wealth lay in spending and sharing it: they didn't have a bank and the very idea was alien to them. Instead, they sometimes bought shiny amusements, trinkets, and other novelties that would soon break or play themselves out like the cheap toys they were.

As fox faded from fashion and the Depression hit, the first wave of cash spent itself on the shores of Gambell. Unable even to buy gasoline for their outboards, the once affluent hunters were forced to return to a more traditional hunting-and-barter economy until Laluremka came again.

The second coming of cash was gradual, quiet, and final. Though it exploded into white men's awareness in the late 1970s, it had established itself as the dominant medium of exchange long before that. In Gambell and the rest of Arctic Alaska, it started when the government came to defend the frontier and expand social programs toward Natives. After the Japanese bombed and invaded the Aleutian Islands, for instance, the Army built an airstrip on Gambell's gravel shore and put a garrison atop Seevookak for a few years. During the war, Eskimos were inducted into the Army, trained, and sent away from their villages to the mainland, where they lived for the first time in the society of white men.

When the war was over, Native GIs returned from the new world with visions, stories, and shopping lists of what they wanted. In some instances, their villages were on the verge of economic development. Near Barrow, for example, the federal government had initiated a major effort to explore for oil and other minerals, and a few years later, the Defense Department began building a chain of radar stations from northwest Alaska to Greenland as a Distant Early Warning (DEW) Line to guard against Soviet bombers from across the Arctic Ocean.

The result of these and other federal projects was to create a demand for a third Eskimo resource: their labor. Some Eskimos had worked before for white men, but they had generally been paid in trade goods. Now, those with jobs worked for wages. Villages such as Barrow, bigger and closer to government and the development action, had many more jobs than Gambell. But gradually, like snow blowing through the cracks of wooden houses, money infiltrated even the remote economy of Gambell.

Before the second wave of cash, when trading ships still came, getting white men's things had been a straightforward proposition. It was much more complicated now, especially for those who didn't have jobs, because a man couldn't pay Sears Roebuck a fox pelt for a new gun. Mail-order companies and even the local Native store wanted cash. So, as Eskimos became more engaged in the network of America's economy, the old Native economy had to give way. Barter had become totally impractical. As a man in Barrow once asked so bitterly: "How do you pay your light bill with a dead seal?"

Money had become as vital as runners on a snowgo: transactions with white men didn't move without it. But where did the villagers of Gambell get their money? As much as they might share the wages of those who worked, jobs couldn't account for the volume of spending. Only three or four dozen people were employed, almost all in public-service jobs, such as school aides. Nor could transfer payments from state and federal government explain such conspicuous consumption, although various programs that pumped in welfare and unemployment checks, food stamps, and other subsidies were turning Gambell into a welfare ward of the white men. Most welfare programs supplemented rather than substituted for the villagers' income. The government could provide the money to build a man a better house than the shack he lived in, but bigger modern homes needed more furniture, more electricity, more heat, and monthly purchase payments to buy them from the government. So where did the money come from?

"Maybe you want to buy some ivory?" The question was posed over and over again to white men who came here, every white man, and it didn't matter whether we were on the beach or inside drinking tea. It didn't matter whether we were enforcement agents or allies, whether they liked us or not. If we wanted to buy, they often found us before we found them, for whenever white men arrived in Gambell they were presumed to be customers. After exchanging a few courtesies, perhaps, the smiling merchants, who varied in age from twelve to sixty-five, would unwrap, unpocket, or unveil an item of ivory or sometimes an array of items, then politely ask, "Maybe you want to buy?"

Over time I held in my hands a menagerie of animals, in every imaginable pose and a wide range of sizes: bowheads and belugas; polar bears standing on twos, walking on fours, copulating, defecating, or digesting dead seals. The carvings came in either milky white "new" ivory or in earth-tone, chocolate-colored "old" ivory that had been dug up out of gravel and water. There were bracelets, cribbage boards, pendants, chess sets, letter openers, and hash pipes; things that surely didn't repose in the underground ruins of ancient ancestors but were created for their commercial possibilities.

Carved, dug up from antiquity, or cut out of freshly killed walrus, ivory meant money. Lots of money. Indeed, if walrus was the staff of life, its tusks were the stuff of which Gambell made a living. Like their ancestors, Silook and the other villagers hunted walrus for food, for hides to make their families' angyaqs, and for the animals' two- to three-foot-long tusks. Only the end toward which they put the ivory would have been foreign to their ancestors, who used it to make such things as harpoon heads, sled runners, and tools. Nowadays, ivory was a commodity, and carving it was a cottage industry geared to white men who wanted folk art.

Ivory dust dropped to village floors in a flurry of snowlike powder as village men and boys carved for money to pay for life's essentials. Whenever he was feeling the pressure, Silook sat down beside his workbench and carefully sorted through a small box full of ivory fragments and leftovers that he saved, piece by piece (ivory wasted was money lost). Like other Eskimos, he had a marvelous ability to envision and to bring out objects that conformed to the limitations of a fragment's shape and size; an oddly curved remnant, for instance, would become the curl of a reclining seal. With a coping saw, he would cut the piece into the rough form of what he wanted. Then he would use a small power tool that looked like a dentist's drill, rounding and shaping the ivory to bring out the flippers and tail. Next he colored the eyes black and scored its body with tiny scratches that he'd rub with cigarette ashes and ink to simulate spots and color patterns. His seals were infused with a spirit of being.

The villagers' ancestors had carved ivory for as long as they had hunted walrus, and looking among artifacts unearthed from the gravel, one could see how magnificently they had blended form with function. Ancient harpoon heads, for instance, were both tools and art simultaneously. Some of today's work was similarly exquisite and expressive, for among the carvers there were inspired artists, men such as Sook's father, Holden, who made fabulous bracelets. But much of the carving was executed poorly because the carvers were either unskilled or, more often, impatient to make money. Eskimos had long ago stopped using ivory to make tools of subsistence, and to many villagers, the value of carving had become extrinsic only. One man, who prospered by his art and prided himself as an artist, called such villagers "money carvers," which was true enough. Yet disdain for commercial art is a judgment best reserved to people who suffer cold and hunger for artistic integrity. When I asked a man with a wife and five children, none of whom had jobs, about the meaning of his work, he seemed amazed by my simple-mindedness. There was nothing abstract in his conception. The meaning, he said, was that without it, there'd be "no more eating, no more sugar, no more milk, no more heat" until the next welfare check arrived. Maybe, he suggested, I wanted to buy some ivory.

The market for the villagers' carvings, whether workman-like or pedestrian, had never been better. It took off in the early 1970s, with the influx of oil workers to the Arctic, and was sustained by tourist shops and galleries in Anchorage, Fairbanks, and Seattle. Silook sold his seals for $100 apiece, while a cribbage-board maker could get $500 for a nicely done, tusk-long game board. Irrigoo's grandson "Crunch" wanted $4,500 for a massive walrus skull and its two attached tusks that were scrimshawed with animal figures. Who the hell was he going to sell it to, I asked? A rich doctor, he said without a moment's hesitation.

There was money to be made, all right. One villager said that he could make $250 a day from carving, and a State Fish-and-Game biologist figured that a carver could earn $1,500 in a week while his supply of ivory lasted. But most villagers made money only as long as ivory buyers came. These were the new traders of the Arctic: they came in small planes instead of ships and with cash instead of trade goods.

Some traders were honest and fair, while others resembled the old-time pirates and traded whiskey and drugs, for which Gambell's demand always seemed to outrun its supply. Complain though villagers might about the traders' cheating or low prices, Gambell received all of them enthusiastically. Traders, after all, were the alchemists, the ones who could liquidize all that ivory.

It was amazing how quickly news would pass through town that traders were coming. Eskimos may not be the most industrious people in the world, but hearing that message immediately galvanized them into action. Suddenly they headed to their workbenches; all night long they stayed up carving, in anticipation of a plane arriving the next morning. Money was coming, like the cavalry, to an outpost that seemed on the brink of financial collapse every time it arrived. I was there one day when a trader's plane flew in. It took off with a load of carvings a few hours later after depositing $17,000 into the villagers' hands. It was a good thing traders came twice a month now, the carvers said. Ivory wasn't any good for food, heat, or running motors. It was only good for making money.

After the plane left, there would be a run on the store. Expenses would eat up the money almost as quickly as it had come. Groceries and gas cost three times more than they did in Seattle, stove oil cost more than twice as much, and the yearly cost of electricity and heating in one of the new homes was more than $3,000. Even Eskimos who made lots of money—and at least some of them did—felt pressed to make more, because now more than ever before, they were aware of what money could buy.

Toward that end nearly every woman and man was involved in the pursuit of ivory. While men hunted and carved, the women dug in summer's thaw for hundred- and thousand-year-old artifacts of their ancestors. With a shovel and pickax, they worked their way down into the four mounds of old village sites that lay to the east of present-day Gambell, closer to Mount Seevookak and the origin of the gravel in which the villages had been built. The digging sites looked like foxholes in a field of skeletons. Thousands upon thousands of bleached-out bones from whales and walrus, which had been dug up from kitchen middens and cast aside by earlier diggers, littered the landscape. The women looked for fossilized tusks; for teeth from walrus skulls that had been used to make the walls of ancient ningloos, and for the belongings found inside the ningloos. Carefully they dug down through floors made out of whale and walrus shoulder blades. Then they sifted through the gravel once it thawed out.

Since the first scientific dig in the 1920s, Saint Lawrence had intrigued archaeologists. Beneath the fertile, grass-growing mounds covering buried villages lay a treasure chest of ancient artifacts and secrets about the origins of Eskimo culture. Numerous expeditions had come here to unbury the relics for distant museums. They hired villagers to help them and bought what relics the Eskimos had already uncovered.

Even after archaeologists stopped coming, the mounds still abounded in heritage, and in what was more important: ivory. Working alone over the course of one summer, Sook was able to dig up a couple of oosiks, a couple of tusks, and a bull walrus skull with its tusks still intact. Handsome earth-colored fossils were much more valuable than new ivory. Silook said he and Sook would hold out for top dollar on the several-hundred-year-old head. The big prize for a digger was finding an artifact, a piece of antiquity in ivory. "Instant cash" was what Silook called it, because the artifact buyers carried big bucks. Leonard was one of the sweepstakes winners. He reportedly found an ivory Eskimo doll and sold it for $10,000.

Seeing Eskimo diggers shoulder-deep in the legacy of their forefathers, we white men lamented the tragedy of it all, for they were selling off their heritage as if this were a yard sale in the suburbs. Surely, we white men thought, they must have found it traumatic. And what did they think? I asked Silook, yet like the others, he too was malleable to suggestion. Reacting sympathetically to white men's emotions, the villagers would be joyful when we were happy, solemn when we were sad, and they would almost always agree with us if they felt that would make us feel better. "Yes," he said. "It makes us sad to see these artifacts sold, but people are digging to make a living." The villagers went about the business cheerfully enough, though—suggesting they shared neither our pain nor our logic.

I could never quite decide whether selling off the artifacts showed Zen enlightenment toward materialism ("All composite things must pass. Strive on vigilantly.") or the strivings of materialism itself. What I decided in the end was that we white people did more thinking about what it meant to be Eskimo than most Eskimos, and that selling artifacts was a choice rather than a decision. Like most of us, the Eskimos followed rather than charted a path through life. When our grandfathers chose automobiles over horses, they were not making a decision to turn fertile farmland into asphalt parks. Similarly, the Eskimos never decided to get addicted to a cash economy, although that was the result of making choices such as snowgoes over dog teams. The Eskimos made practical choices based on what was at the time self-evident. And the choices seemed obviously right to all but the white men, who looked at them in retrospect and wanted to think they were tragic.

11. They Shoot Walrus, Don't They?

I found it hard to avoid the conclusion that Gambell was plagued by a crisis of too little cash for too modern a society. Other white men made the same assessment, and their solution, which I shared at first, was that Eskimos should de-modernize. Never had the subterranean sod houses or the dog teams seemed more appropriate, we thought, hoping that Natives would return to their soft, small-is-beautiful, fuel-efficient past. But Eskimos had a different view. To them the problem wasn't that they were too modern. It was that they didn't have enough cash for what they needed. And the solution was to make more.

Ivory alone was what the villagers could sell to white men. So when the time came, in the 1970s, when they needed still more money, many of them began hunting walrus for tusks more often than for meat. It was an unprecedented action by Eskimos and a shock to white men with preconceptions about the Natives' way of life. Killing a fifteen-hundred-pound walrus for no more than its two eight-pound tusks turned men into headhunters, and Eskimos weren't supposed to be like that at all.

"Some people are admired only on closer acquaintance," wrote Kaj Birket-Smith in his heralded account, *The Eskimos*. "The Eskimos cannot complain, for on many occasions they have been given most praise by those who knew them least."[8] Whenever I traveled far to the south of Gambell, I knew that statement to be true. Beyond the fur parkas and snow houses to which we assigned them, the defining image of Eskimos in our minds was that they wasted nothing. White men who had never met them acclaimed Eskimos for the ingenious and thorough use of every animal they hunted. It was a quality that endeared them to a society that was the world's most wasteful.

Several generations of writers, reporters, and filmmakers had acclaimed the same quality, so it was not at all surprising that Eskimos themselves adopted our image as fact. "We use everything," villagers would say. "There is no waste." And, dutifully, many white men who came here would report that. Perhaps they never stayed long enough, but if they had, they might have learned otherwise. It was obvious even to them that blubber was no longer needed for fuel or light, that bones no longer built houses, and that gas-fed snow machines had replaced walrus-eating dog teams. It was also true, though they may not have seen it, that people liked to eat certain parts of animals better than others, and that meat often spoiled because it had been stored too long. Of course, by only the most stringent definitions could these things be called wasteful, but that was precisely what most white men would have called them because our expectations were so sanctimonious.

Our belief that Eskimos were thrifty subsistence hunters led at first to favorable special treatment, as when we passed landmark legislation on behalf of wildlife and environment.* Eskimos were allowed to hunt marine mammals and to possess uncarved tusks ("raw ivory"), while white men were ordered not to. Moreover, as long as they were under federal jurisdiction, there were no regulations or restrictions on the Eskimos' hunt for walrus, seals, polar bears, and belugas. And since federal law banned imports of marine mammal products, Natives had a monopoly on the market for carvings.

No one could legitimately question the villagers' dependence upon walrus, and no one will ever convince me that white sportsmen or commercial white hunters should have an equal right to walrus. Without walrus the people of Saint Lawrence

*The Marine Mammal Protection Act of 1972 and the Endangered Species Act of 1973.

Island would go hungry, as I learned in Silook's household. While I was there, his family ate walrus almost every day, and when the store of frozen walrus ran low around the village, people became noticeably uneasy.

Our concept of subsistence did allow the legitimacy of Eskimos selling carved ivory, since that was an "authentic Native article of handicraft." On the other hand, we prohibited the sale of raw ivory to white men, presumably because we didn't think that was Native. But it was only because we recognized Eskimos as subsistence hunters in the first place that we allowed them to sell carvings at all. We expected carvers' raw material to come from walrus that they killed for food and fully consumed in the traditional manner.

For the villagers, subsistence laws cut both ways, conferring the privilege of nearly unregulated hunting while at the same time perpetuating a mythology that undercut economic opportunity. The villagers needed both food and money, but it took far fewer walrus to fill their appetites than to fill their wallets. So, at times, many of them became commercial hunters and took little more than heads. But since this was against the law's intent, they had to hide, camouflage, or deny the real reason for killing so many more walrus than they had ever killed before. And to this end they learned to use imagery that would fulfill the white men's expectations. By the Eskimos' account, they were simply hungrier now.

Nobody really knew how many walrus the hunters were taking now, and the hunters themselves weren't keeping score. The State of Alaska tried to keep track for a while in the late 1970s, after the federal government granted it jurisdiction over the walrus.* The state had a plan to manage the hunt, but that

*From the time of statehood in 1959 until 1972, the State of Alaska had managed the walrus with great success, restoring the depleted herd to a healthy size. Then, with the passage of the Marine Mammal Protection Act of 1972, the federal government declared a moratorium on the taking of marine mammals and the importation of marine mammal products. This effectively took management authority away from Alaska and the rest of the states until they could propose management plans that would satisfy federal authorities. In 1976, three years after the State of Alaska filed its petition, the federal government returned its management authority for walrus, but with several conditions. One of the most important was that the state could not allow any more than three thousand walrus to be harvested a year.

didn't sit too well with Eskimos, because under the feds, they had hunted with neither limits nor controls. In order to meet federal requirements, however, the state imposed quotas that limited each village's catch. For the 1978–1979 season, for example, Gambell was allowed to take 450 adult walrus. That translated into about one animal for every man, woman, and child; and

Walruses.

to call that an adequate stock of food would be understatement, because an average female walrus weighs fifteen hundred pounds and an average bull weighs at least twice as much.

Of course, it wasn't always possible to salvage all the food from every walrus, especially now that Eskimos hunted them from aluminum boats. Aluminum "speedboats" were faster than walrus-skin angyaqs, but they were also smaller and less seaworthy. Because they carried less weight than the angyaqs, hunters were afraid of overloading them. But even if the hunters took only the best meat, blubber, and organs—about 25 percent of the animal's total weight—the quota still provided them with at least four hundred pounds of food per villager (and probably over six hundred pounds), just from walrus. And that didn't include all the baby walrus they took, which weren't counted against the quota since the orphans would probably die anyway if their mothers were killed.

THEY SHOOT WALRUS, DON'T THEY?

The quota provided Gambell with a bellyful of walrus, but the hunters wanted more. Before the start of the 1978–1979 season, they officially asked for six hundred walrus. The previous year's hunting was more indicative of what they really wanted. In the first half of 1977, when the quotas had not yet been imposed, they took seven hundred adults. The same thing was true in other villages. When the roller-coaster ride through the 1970s started, Alaskan Eskimos took an average of fifteen hundred walrus a year. In 1976, they reported killing three thousand, and after the state initiated village quotas midway through 1977, villagers had even less reason to count any further. They had already reached their legal limit.

It was like that for the next two years. Each year the state set a quota of 450, and Gambell's hunters asked for more; when they were refused, they found little incentive to keep counting after 450. How many of them took more than their "legal" share was hard to know. How many of them were headhunters was even harder to determine. Each spring, the state put a young white monitor in Gambell just to collect the numbers from villagers. The results were predictable. The monitors got along famously with most of the villagers, and their reports never added up to much more than 450.

At the beginning of the season, and whenever the store of walrus ran low, the hunters took nearly every part of the walrus they killed. It was magnificent to see how resourceful they could be, as they were that time we shared warm clams from a walrus's stomach. All they left behind them that day was the blood on a crimson-stained ice floe. But as more and more walrus were hunted each spring, the crews brought back higher grades and lesser quantities of meat. The over-quota ivory came ashore hidden in the bottom of boats or put ashore somewhere else or otherwise smuggled home when the monitor wasn't looking. There were all sorts of ways in which hunters tried to escape notice. The monitors knew that. They weren't enforcement agents, but they could see what was going on. They also understood the Eskimos' need for money. But since what they were doing was against the law, the hunters continued to act out their charade. Some of them enjoyed getting away with the deception and a few were plundering rogues, but even they were mostly just victims, doing Stepin Fetchit routines and stealing chickens from the white men's henhouse (as if white men really owned the chickens) because the world wouldn't let them make enough money legitimately.

Although the quota wasn't and couldn't be enforced, most villagers didn't like the idea of breaking it. Isolating an Eskimo from public favor causes him great embarrassment and agitation, and isolating an entire village can have the same effect, especially in a society where isolating someone had always been the greatest punishment. In spite of widespread resentment, there were few militants in Gambell while I was there. On the contrary, the villagers could be impressively patriotic. Nearly every family had one and sometimes several men enlisted in the National Guard; you could see the GET UP YOUR GUARD bumper stickers pasted on their snowgoes. They didn't want to break the law, one of them told me, because, after all, they were American citizens.

They didn't want to break the law, so they asked for higher quotas. But since they were unable to state the real reason why, they resorted to more powerful reasons of "hunger" and "struggle." At a meeting with the State Fish-and-Game manager, for example, one hunter pleaded, "Without eating walrus we cannot stand this cold weather." The manager, who knew the statement was both true and irrelevant, responded that if the villagers took only what they needed for food they couldn't possibly eat 450 walrus.

This was the sort of reaction that explained why Alaska's Eskimos wanted the feds to take back jurisdiction over walrus. Arguments of hunger and struggle found more receptive ears in the Lower Forty-Eight, where people still rallied to the cause of subsistence. In the Lower Forty-Eight, most of us would be overwhelmed by such poignant words as "Hunger knows no law." Yet the real hunger was for money more than meat, and the evidence was all too clear: too many of the walrus washed up in the wrong places without their heads on. The Soviets, who found them by the hundreds, complained about litter on the shores of Siberia.

In response, Eskimos often reacted with denials and countercharges. Some of them blamed the wrongdoing on white men, claiming that men in planes were landing on beaches and cutting heads and tusks off dead animals that washed ashore. Some white men were in fact doing that, but not on the Soviet side. Under criticism from outsiders, villagers banded together in a solidarity that veiled the real truth. Yet, in the absence of white men's criticism, villagers would acknowledge the practice of headhunting, in subtle and quiet ways.

When there was no shortage of meat, it was apparently acceptable to take only the choicest parts of walrus, like Indians high-grading buffalo. And if such hunting wasn't very resourceful, the villagers were at least taking food (and in a way that allowed them to eat well and collect more ivory at the same time). But taking no more than the heads was hardly inspired, and certainly not inspiring. Most of the headhunters themselves were, I think, uneasy about what they did, because their actions clashed with the avowed values of the community. What was an Eskimo, after all, if he turned away from carcasses of animals that offered themselves up to him? Many of the villagers disapproved of headhunting, although their disapproval, like all Eskimo dissent, was quiet. A man's name would arise, for instance, and someone would tell me, "That man is a headhunter." After some friends set out on a hunting trip around the island one day, Silook scoffed at their intentions: there was only one reason, he said, why men would travel nearly four hundred miles over a week's time, and it wasn't to fill their boat with meat.

Among elders and middle-aged Eskimos throughout the Arctic there was a collective memory of hunger. To different villages it may have come at different times and for different durations, but hunger came to all of them, and the villagers never forgot. By plundering the walrus herd for its blubber and ivory, Yankee whalemen had helped bring about outright starvation in many villages. The shortage of walrus had lasted well into this century. Yet what was this Eskimo headhunting if not plunder, just like the white men's of long ago? Both Eskimos who disapproved of headhunting and at least some who engaged in it felt a sense of shame whenever it was discovered.

As unpopular as its quotas might be, at least the State of Alaska understood why Natives needed so many walrus, and it alone tried to accommodate them. But fearing the state would jeopardize its wildlife, the federal government had placed a limit on how many walrus the state could divide among its villages. So the state had to petition the feds for a higher ceiling.

To justify its request, the state wanted to create overseas

and domestic markets for surplus walrus meat and hides. This way, the hunters would have an incentive to use animals more fully, which would in turn protect them from charges of being wasteful. (And that would get them closer to their main objective: getting more ivory.) Of course, the state's idea would engage Eskimos in an openly and self-avowedly commercial enterprise.

"What difference does it make if you're called commercial hunters instead of subsistence hunters?" a state biologist once asked of the villagers. What was important, he said, was getting higher quotas, and the state managers thought they could get them by calling the hunters commercial. Indeed, in moments when reason outweighed experience, it seemed that Eskimos would be better off if they were called commercial or, better yet, part-time commercial hunters. They would be freed then from the big lie, the lie they used, and which in turn was used against them.

Though the logic seemed reasonable, historical experience was less convincing. If they let themselves be called commercial hunters, Eskimos would forfeit exclusive privileges and special treatment that accrued to them because of federal protection and popular myth. State wildlife managers might understand their needs, but the decisions on quotas would be made by state game boards dominated by a generally ill-tempered lot of white, don't-tread-on-me states' righters who thought things had gotten out of hand and wanted to restore equal hunting rights to white people. Once white men got into the act, they might be competing for the share of ivory, a scenario that caused the greatest fear among Eskimo villagers. So the villagers wanted to be called subsistence hunters, and they wanted a return to federal management and a world of myths that they might use (and also be abused by) to get more walrus to make more money.

The situation was absurd. The State Fish and Game Department, which Eskimos mistrusted, wanted to increase the quotas but couldn't because the feds, whom Eskimos favored, feared the state would mismanage the resource. Yet the ultimate absurdity was that the North Pacific was in fact wallowing in walrus.

Far from being threatened with extinction, the Pacific walrus was more abundant now than at any other time in the last hundred years. There were 200,000 of them, as many as there had been when white whalemen first sailed into the Bering Sea, as many as before the white man's dreaded guns were introduced. If ever there was a case for higher quotas, indeed if ever there was a case for a hunt regulating itself, this was it. There were so many walrus, in fact, that they seemed to have outrun their food supply. Eskimos were reporting a much higher proportion of thin and lean animals in the herd, and they saw walrus "hauling out" (pulling their massive bodies out of the water and onto land) in places, numbers, and at times that they hadn't seen in a lifetime.

In fall 1978, a tidal wave of walrus, the likes of which not even Irrigoo or Oovi could remember, came ashore at the eastern end of Saint Lawrence Island. Amazed by what they saw, and frightened by what it meant, the villagers sent word to a scientific expert, Dr. Francis Fay from the University of Alaska, to come and investigate. After traveling to the island, he estimated that over seventy thousand animals had hauled out of the water at just two of the congregating spots, or *uglit*. Near the ancient village of Kialegak, which had been wiped out a hundred years earlier by the Great Starvation, walrus packed the shore body-to-body in an awesome group grope that ran for two miles down the beach and thirty-five yards inland. So many walrus lay atop the mound of Kialegak itself that the frozen tundra thawed beneath them. Coalescing off another *ugli*, observers said, thousands of milling walrus turned the sea into an extension of land that was reddish-brown with life and stretched unbroken in a peninsula to the horizon.

Yet the hunters who saw such things were told they could only take 450 in a year.

One morning, islanders found twenty-five walrus trampled to death by a stampede of animals. The victims may have been the slowest among a beachful that had suddenly charged into the sea the night before. There on the beach lay their bloodied bodies with fresh ivory tusks for the taking. Legally the villagers weren't allowed to take ivory unless they reported it. If they reported it, it would be counted against their quota. After all, we didn't want them to be wasteful.

Eventually, the state threw up its hands, and in the summer of 1979 it gave back management authority to the feds, who had no management plan at all. Instead, the feds allowed Natives exclusive, unrestricted, and unmonitored hunting (after having so sanctimoniously questioned the state's commitment to conserving its walrus). Freed of quotas, Eskimo hunters returned to a hunt regulated by Nature instead of white men. They returned not to the past, however, but to a myth that was based on the past. Nobody really knew how many more walrus they took for ivory instead of food. The Eskimos themselves weren't letting on, because they would be safe that way, until and unless the rest of the world found out and joined forces with the animal-protection zealots. Eskimos were back to the big lie, the lie of using everything that they killed, of wasting nothing that they hunted. And to that end they took all sorts of precautions.

"No pictures of dead walrus," Johnny told me one day. I wanted to go out hunting with him in late spring of 1980. I wanted to travel across the straits in a speedboat closing in on Siberia in search of walrus. But he wasn't going to take me if I took pictures of dead animals. There had been stories printed about headhunting and, worse than that, there had been pictures, which made for bad publicity. Yet for $500, Johnny said, he'd let me come along. There would be only one other condition. When we came upon our target, he'd make two passes. The first one would be for me, so I could shoot walrus with my cameras. Walrus at rest, walrus at play, walrus at work being walrus. But on the second pass, I'd have to stop, because that's when the hunters would do some shooting of their own.

It seemed foolish, yet he knew better than I did how white people would react to pictures of dead animals. I found out when I got to the Lower Forty-Eight and showed what I had shot earlier that spring with the Apangalooks. It didn't matter that the images were of villagers butchering walrus for food. Nor did it matter if the captions read: "Eskimos Harvesting Walrus for Food (They Ate the Whole Thing)." Most white people might support the idea of Eskimos killing for food—they might even romanticize it—but they did not want to look at it. They looked at the big soft eyes of dead seals, all lambent and sad like the eyes of Mexican children painted on black velvet, and they were overcome with emotion. In the darkest of moods caused by my friends' reactions, I wondered if the war in Vietnam would have ended sooner had we been shooting at animals instead of Orientals. And how much worse would it have been had these same friends known about headhunting?

"No pictures of dead walrus," Johnny said. I remember the conditions well. The first pass was for Disney, Marlin Perkins, and Jacques Cousteau. The first pass was for the wonderful world of wildlife, because as Merlin Koonooka once complained jokingly, always jokingly, "People in New York want us to feed walrus rather than kill them."

In Western society our meat is raised by agribusiness and the wails of dying livestock are muffled by the slaughterhouses that do our butchering. We are removed from both the need of killing wild animals and the act of killing our own, so our attitude has changed. Letting wild animals live has become an ultimate value for many of us.

But for Silook and other Eskimos, killing individual animals was no different from harvesting renewable crops. Indeed, he chose other words to describe an animal's death because he didn't like the connotation of *kill*. The only time he used the word in his language, he explained, was when a captain commanded a crewman to put an end to an injured animal's misery. The rest of the time the hunters would use another expression, such as, "I'm going to shoot this one" or "I'm going to hit that one." Killing was different from hunting, Silook added, because the hunt was for food, and killing wasn't.

His people had gotten their food, warmth, and shelter this way from the very beginning. It was as if the Eskimos were imprinted with the hungry experience of their ancestors. Up along the slopes of Mount Seevookak, boys might climb with poles and nets to catch auklets or to pull chicks from among loose rocks and bite through their necks or crush their hearts with little thumbs. Like foraging cubs, they often learned about killing by playing at it.

As boys grew older, they stuffed gunnysacks full of broken-necked auklets and gunshot ducks; they jigged scores of tomcod; collected dozens of eggs; and they prepared for their first seal kill, which was the bridge to manhood. From their first boyhood adventures they had abided by the ancient rule of killing whenever they could and whatever they saw that was edible. The animals they hunted had always come and gone in short-lived seasonal migrations that varied in size from one year to the next.

GAMBELL: THE VILLAGE

They were like waves that swelled, crested, and dissolved back into the sea with no indication, until it was too late, of how big they would be or how long they would last. And not knowing how many animals would come to them, Eskimos never worried about killing too many, because the real danger lay in killing too few.

We white men who came to the Arctic found out the hard way that the Eskimos' instincts often ran counter to ours. Standing on the shores of Gambell one day were a hunter and a couple of birdwatchers. A fabulous diversity of birds roosted or bred here or in summer were occasionally blown eastward from Asia by strong Siberian winds. Spotting any of these rare or exotic species would be the highlight of a birdwatcher's journey, and the birdwatchers traveled farther than the birds themselves to get here. To the hunter and other Eskimos, the sky was clouded with birds—in springtime there were tens of thousands—but for the birdwatchers, the same sky was empty save for a few rare birds they had come to add to their lists. They came with powerful binoculars, expensive cameras with motor drives, U-2 lenses, tripods, and walkie-talkies for reconnaissance of rare species. At times they looked like a cross between an army of occupation and a far-flung Radio Shack convention, as in 1980, when ninety watchers rendezvoused in this village of about four hundred.

"I think that's a rare bird," exclaimed one of the birdwatchers, for he thought he might be looking at a Siberian species. My Eskimo friend shouldered his shotgun, aimed as the bird passed overhead, and shot it out of the sky in one fluid motion, to see what it was. The birdwatcher was right, the Eskimo confirmed, when we got to the dead bird. "We sometimes see this kind when the wind comes from the southwest."

Traveling downriver in an Eskimo village another year, a Californian who was new to the Bush saw a beaver nearby. Delighted, he pointed it out to his Eskimo companion, who was equally delighted. The Eskimo reached for his gun, shot the animal dead, and threw it into the boat, thankful for such a serendipity. "But it was my first beaver," the Californian moaned.

As for Johnny's price for taking me hunting, it started at $1,500, dropped to $500 when I laughed, fell to $50 over the next few days, and eventually disappeared because, after all, we were friends and Johnny was easygoing. (Though I don't for a minute doubt that had I agreed to any of those figures he would have taken it gladly.) We never got to go walrus hunting together. It was too late that spring, so we took off seal hunting instead, and I got some great shots of him dragging dead seals over spring ice glistening with pools of melt water. Why he didn't mind the pictures I'll never know.

After the feds took over, the villagers' hunt was as unfettered as their ancestors'. But a new problem arose when the feds decided to stop Eskimos from selling raw ivory to white men. Even though carved ivory sold for much more, some villagers were often too desperate, too eager, or too unskilled to carve the tusks first, so they sold them raw. This had been legal under state management, but it became illegal once again when the feds took over, because it was deemed too commercial an activity for subsistence hunters to engage in. Making it illegal, however, had only created a black market, thereby raising the price of raw ivory and the villagers' willingness to sell it.

In February 1981, a year and a half after the feds took over management of walrus, enforcement agents posing as buyers seized nearly half a million dollars' worth of raw ivory from Alaska. The fact that only white businessmen were arrested gave little consolation to Eskimos. By cracking down on the black market, the feds were shutting off a sure supply of money for Gambell and a half-dozen other villages. In the Lower Forty-Eight, conservationists applauded such vigilant protection even as the walrus population had long since grown too big.

Who knows why the feds had suddenly cracked down on the sale of raw ivory? White men were like the ice. We were powerful and we could bestow upon Eskimos the products of our power like pack ice bringing animals to the hunters. We could provide economic opportunity, but like the ice, we were unpredictable and could starve them just as easily. So while the Eskimos stalked our modern world for its advantages and our welfare system for its handouts—and they did these things at least as skillfully as they hunted—they stayed as suspicious of us as if they were on the ice. We were powerful, and dangerous in our vacillation.

12. "We Must Go Forward"

Silook and Sook had grown up in one era and married in another that was faster, richer, broader in opportunity, and deeper in confusion than the first. This second era brought them to the threshold of still a third era that was full of promise. They were impatient to cross over, although crossing into the newest realm meant they might have to leave the oldest one behind. "Our world is ending today," Silook's uncle Roger said to him and to the other villagers one night. "We must go forward to meet a changing world."

Everywhere in Gambell I sensed this imperative: "We must go forward"; "We must become modernized." I often wondered what the villagers imagined when they heard such things. But if the meaning was vague, the villagers' intentions were clear. Over a third of the village's population in 1958 had emigrated to the mainland as of 1972, often in whole families (for even in leaving they were still a product of tradition). They left to seek work and the Great Society, as they were encouraged to do by the federal government, which even paid their expenses out. Some were absorbed or swallowed up in city life; those who stayed behind, and those who came back, after deciding they couldn't or didn't want to be autoworkers in Illinois or carpenters in California, hoped the Great Society might offer itself up to them like a whale sent by God.

Roger Silook (his surname was the same as his nephew's Eskimo name) was a sly, smiling, and altogether charming man of middle age. He'd lived on the mainland for a number of years, as a postmaster in Nome and, it was alleged, as an autoworker in the Midwest. He'd come back with his family in the mid-1970s in order, he said, to show his children the ways of Eskimos. An enthusiastic captain, he was the first to arrive on the beach, and, along with his crew of sons, he was the first to launch his angyaq, often sailing outward when no one else would venture. In contrast to the composed, almost phlegmatic captains around him, Roger so tensed with excitement at whaling time that his stomach rebelled and he had to take a steady dose of antacid.

Because Roger knew how to communicate with white people and, more important, how to deal with them, he proved an effective ambassador when it came time to lobby against quotas and the attempt to ban Eskimo whaling. Fellow villagers made him the local whaling commissioner. Roger spoke just as capably when talk turned to economic development. With the enthusiasm of a builder, he talked to villagers about starting up a commercial fishing industry for crab, halibut, herring, and shrimp, species heretofore caught, if at all, with hooks and lines. His outlook was overly optimistic (wildly so for a remote village with no experience and no sure supply of fish to support a fishing industry). But Roger was eager, nevertheless, to get on with the job of going forward, and toward that end he manifested a refreshing ambition and a degree of initiative that were generally missing in Native villages. Sparked by the same can-do confidence of white Alaskans, Roger was a reminder that not all Eskimos were helpless victims of white society.

With the same expectant initiative, Silook had gone off to school on the mainland. And perhaps he would have stayed there when he got his diploma had his father not ordered him home. In order to go to school in the first place, he had abandoned his apprenticeship as a hunter and had had to start over again when he came back to the island. He was different from most villagers now, and, recognizing this, they had put him in charge of jobs that gave him the duty of dealing with white men, as they had with Roger and others who had been off the island. He administered a federal contract, became the village policeman, was appointed to the federally recognized tribal government, joined the "city" council; and the year I met him, he became mayor. He was bright and enthusiastic, and one of my white friends used to predict that someday Silook might be governor of Alaska. Silook had come home with an idea of what could be and a zeal for making it so. But he ran up against a wall of resistance and inertia.

When Native children left home for high school, they carried the aspirations of their communities, but when they returned, they were often regarded and resented as misfits. "Hey, Sam," a teenager would be encouraged, "we need educated people like you to help society." Once Sam returned home, eager to change the village that now seemed backward to him, the village resisted. "Hey, Sam," the villagers called, "who do you think you are, a smart aleck?"

And so it was for Silook. With each new job, he charged forward and then "burned out." He talked of going to college so he could become a more capable administrator, but at the same time thought about dropping out of the "system" so he could hunt like the others. Hunting was something that brought him confidence, self-esteem, and success. Indeed, he had been given few opportunities to succeed within the system.

"We must go forward," they agreed, for it seemed that Gambell couldn't get enough of what we had and it wanted. They wanted to go farther faster. But on the threshold of this new era, the villagers clutched the past even as they grabbed for the future.

Sometimes, in their growing affluence as consumers, Eskimos seemed to share our idea that using white men's things would transform them into white men. No matter how practical they were, the choices they had made—to use electricity and gas, to watch televison, wear manufactured clothes, eat white men's food, attend white men's schools, and seek help at white men's hospitals—all served to diminish the differences between their culture and that of the outside world. Their choices inevitably affected Eskimos' ways of thinking and acting, and the recognition of this when it came to them led villagers into a brooding ambivalence.

In the past, Eskimos had wanted to be accepted like white men, only to be denied, segregated, and discriminated against because they were Native. Today, villagers still sought our approval in all sorts of ways that might prove they were like white men, from serving us TV dinners to showing off big color televisions. Only, nowadays they were often disdained for being too much like us. Among the young, however, it was more important to know they were different, for reasons of pride and politics. The number of similarities with white men was growing, and the world was reminding the young that Eskimo culture was dying, a pronouncement that only nurtured their insecurity.

"I guess there can be modern Eskimos too," Silook once replied to a question I asked of him. Yet he himself vacillated between faith and doubt, a doubt he once expressed in the sad assertion that "our ancestors probably wouldn't recognize us."

By 1980, Sook and Silook had moved into a new home and a new neighborhood. It was still Gambell, but now they lived in one of sixty government-subsidized houses; the last thirty had just been completed. The home they abandoned belonged to the old village, huddled on the crest of Gambell's western shore, looking seaward. The new one, which lay a half-mile inland, had no view of the ocean. The old village was effectively, almost symbolically, isolated now.

Perhaps it didn't matter, since it was being evacuated. The houses there were ramshackle and drafty, and villagers preferred the new ones, even though the first lot were poorly designed and expensive to heat.

Sook and Silook were delighted with their new house. It was a five-room box with a big fuel tank outside, two bedrooms, a bathroom, a furnace, a wood-burning stove, an automatic washer-wringer, and a kitchen. In the next few years, they hoped to get running water and plumbing too. Sook stood proudly in her bright, clean kitchen when I entered. "You can have your own room and bed now," she said enthusiastically. A big smile showed how pleased she was by my reaction.

Though it was superior to the other house in many ways, I felt a twinge of nostalgia for the old neighborhood. Apparently some of the elders felt the same way, for I used to watch an old man trudge across the gravel to his former home each morning; he'd spend his daylight hours there, then trudge back to the present at night, a present that was warmer if also less assuring. I felt guilty for feeling nostalgic. After all, I wasn't the one who had to spend winters in the old house, where standing water sometimes froze and my hosts complained of the cold.

I did have some trouble sorting out Silook and Sook's home from twenty-nine other homes that were all cast in the same mold, painted one of four or five colors and arranged in neat, perfectly spaced rows and gravel lots. Realizing I was disoriented while driving home one night, Silook nudged me from behind on the three-wheeled Honda. "I live on Third Avenue," he chortled. Ha! Third Avenue in a village with no roads. I felt his weight lurching around behind me and thought we'd surely tip over. Coming to a sudden stop, I turned to see him laughing with a full set of gleaming teeth.

Beneath the joke of Third Avenue lay the Eskimos' brooding ambivalence and confusion. They were possessed by contradictions and inconsistencies not unlike those that held me and my comrades in the 1960s who talked of going back to Nature while indulging in electronic and chemical pleasures.

"I can still go out on the island and lead a good life," Sook said one day. "I don't think many people would like to live that way, but I for one would like to try. I am Eskimo, after all." It was the idea of being "Eskimo," of living without money, without the complications of schedules and bills and social upheaval, that captured her heart. Silook felt the same urge. As a boy he had lived that way when his father took the family out to their camp. They had stayed there for months, without any cash—indeed, they had gone there because they had none—supporting themselves instead by hunting and by trading sealskins at the store when they needed staples. Necessity, not choice, had driven his father, but Silook sometimes thought of choosing the same thing, perhaps to prove he could still do it.

Confusion twisted and turned inside them like a bone blade inside a polar bear's stomach. Long ago Eskimos had hunted bears by hiding a coiled splint carved from a whale's rib inside a piece of blubber and setting the frozen ball out for Nanook to eat. Once the bear swallowed the bait, the blubber thawed and the sharpened splint unwound like a scythe inside its stomach; to find their prey, the hunters followed the trail of an agonized death. Would the stress of uncoiled change work the same way in today's Eskimos?

To turn off the confusion or at least tune it out, many Eskimos, now that they could get booze more easily, drank as if there were no tomorrow. Which for some of them there wasn't. Booze only magnified the confusion and, when mixed with the stress already there, often led to madness. Several times I saw Gambell possessed by it.

The National Guardsmen had come back from "war games" on the mainland; someone had flown in from Nome with a couple of cases; someone had ordered a liquid shipment by air. It all meant the same thing: booze was coming to town. For Gambell that was always bad news.

Whenever booze came to the Bush, and it was arriving more regularly now, whole villages would go on a bender, drinking whatever they had until there was no more. As anywhere else, drunks in the Bush could be easygoing, quiet, sloppy, loud, belligerent and explosive, or any combination thereof. What was striking among drunken Eskimos was that this range of emotions emerged from a normally completely opaque exterior.

Unless someone had been drinking, I seldom saw an angry-looking villager. He might very well be angry, but his anger would be cold and introverted. When such traditional controls were short-circuited by liquor, the party turned sour. If someone didn't like me, all of a sudden I was hearing about it face-to-face, sometimes with an added message that I better get out of town. One of the most gentle people I knew threatened to slit my throat one night, only to return the next day, embarrassed and contrite about his behavior. With a flair for a well-turned—if in this case self-serving—phrase, the local missionary called booze "a return to shamanism." It was unquestionably magic and it worked with dark effect, temporarily transforming people who were normally courteous and hospitable.

Villagers had long ago outlawed the sale or possession of alcohol, but the law had not stopped a rising tide of it or its periodic waves of destruction. When the party kicked into over-drive, the terror started. Someone might go off and shoot up the school or bust a few heads. Someone would come down on his wife or, more truly horrible in the minds of Eskimos, beat up the kids. Or turn the barrel on himself. In the Bush, there were ample statistics for each occurrence.

No one had ever locked his doors until the last few years, when drinking sprees became more frequent. I went to visit old Oovi one night only to find his door boarded up, to hear a voice asking who it was, to see a face peering out the window. Welcoming me inside, he apologized, explaining that he'd heard there was going to be drinking that night.

Sober or drunk, villagers came to Silook for help. He was the mayor, but what could he do? There was one cop in Gambell, and somehow he was supposed to exercise civil authority in a village that had been run by clans and traditional, decentralized controls. What do you do with wife-beaters, child-abusers, and kids that beat up on their parents? There wasn't a jail to hold them, and their families didn't want to press charges and have them sent away to be locked up on the mainland. When the pressure came off and the booze dried up, the drunks would turn remorseful. But until then, what could the cop do with them other than baby-sit, and how could he do that by himself, when on the nights of binge drinking, the whole village was overrun by drunks?

When people were busting up the place and bad blood flowed, those who were still sober would call in the Alaska state troopers. They were two hundred miles away and would fly in the next day if the weather was good. If the booze wasn't gone by then, they'd mop things up. If someone ws still on a tear, they'd arrest him and fly him out for a while. That's what they did with a disaffected teenager who fired a half-dozen rounds of his semi-automatic into the home of a white schoolteacher one night (also causing a temporary evacuation of white people to the mainland). By 1981, drinking had become so disruptive to village life that Gambell asked that a state trooper be stationed there permanently.

Meanwhile, the cop and other villagers came to Silook whenever things went out of control. Off he would go to deal with another crisis: sometimes nothing more than a bunch of rowdies and a few bruises. Other times it was worse, as when he found a friend who'd put a rifle barrel in his mouth and blown part of himself onto the ceiling. To portray Gambell as a village yearning for the simple past is sheer romanticism. To portray it as a model of pleasant transition into Western progress is equally naïve. As mayor, Silook saw the twists and turns all too well. He too was a victim of them.

"We should decide either to return to the past or become like white men," he would say, embodying this seesawing ambivalence. Implicitly, he was asserting that if they wanted to, his people could turn back, that they could survive by subsistence hunting, without food stamps, jobs, and welfare. Yet even while he spoke, Silook remained excited about his own plans to institute sewage collection, to install home-to-home telephone service, to construct a laundry/lavatory complete with running water and plumbing. There were also plans to build a supply line to distribute water to houses in summertime, thereby saving villagers the task of collecting and hauling it homeward as they did now.

Looking beyond the obvious improvements, I wondered how many villagers could afford the new services when, as it was, some couldn't even make small home-purchase payments to the feds. I supposed they'd find a way. They'd have to. But the solution would not be going back to the past. Yearning for simplicity was an emotion that would coexist with telephones and running water. Fantasy or not, that yearning had a real function: the thought of being able to live the old way made the new one seem less threatening.

Eventually Silook quit his job as mayor; he simply did not like the responsibilities. Every time he left the office, paperwork had piled up, making greater demands on his life when he returned. He had felt overloaded with work, trapped by routine, discouraged and unsure of himself as he treaded water in an alphabet soup of government agencies and village problems. But afterward, he felt liberated. He had once again become master of his own day. He now hunted far from shore, or gathered driftwood along the northern coast, and felt happier than he ever had before. Hunting was more enjoyable because he did not have to succeed every time he went out. Hunting, carving, part-time work, and digging for old ivory would allow him and Sook to support their family.

In this blend of subsistence and cash, life was rewarding, though hardly secure. There were times in winter when they didn't have enough money to buy heat and their house was bitterly cold. There were times too, in bad weather when Native food was scarce and the ivory market dropped, that Silook regretted ever having acquired a taste for things like steak. A chronic, sometimes acute anxiety over money reminded him of the price he paid for independence. But despite the hard times, he and his family endured.

Watching him come home, I envied his ability to provide so much. Standing on the north beach in late-spring evenings would be brothers and sisters, nieces and nephews, waiting to help pull the aluminum boat up a steep bank of shore ice and unload walrus and seals. Once on the ice, the meat, organs, máhngoona (the blubber and hide of walrus), and braided intestines would be divided up, then shared among the families. Providing such food was a man's greatest achievement in Gambell; it had always been.

Though a man might make lots of money, that didn't assure him of respect and often brought just envy. Respect went to those who shared most, and food was the greatest gift of all. Leonard, who was Silook's captain, owned the boat, the engine, and the gear, and was affluent in comparison. But despite all this, he depended upon his younger brother because he himself was often too busy tending to business at the store to go hunting. Though Silook had little money, his success as a hunter made him a wealthy man.

Working at his meat shed one day, Silook was approached by a Chinese-looking priestlike man with whispers of gray hair hanging from his chin. His name was Conrad and he was a widely respected hunter. Talking to Silook, he seemed oblivious to my presence until, having finished his story some fifteen minutes later, he turned to me with a gentle smile and apologized. He didn't mean to be impolite, he said, but he couldn't possibly have explained such things in English.

Later, Silook told me what Conrad had said. Far offshore, the current never shifts in late springtime; it shoots north, which means if a hunter is north of the island, he can get caught in the pack ice and be carried away quite fast. Conrad instructed Silook about making judgments and told him how he, Conrad, had come home from Siberian waters through the fog. Following the compass bearing was not enough, Conrad said. Because of the currents, a man might miss the island altogether. No, a man had to gauge how much fuel he had used and how much time he spent going in certain compass directions around the ice, and then compensate for the northern-shooting waters. These were things, Conrad said, that he had learned from his own experience. It was an education of a lifetime, and he wanted to share some of this with Silook, who was honored by such a gift and the recognition it conveyed.

Whether Silook would ever go to college or find a career and move away from hunting, I didn't know. He saw his options narrowing "like a twenty-four-second-shot clock running out in a basketball game." In quitting his job as mayor he had made a commitment to hunting, which, he discovered, was the thing he did best. He hoped that his children could someday choose from a greater range of opportunities than he had had, and I was sure he would want them to have a fuller education, too. But Silook wasn't at all unhappy with his own life, as I well understood after three years. Standing beside seals and walrus, birds, and—in his greatest glory of all, the whale—that gave themselves up to him, he, like ancient Eskimos before him, could surge with triumphant joy. For indeed, Silook had learned well.

His ancestors probably would not recognize Gambell or the people in it, for the history of the last hundred years had been a series of changes, reactions, and adjustments to the coming of white men. Heritage, however, did not come from the history of change. It came from the prehistory of hunting, and the last century had not destroyed that memory. Hunting was still the villagers' source of life and the heartbeat of their identity.

Some, like Silook and Conrad, who were everyday hunters, might be more recognizable than others to their ancestors. But in springtime, the hunt for bowheads reunited everyone with the past. That was one reason why the hunt lived on in Alaskan villages. If only for a few weeks, and in a momentary stay from the complications of modern life, they all returned in their angyaqs to a place where they did not have to think about money but instead could sail among the ice, reenact the struggle of their ancestors, and triumph in the glory of capturing the whale.

Part Three: The Hunt, Continued

13. "Save the Whales"

In 1978, my first year in Gambell, the hunt for bowheads began in mid-April. On a Sunday, the day after I arrived, Leonard Apangalook's crew came close to harpooning a whale. Then a few days later, on Wednesday, another crew struck but lost a whale. Had the villagers been able to continue that day, they might have had many more chances to capture one because the number of bowheads migrating past Saint Lawrence Island was reaching a climax. It seemed only a question of when, not if, a whale would come upon us. But Pacific storm waves had forced the hunters to return home. "Pacific swells" were protecting Aghvook. Nature had always regulated the hunt this way, bringing whales close in some years and keeping them far away in others. Eskimos considered it the sole authority. But on that Wednesday another authority materialized. Two white men sent by the federal government to enforce regulations of its own were on the beach questioning the returning hunters.

They had been sent because the International Whaling Commission (IWC), a regulatory organization to which the United States belongs, had decided the Eskimos were killing too many bowheads. No one knew how many bowheads there were. Varying estimates of the population ranged from a thousand to three thousand animals, but no one had ever actually conducted a scientific census. Indeed, whale researchers were being sent north in 1978 to determine if it was actually necessary to have the quota the agents had been sent to enforce. And not knowing how many whales there were, no one knew if the population was increasing or decreasing, either. Scientists knew little at all about the bowhead. In fact, few of them had ever seen one.

From hunting statistics submitted by the federal government, however, the IWC's scientific advisers feared that the population was nearing extinction. During the last three decades, Eskimos had caught an average of ten bowheads a year, but since 1970 they had been landing twenty-nine a year. And even more disturbing to IWC scientists were the large numbers reported to have been struck with harpoons and bombs but lost at sea; for several years the losses appeared to be increasing. Then, after the spring hunt of 1977, the United States reported that the Eskimos had struck and lost a staggering total of seventy-seven bowheads in addition to capturing twenty-six more. Appalled by the report, the IWC's scientific advisers recommended what the IWC executive secretary would later call "drastic measures" against a "desperate situation."

Without having a good estimate of the population, of course, the scientists couldn't know the actual effect of the Eskimos' hunting. But having accepted the "guess" by a fellow adviser that there were no more than a thousand bowheads left, the IWC's scientists assumed that the herd was in imminent danger. And declaring that this imminent yet unproven danger must be stopped, the advisers warned the IWC's commissioners that "the taking of any bowheads could adversely affect the stock and contribute to preventing its eventual recovery, if in fact such recovery is still possible." *Could* and *if*.

The advisers' recommendation made an international issue out of a hunt that was as obscure as the bowhead itself to the Western world. IWC commissioners from as far away as South America, Europe, and South Africa were examining the question of whether Eskimos should be allowed to continue hunting, and nothing typified their distance from the hunt so much as where they were meeting in June 1977—Canberra, Australia—when they deleted the exemption that until then had allowed Eskimos to kill bowheads.

The Eskimos had reacted to the ban with surprise and anger. You could have counted on your fingers the number of Native hunters who had ever heard of the International Whaling Commission before 1977. No one from the IWC or from the U.S. Commerce Department (which oversees management, research, and protection of marine mammals) had informed any of them until a few months before the ban was passed that the IWC was concerned about the number of whales they were killing, though it had been urging the United States to take action for five years. Now the IWC seemed to be punishing Eskimos for the federal government's negligence. Instead of working to persuade the Eskimos that the hunt must be scaled down and improved, the IWC had decreed an outright end to hunting, an action that virtually precluded any future cooperation and compliance by hunters.

After the vote by the IWC, the Eskimos demanded the United States file an objection, which would have had the effect of overriding the IWC's action and allowing the hunt to continue. This forced the federal government to decide between protecting whales and protecting the rights of Eskimos. To the Eskimos' shock, most conservationists insisted the federal government abide by the ban. In a scene burning with racial overtones, white spokesmen for some of these groups claimed the Eskimos' use of Western tools and weapons had turned them into a "bastard culture" and thus deprived their hunt of any legitimacy.

Lost in the rush to save the whales was the question of whether the IWC's scientists were right. For many, the cause overcame any doubts. In its largely embarrassing history, the International Whaling Commission and its predecessors had presided over the depletion of blue whales, humpbacks, and sperm whales. In one of its first acts, its predecessor had prohibited the commercial hunting of bowheads, a commendable enough action except for the fact that it came two decades after the last bowheads had been hunted by white men. For most of its history, the International Whaling Commission had proved no more effective, almost always regulating to the whalers' advantage; indeed, the IWC had been a sort of whalers' clubhouse.

In recent years, however, conservationists had disrupted

the fraternal atmosphere. Under U.S. leadership, an alliance of countries had successfully fought to increase the scientists' role in setting catch quotas and demanded a tougher approach that would err, if at all, on the side of conservation rather than commerce.

There was a difference, however, between commercial and subsistence hunting. Erring on the side of the conservation of sperm whales, for example, would only cost the commercial whalers money, but erring on the side of conservation of bowheads would cost subsistence hunters food and a way of life. And it had been the commercial fleets, not the Eskimos, that had made both the sperm whale and the bowhead endangered species in the first place.

The debate as to whether the United States should accept or object to the ban on Eskimo whaling was nasty and ideologically troubling for many white people. It pitted against each other two of the most romantic causes of our time: Native Americans and whales. Native Americans, particularly Indians, who had been more popularized than Eskimos, were seen as the embodiment of Old World ecology. All the ideals of modern conservationists—soft technology, back to nature, and small is beautiful—were epitomized by Indian and Eskimo culture. Many Americans, myself included, were drawn to Native culture because we infused it with virtues we sought for ourselves. We were also drawn out of guilt, for if ever there was a symbol of America's inhumanity to man, it was in our treatment of Native Americans.

Yet if ever there was a symbol of man's inhumanity to his planet, it was the slaughter of whales. In the heyday of young America, the seafaring hunt for leviathans was a glorious industry rich in the legends and symbols of conquering the frontiers. In the current age, however, it had come to represent a purposeless technology unleashed by greedy commerce. The emptiness of much of Western civilization might have been epitomized by the butchering of whales for dog food and eye shadow. The commercial hunters had become beasts, and the beasts had been transformed into "gentle giants."

More than a sense of conscience tied many Westerners, especially the younger generation, to the whales. Lost souls in search of meaning, they beheld whales with a reverence reserved for few other things or people. They saw transcendence in their skyward leap and felt ecstasy in the whales' close presence. The eerie, haunting song of the humpback struck many Westerners as profound: Was it the plaintive song of a species on the verge of extinction, and did it have a meaning for humans too? They responded as if it did.

In the whales' reflection many Westerners saw man as killer. But also as savior. To protect the whales, some braved Soviet and Japanese harpoons. Others rammed whaling ships or threw blood on Japanese diplomats. And when whales hurled themselves onto land, some people tried to tow them back to sea, often against their will, and then cried in agony as they ran aground once more and died. People who had never come close to a whale boycotted the products of whaling countries; marched, ran, and walked with their children; wrote letters; sang songs; and prayed fervently to save the whales. Indeed, saving the whales had become a modern-day religion. For the true believers, it was not enough to conserve whales; they wanted no killing whatsoever. To them, killing whales was an atrocity against life and must be stopped.

In the clash of symbols, the need to save the whales had won out. Not one of the major conservation groups had sided with the Eskimos and called for the United States to file an objection to the IWC ban, though many conservation spokesmen tried to express an understanding of what whaling meant to the villagers.* Some said they didn't want to stop the hunt forever; they expressed a hope that some year soon the ban would no longer be necessary. A few favored a compromise, expressing hope for a scaled-down, supervised hunt (although only Friends of the Earth actively lobbied for one). But most conservation groups urged the United States to enforce the ban.

It would be unfair to characterize the conservationists as callous. Many of them agonized over their decisions. They weren't going to let the Eskimos go hungry. They expressed sympathy and sought to implement their social concern through

*Friends of the Earth originally called for an objection, but changed its policy after learning that the IWC would hold a special meeting in December 1977 to reconsider the ban. The group then advocated that the United States seek a compromise that would allow Eskimos a "reasonable" quota.

federal welfare programs. Thus, while insisting the United States abide by the whaling ban, they also called for alternative food supplies directed at Eskimo villages.

Some talked about substituting food stamps for bowheads. One save-the-whales activist, the head of a California-based group called Project Jonah, suggested that walrus carcasses found washed up along Alaskan shores should be flown out to the villages. (She presumed, I suppose, that because Eskimos have a taste for fermented meat they must enjoy rotting flesh, too.) Other conservationists wanted the government to provide the villagers with beef, mutton and pork. But recognizing that the Eskimos had ancient traditions of communal sharing, the Society for Animal Protective Legislation proposed that the frozen whole carcasses "should be divided by the villages in the same way as whale meat is allocated among them." What remained to be solved was how frozen, forty- to four-hundred-pound carcasses could be butchered and shared in the same manner as the forty-thousand-pound carcass of a freshly killed whale. One conservationist, worried about the effect of the ban on the Eskimos' cultural well-being, recommended that the actual hunt be replaced by symbolic killing and urged the feds to send in cultural anthropologists to maintain "an optimal cultural state" while the whaling was being phased out.

In the end, the United States chose not to file an objection to the IWC's ban because it didn't want to lose moral leadership of the movement to stop commercial whaling. The government agreed with the conservationists who claimed the bowhead issue was a test of our sincerity and commitment to save whales. In the past, the IWC had failed because whaling countries such as Japan and the Soviet Union could avoid its quotas by simply filing an objection. Then, in the 1970s, the United States had fought for and won a general agreement to abide by the scientists recommendations. As a result, Japan and the Soviet Union hadn't filed an objection in the last five years, though the IWC had cut their catch in half. How hypocritical for the United States to file an objection now, the conservationists argued. Such a move might jeopardize whales all over the world! And what was the "temporary disruption of nine Eskimo villages," as one group called it, when matched against that?

The meaning of the federal government's action was clear

to many Eskimos when they lost an October 1977 court fight to force the United States to file the objection that would save their subsistence hunt; they came to believe, as Barrow activist Charlie "Etok" Edwardsen put it, that white men were "very selective about which species they choose to preserve. . . . Evidently, [Eskimos] are among the species they have destined for extinction."

Though the United States did not file an objection, it did seek a restricted hunt for a small number of bowheads, and at a special meeting in December 1977, the IWC relented. Citing cultural and nutritional considerations, the IWC voted, over the objection of its scientists, to allow a special, limited hunt in 1978. To the Eskimos it was a small concession, in part because the quota fell far short of what they said they needed for food. But because the whaling captains were confident that a count of the whales would show there were far more than the IWC believed, they expected the IWC to go away after the study was made. In spring 1978, the organization of Eskimo captains, the Alaskan Eskimo Whaling Commission, conditionally agreed to abide by the IWC's restriction. Grudgingly, the Natives worked out with the federal government an allotment of the quota that would allow nine villages to land a total of up to twelve bowheads. In trying to catch the twelve, Eskimos would be allowed to strike no more than eighteen with their darting guns. Since 1970, the Natives had taken an average of twenty-nine bowheads a year. In Gambell, which would be permitted to land one whale or strike two, whichever came first, Silook said he felt as if his family were under attack by white men.

Although the temporary quota had cooled the crisis by a few degrees, there was bound to be friction when, in April 1978, two federal enforcement agents, two scientific reseachers, a handful of brief-visiting bureaucrats, a wire-service reporter, and a journalist showed up in Gambell, a village that wasn't used to having white people stay for very long. One villager called us "sons of the whale men," an apt, if unflattering, reference to this, the second coming of white men with a vested interest in the whale.

Though none of us white men was ever hard to spot, the enforcement agents stood out most of all: they dressed alike in green parkas and pants, with woolen watch caps to match, and they both rode shiny new yellow snowgoes. Understandably, they did not like the attention that pressed upon them. And who could blame them, for the situation was tense and they were apprehensive. What were they going to do if the hunters violated the quota and continued whaling? Everyone knew that if it came down to it, the agents could not enforce an unpopular law in a far-off village.

A federal wildlife agent had proved as much in Barrow back in 1961, when he tried to enforce the Migratory Bird Treaty of 1916. The treaty had never been enforced in northern Alaska and for good reason: it prohibited the hunting of wild fowl during the only months they were present in the Arctic. Because ducks and geese were an important part of the Eskimos' diet, arresting someone for shooting them out of season was tantamount to raising the Jolly Roger. A day after making his second arrest, the agent was met by 138 Eskimos bearing 138 pairs of dead ducks and sworn statements they, too, had shot them out of season. Faced with the prospect of arresting a whole village, the government relented. This dramatic show of civil disobedience had won what became known as the Barrow Duck-In.

No, the enforcement agents could not enforce the whaling quota without the Eskimos' compliance, and they knew it better than anyone else. The only way to stop the Eskimos if they challenged the law was to call in the troops. That possibility had actually been raised back in Washington, where it was always easier to talk tough. But what was the federal government going to do? One of the Alaskans in charge of federal enforcement had been the first to ask. The government could hardly send PT boats to patrol the ice fields, he had pointed out. This would not be a job for the Coast Guard or the Navy: nothing short of a military airlift would do. Shuddering at the thought, in June 1977 he had turned to William Aron, U.S. commissioner to the IWC, and asked if he was actually ready to consider that. Yes, Aron said, probably to impress the Alaskan with his influence, he could get congressional support for an airlift.

Imagine troops parachuting onto shore-fast ice to intercept the hunters. Or maybe they'd try to advance by motorized transport. And who would the federal government send? The National Guard would be the logical choice—the Guard had the only special force that knew the ice and was trained to move over it. This force was called the Scouts. The Eskimo Scouts. In civilian life they were hunters, and they lived in villages like Gambell and Barrow. Using them would create a problem, though: after all, the feds couldn't very well send the Scouts out to arrest themselves.

Perhaps the idea of an airlift was no more than bluster. Aron later told me that if he had said such a thing he was joking. Yet the thought of making arrests, with or without reinforcements, was not funny to the Alaskan agents who would have to carry out Washington's directives.

Although angry and troubled by Outside intervention, most Eskimos were not belligerent. Traditional Eskimo society had always sought to avoid confrontation, stressing instead the restoration and maintenance of peace among its members. Public opinion was its greatest control; to be isolated from the whole in a land with so few people was its greatest punishment. The Eskimo Whaling Commission, which represented all nine villages, pledged to abide by the quota for this one year. For its part, the federal government lauded the spirit of cooperation and privately assured Eskimos there would be no heavy-handed attempt at enforcement. The possibility of a violent confrontation seemed minimal, especially in Gambell, where villagers were more acquiescent than villagers elsewhere.

Furthermore, the agents in Gambell—Andy and Bill— were far from gun-happy marshals. Seeking to avoid confrontation, they went about their job with commendable tact. Outgoing and friendly, they did all they could to be "just folks." When some of the villagers had mechanical problems with their snowgoes, for example, Andy, the lead agent, helped repair them. The big man, Bill, was equally accommodating. He had an easy laugh, always an endearing trait to Eskimos. Both seemed to get along well with the villagers, but beneath the surface, they and all the other whites who had come north were deeply troubled. Like soldiers abandoned at an outpost, they were charged with a mission they grew to resent.

At the headquarters of the IWC in London and in the command centers of Washington, it was not hard to believe in the mission. But at an outpost far from the security of consensus, the rightness of the quota inevitably came into question. Living among the villagers made it harder for even the most zealous protectionists to believe in the cause. (So it was that, after visiting Point Hope and Barrow that spring, two representatives of the Greenpeace Foundation, the most dramatic and well-publicized antiwhaling crusaders, came away from their experience supporting a subsistence hunt that other members of the organization totally opposed.)

In Gambell, it was easy to go over to the other side. It was hard to dislike the villagers. Eskimos were courteous and gracious hosts. They invited us into their homes for tea and crackers and Native foods, and they were just as generous in sharing their knowledge. "Watch out for that kind of ice"; "Never go off without food"; "Navigate by the direction of the snowdrifts because they run east and west." On the trail or out in the angyaqs, they were always helpful and always concerned about our well-being, which was almost totally dependent upon them. Were we warm enough? they would ask. "Here, wear this." When most of them talked, they spoke softly, simply, with a cheerfulness that came more easily to them than to us.

It was hard not to like the villagers; it seemed easy to dislike other white people. The battles among us whites were more open than any waged with the hunters. Strangers in a foreign land, we were pulled toward one another by curiosity and the need to communicate with other whites, but, because we were competing for territory, we circled each other warily. Even when attraction temporarily overcame repulsion, we tried to avoid being seen together by the villagers.

I think all of us wanted to be different from other white men in Gambell and, hence, be "more acceptable" to the Eskimos. I did. That's why I kept my distance from the AP reporter on the boat that day. That's also why I took big helpings of mungtuk, whale gum, clams from the walrus's stomach, and meat dipped in seal oil, all with a big smile on my face, though I sometimes pretended I was less hungry than I really was.

There were other ways in which I found myself and other white men competing. I and perhaps some of them came to believe that the villagers must be protected from Outsiders, which meant from other whites. Like prosecutors stalking a defendant, we cross-examined each other's rationale for coming here. We accused each other of dark motives and damaging effects. To me, for instance, Andy and Bill were at first the agents of an unjust and heavy-handed intrusion, while to them, I was the intrusive Press out to sensationalize Trouble in Paradise. Just as I made sure everyone knew I was not a cop, one of the agents counseled whaling captains not to trust me because of the damage I might do to them.

On the surface, our dealings with the Eskimos seemed so much friendlier than our dealings with each other. Amid the banter and cheerfulness, it was easy not to see their resentment because it was difficult for the villagers to express it. Members of perhaps the most traditional of Eskimo villages, Gambell's people had been bred with a sense of courtesy and a lack of assertiveness. They shunned aggressiveness, and the display of anger was considered childish. Hard pressed to give orders, they preferred the modest and suggestive tone of *maybe*, as in, "Maybe you should do that differently." And if they failed in their first endeavor, they might patiently allow experience itself to command by example. Except for some who had spent time in white society or were drinking, they never criticized anyone loudly or directly.

The combined effect of these traits was to surround the Eskimo in an aura of peacefulness, an aura that two and a half centuries of white men had beheld with the most romantic admiration. It helped, of course, that the traits made the Natives seem acquiescent too. Straightforward requests and straightforward refusals were considered impolite, so when white men made their requests, the villagers shrank from saying no. But never hearing *no* caused a great deal of cognitive confusion for white men, who never learned that *yes* meant *maybe* and *maybe* generally meant *no*. Instead of arguing with people who could be childishly demonstrative, Eskimos preferred to agree, then go about doing things the way they wanted. As a result, two and a half centuries of white men had concluded that Eskimos were not only acquiescent, but slow-witted as well. Learning the ballet of nuance and suggestion might require a lifetime's apprenticeship, and most white people did not have the time.

Within traditional society, the dance of social norms was gracefully effective. Beyond the village, its subtlety was lost on white bureaucracy. The villagers' patience and lack of assertiveness weakened them politically, a handicap aggravated by language. Many of them could not read, and very few were comfortable speaking before a crowd of white men.

Paradoxically, Eskimos had to act like non-Eskimos to

defend their way of life. When the IWC had proclaimed its ban on Eskimo whaling, for example, Barrow Native leaders had counterattacked with organizational skills, angry political action, and a team of corporate lawyers. From Barrow, young hunters regularly traveled to Juneau and Washington, DC, where they worked as aggressive, hard-willed lobbyists. Had it not been for Barrow's activists, the federal government would never have been pressured into helping overturn the hunting ban.

But they had succeeded with just the sort of assertive, outspoken, and forceful behavior that would have been shocking and unacceptable within a traditional Native community. Charlie Edwardsen expressed the dilemma well: "To stay the way we are, we have to fight. But if we fight we are no longer the way we are."[9]

On Saint Lawrence Island, it was easy not to see people's resentment because they often expressed it through jokes and laughter, which were traditional, socially accepted forms for airing grievances. From previous experience, for example, Silook always expected white men to ask about igloos. White men's stereotypes (for example, that Eskimos live in igloos, rub noses, and share wives) irritated many Natives. Though the questions seemed innocent to white men, they were tantamount to asking black people if they really liked watermelon. Yet when asked the offending question, Silook would explain, "We used to live in igloos, but they burned down." When he was off the island, he would preempt the question by telling people that he sold "prefab igloos" for a living.*

The Eskimos threw verbal spears with an endearing smile, and we who were their targets laughed along with them.

"How do you spell *mahngoona?*" I once asked.

An older man looked at me incredulously. "We don't spell mahngoona. We eat it."

"Hee-hee-hee, hee-hee, hee-hee-hee." An explosion of giggling burst over his audience, who repeated it again to each other as if they'd never heard it before. One of them leaned forward as

---

*One further and last note on igloos (the word means "house" in Inupiaq): the image of Eskimos typically living in dome-shaped homes only held true in central and eastern Canada. Alaskan Eskimos never lived in, made, or even saw such houses.

if he were going to break in half, biting his tongue to stop laughing. Others hurried over—they loved to share in someone else's laughter—and like a piece of mungtuk, the joke was chewed again and again. When it seemed that it was about to be swallowed, someone smiled at me affectionately and commented, "Aapghuughaaq, you sure are a *soospuk* [nitwit]," and it started all over again.

One of the whale researchers came by with a notebook later on, and oh, how one of the villagers marveled at it. "Imagine," he said, "I spend my day hunting and you spend your day dirtying up little pieces of paper." Again, the audience fell into hysterics. Could such infectious little-girl giggles really be malicious?

Silook's uncle Roger, one of the more urbane citizens of Gambell, loved to inform the white men who sought him out, "I have a master's degree in Eskimo studies." Scientists, administrators, and agents all gravitated to him. Afterward, Roger would announce: "Our knowledge exceeds the biologists'. They're asking us questions, so we must know more." The villagers could hardly contain their glee.

As we motored home through heavy ocean swells on that Wednesday only a few days after my arrival in Gambell, I wondered why the whale had been lost.

Its loss made me uncomfortable—as it also made the researchers and enforcement agents. We had all hoped the hunters would kill and land the first whale they struck. It would have made things simpler for all of us. Then the enforcement agents would not be in the position, as they might be now, of having to declare an end to this spring's whaling before a bowhead was landed. If villagers had gotten the first whale they struck, we could all believe in the tidiness of the hunt and in the hunters' skill.

The question was posed merely by our presence among the returning hunters, who made no attempt to hide the fact they had struck and lost a whale. The whale had gotten away for two reasons, the captain said: the gun had fired the bomb, but the bomb hadn't exploded and then the harpoon came out. So the whale escaped, probably with a bomb the size of a horseshoe stake lodged inside its body—although other reports were that the bomb may have grazed off it altogether. Whether or not the whale escaped with its life, it had definitely escaped the hunters.

The captain's answer seemed sufficient enough for the other hunters. "Our food is hard to catch," the captain said softly. He said this with great sincerity and a dignity that underlay his every expression.

"Our food is hard to catch," he repeated. "It is an Eskimo custom." His grand equanimity impressed the white men who spoke with him.

He regretted that the gun hadn't worked, but, "We can't help that," he said. Surely these white men who lived among them would come to understand how hard it was to capture Aghvook. Putting the loss of the whale out of their minds, along with most other things that were already relegated to the past, the villagers went about living. They had come home safely through the ice. It was spring and the whales were coming north. It was a time to be glad.

At the basketball game that night they cheered and laughed and marveled like kids at the movies.

Watching them, I began to brood. When asked why the whale was lost, it was enough for them to answer the gun didn't work. It wasn't enough for me. After several days amid the ice, I understood how injured, harpooned whales could escape from the hunters. The ice was beyond mastery, and it offered a comforting explanation why the whales were lost. But the gun was a human contrivance, and its mechanical failure was banal and unsatisfactory.

Sitting among the villagers, I wondered if the whale was still alive. No one knew, for there was no way of knowing whether it survived the wound, unless and until it was found belly up somewhere in this ocean of ice sometime in the precious few days before putrid gases escaped its bloated corpse and Aghvook forever sank out of sight. There was little chance it would be found, for in the Arctic, smoking guns always outnumbered corpses. If the bomb had severed an artery or pierced a vital organ, the whale must surely die. Maybe it had lodged inside a muscle, I thought. Maybe the whale was all right. But what if the wounds were septic? One of the hunters had said a wounded whale will die from infection in two or three days. I

             GAMBELL: THE HUNT, CONTINUED

hoped he was wrong. The game went on, and around me my friends cheered and clapped with a delight I chose not to share.

The loss of one whale would be inconsequential if there were lots of bowheads. And even if there weren't, it would have been insignificant in any other year than 1978. Under the circumstances, however, it *was* important, because Gambell was allowed to strike and lose no more than two whales. Why no one seemed anxious about this that night puzzled me. "Why," I asked myself, not wanting to alienate myself still further from my hosts, "why didn't the gun work?"

Early Friday morning the Apangalooks placed the darting gun and a wooden box of bombs into the angyaq. We pushed the boat over gravel shore uncovered by the Pacific swells and launched into calm seas, for the storm waves had died. We sailed westward, under gray skies, past gray slush, into gray fog and snow. The world closed in.

Opening the wooden toolbox, Elmer took out a bomb as his uncle Leonard commanded. Although it was a school day, Elmer and the rest of the high school basketball team—and most of the male students, for that matter—were out on the water. He clutched it at the bottom and passed it forward like a baton, making sure I had a hold on it before he let go. It was packed with a half pound of powder and, had he dropped it, the bomb might well have blown up. I passed it carefully to Silook, who loaded it into the barrel of his darting gun. He lifted the gun by its long wooden shaft and moved it into position. The barrel rested atop a small triangular foredeck so that the bomb pointed over the bow and the harpoon jutted out of the boat like a bowsprit. To the walrus-skin harpoon line, he attached a float made from an eviscerated seal and another made from red polyethylene like the ones used by commercial fishermen in the Gulf of Alaska.

There was nothing to do now but sail among patches of ice that lay like leaves on a pond. We sailed westward, lulled into reverie by a listless breeze and the rilling of water against our hull.

Elmer, who was monitoring the walkie-talkie for reports from other crews, switched channels. He passed through conversations between Japanese fishing boats somewhere in this same vast ocean, though certainly not nearby. The villagers thought Japanese was comically frenetic. Hearing the same transmission, a crewman aboard another boat broke in with his own imitation: "Yuka-tuka-ta, yuka-tuka-ta." Silook and his brothers burst out laughing when they heard it.

Not so far away as the Japanese were Soviet broadcasts to the Yupik-speaking people of Siberia. From a radio broadcast in Nome came Roberta Flack and Donny Hathaway singing "The Closer I Get to You." We sailed westward, in a translucent leather boat with a gun barrel poised on its bow like a missile. I gazed at our little shell of steel and stone age, naïvely trying to decide if it carried us backward or forward: to Old World Asia or the modern West. Like Saint Lawrence itself, we were an island in between, yet our direction was irreversible.

Far to the west, when nothing was behind us and nothing was in front, when the sky fell down and the cold scraped my bones, when we seemed like a tiny boat in a primordial ocean, we began to see bowheads. They were surfacing on both sides of us in an eerie silence broken only by their breathing and the rustling of wind in our sail. Silook turned and flashed me a quick smile. He was the boat striker today because Preston was back in Gambell, minding the Native store while its manager, his brother Leonard, was out with the crew. He was smiling because Leonard had a good chance of steering us onto Aghvook's back to give Silook his first chance to harpoon a whale.

We were sailing through a corridor of ice cakes laid out like flagstone in a garden. At short intervals, wide black tails rose skyward, brushing the air like the lazy wave of a fan on a summer's day. Did they know we were here? Unexpectedly, the bow-shaped snout of a big, black head cut through the ocean's dark surface as if it were a submarine ascending. "Puhhh! Puhhh!" Sucking in the Arctic air, it went under for a few seconds and came up, went under and came up, on a northward path to an uncertain destination.

Tense, still, and intoxicated with anticipation, I sat upright, unmindful of the cold and suddenly intent. The Eskimos were tracking down food, and their attempt to catch it was made no less serious by the fact that they were tingling with excitement, like schoolboys at a basketball game.

Like Eskimos, the whales seemed less intent on motion than white people were. During the spring migration they could travel at a casual pace, stopping along the way to rest or perhaps to copulate or give birth. Sometimes, as when their path through the pack bottled up, whales had to wait at its southern edge for the ice to disintegrate further so there would be passages or breathing spaces while they moved north. There was a time to play, too, and in one spot of a pondlike ocean where yesterday there had been a sea, three bowheads were playing when Isaac's crew came upon them. It was his crew that had struck and lost Aghvook two days earlier.

Through the binoculars we saw the striker raise his darting gun. He looked like a foremast with its yardarm tilting forward. As the boat drifted closer to a pair of whales, one lying atop another, he cocked his arm and hurled the gun from nine feet away. The whale underneath was already alarmed, but it was too late for the whale on top. In pain and fright it lurched high out of the water, its head, jaw, and chin straight up, quickly looking about for its assailant before it dove.

"Aghvengukuut!"

Silook and our crewmen let out a great yell. Still cheering, they hurriedly struck the sail; it tumbled down on us like a tent collapsing. We furled the canvas around the boom as Mike and Leonard secured the Evinrude into its motor well, then primed and jerked it to a start. With Leonard at the tiller and Mike, our motorman, opening the throttle, we dashed off in whining pursuit of Isaac's whale.

At the time we didn't know that the gun, the same one that hadn't worked two days earlier, had failed again. The triggering rod had sprung the gun hammer, but this time the shell hadn't gone off and the bomb had never left the barrel. As a result, the whale drove into the ice with only the harpoon embedded in its flesh.

This was the way the hunt had been before the coming of guns and white men. We were chasing a whale as it dragged the speckled sealskin floats toward Siku—the ice—its great protector. Isaac's angyaq was nearest, but his crew was slow getting the motor into place—they had to move around a small cake of

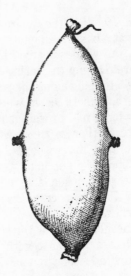

Sealskin float.

ice—and they lost precious time. Other boats converged on the scene, racing through open water, into slush ice that had already set up as young ice farther in. Leonard's angyaq smashed it into shards as we plunged forward. Farther in, when the motor started grinding like a worn-out blender and the captain worried that ice might cut into our hull, we reached for boat paddles— they were tucked in along the rails—to punch through thicker ice. On the other side of the sheet ice, we came to a zone of broken ice that was congested with small slabs like a pond with water lilies. Taking long, deep strokes, we paddled canoe-style, although the gunwhales were designed more for ocean sailing than paddling. My arms ached from exertion, yet I hoped we might reach the whale and I thought we must.

Someone saw a pair of sealskin floats moving through the ice a quarter-mile away. All eyes turned in their direction, and soon after, the whale surfaced in the same vicinity. With their binoculars the men saw it roll onto its side. Because the shell hadn't fired the bomb out of the barrel, the men thought the gun might still be attached to the harpoon. But it had apparently been sloughed off and deep-sixed. Only the harpoon was affixed to the whale.

GAMBELL: THE HUNT, CONTINUED

We went back to paddling for a few minutes more until by silent agreement the others stopped. It was no use. The floats that led to the whale were traveling farther into the ice. The whale was driving itself deeper into safety.

Sometimes, if the ice was thick enough, the men could give chase. If the ice was also flat, they could push the angyaq's ivory-lined keel over it. Or they could run after the whale, as Leonard and Roger Silook did once when John Apangalook was still captain. On that occasion, the injured animal had been lying a half-mile away under a sheet of ice that heaved upward like the earth's crust, releasing a volcano of steam whenever the whale surfaced to breathe. Climbing atop the mountain, the two hunters had lifted a chunk of ice and driven their gun into the black turbulence below. The whale smashed through the wall and died there when the bomb blew up. Leonard still had the home movies to show it.

But now the ice was too thin to stand on and too thick to break through. "We made a real good strike," Isaac said several days later. "If that shell had gone off, we would have gotten the whale even if the bomb didn't explode."

At the edge of the ice field, the boats stayed on a while longer to search for a sign of the whale. We drank tea and coffee and ate granola bars and Spam. Two hours after the whale had been harpooned, we dismounted the motors and raised our sails. Giving up the chase, we drifted off.

14. Silent Guns and Other Omissions

Once they had given up hope of capturing the second whale, Gambell's hunters sailed on in search of another, to be hunted with these same suspect guns. It hadn't always been this way. The first white men who brought guns must have seemed to the Eskimos like gods throwing lightning bolts. They could kill walrus and seals and white whales from a distance that amazed hunters who often had to come within arm's length of their prey before striking. Eskimos must have beheld firearms with a combination of fear and delight. Metal had long captured their imagination. They had seen it in precious knives and spears obtained through Siberian traders before the coming of white men, and after Laluremka came, they saw it in harpoons; they marveled at the cold, sharp steel that was as strong as the sea and held its edge like a long Arctic shadow. But the guns manufactured from metals were as yet unknown to them and fearsomely effective.

> A people are coming who will take the strength of thunder. All will be metal and their power taken from the thunder will be metal.[10]

It didn't take long for the Eskimos to discover how the magic worked. They had a fine sense of mechanics that had allowed their ancestors to fashion ingenious, sometimes elaborate traps and snares and tools that proceeded from A to B to C in workmanlike order. Indeed, it has been said by some that Eskimos understood how the gun worked even before they saw it; what they didn't understand was the gunpowder. Watching Silook take apart watches and motors and even my camera, I marveled at such innate ability. I saw it among the others too, and I was especially attuned to it because I am a true technological Neanderthal. Silook had never taken a camera apart before the day he fixed mine. When I expressed my admiration, he shrugged off my compliment, telling me, "We have an expression around here: 'If the Japanese can build 'em, the Eskimos can fix 'em.' "

Eskimos were quick to adopt guns. Before 1848, there had been no more than a dozen guns in all of northern Alaska, because the few white men the Eskimos met had been careful to keep guns out of Native hands. But thirty years after the whalers came, most of Barrow's hunters had guns, and the kind they wanted most in springtime was whaling guns.

Captain Ebenezer Pierce's "harpoon bomb lance gun," as the darting gun was first called, was especially designed for the Arctic. Hunting in open water, Yankee whalemen found killing and catching whales a straightforward business. They used a harpoon with a long, heavy rope line that was fastened to their whaleboat, so that after the whale was struck and was struggling to get away, whalers and boat were pulled along on a "Nantucket sleigh ride"; when eventually the line could be reeled in, the hunters would come alongside the animal and could thrust their lances into its vitals.

Hunting bowheads among northern ice, however, posed greater problems. Tying on to the struck whales meant being dragged through a deadly obstacle course. And all too often the struck whales would swim under the edge of nearby ice fields and escape, taking the Yankee harpoons and lines with them.

As far as the Eskimos were concerned, the escape of whales was an event ordained by supernatural forces. To the Yankees, however, losing whales was a technical problem. And so, while the Eskimos tried to devise more powerful songs to lure the escaping whales back, the Yankees engineered a scientific solution. By inventing a gun that allowed whalers to shoot and harpoon the whale in a single motion, the Yankees dramatically reduced its chance of escaping.

Pierce's darting gun had an elegant simplicity that made its design ingenious. Pierce put a gun barrel at the end of the wooden throwing shaft where the harpoon used to be and then put the three-foot-long harpoon above the barrel so that it projected beyond it, like a bayonet. To the firing mechanism at the back of the barrel, where the gun was attached to the throwing shaft, he connected a long, thin triggering rod. The triggering rod extended along the barrel's underside and beyond it as well. When a hunter threw the darting gun, the harpoon lodged into the whale, thereby securing the line and floats. And in a separate but simultaneous action, the triggering rod recoiled against the whale, causing the rod to push back and spring the gun hammer in the breech of the gun. It was as if someone had pulled a trigger. The hammer sent the firing pin into the primer of a brass eight-gauge cartridge filled with black powder. Its explosion shot the bomb out of the barrel and into the whale like a bullet, and if all went well, the bomb would blow up and might kill the whale instantly, while the darting gun, kicked free of the whale as the bomb shot out the barrel, could be retrieved and reused.

The truth of the darting gun was that it worked well in the hands of capable hunters—and the Yankees were among the world's greatest. Using it while roaming northern waters, they were able to catch nine out of every ten bowheads they struck.[11] And though that average dropped sharply when they began to hunt from shore-fast ice as the Eskimos did, their losses had little to do with the gun itself. In Yankee hands, the gun seldom failed.

Metal lightning, metal thunder. Darting guns must have once worked well, too, for the Eskimos who got them from Yankee whalers; after having (in several noted instances) rejected Yankee harpoons as inferior to their traditional weapons a few years before, in the late 1880s and the 1890s the Eskimos adopted the darting gun as universally as the Yankees had.

Then why did the whaling guns fail today, when they had once worked so well? Had I known the history of the gun's performance I would have asked that question sooner. But I

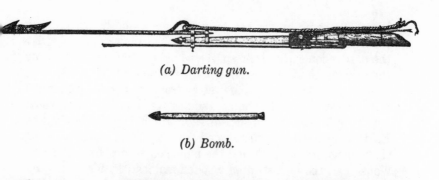

(a) Darting gun.

(b) Bomb.

Diagram showing inside of bomb.

didn't. I had come to Gambell believing there was something wrong with the gun.

Conservationists and people in the federal government portrayed the darting gun as obsolete and unreliable. They pointed out that its design was over a hundred years old and that in many instances Eskimos hunted with the very same guns used and left behind by nineteenth-century whalemen. Today's villagers were loading old guns with bombs and primers designed for newly manufactured weapons, Andy, the enforcement agent, explained. "It's like mixing Chevy parts with Ford parts, and then they wonder why the bomb didn't go off."

When I asked the hunters why the gun failed, they offered even more answers. Some said the spring on the older gun hammers wasn't strong enough to drive the firing pin into the cartridge. Others said the copper primers on the cartridges were too hard or that the primer pocket was too deep, or the rim of the cartridge was too thin so it sat too far down in the barrel. The result in each case would be the same: the cartridge would not explode, and the bomb that rested on top of it would stay in the gun barrel.

The hunters listed other reasons as well. I listened to Oovi explain why the bomb might not explode even when the gun shot it into the whale. Inside the bomb, he said, was a percussion cap.

When the bomb hit the whale, a plunger would be driven from the front of the bomb toward the back. The plunger would strike the percussion cap and the sparks would ignite a fuse to blow up the powder. But until the bomb hit the whale, a thin wooden peg, "the keeper," kept the plunger away from the percussion cap.

In store-bought bombs, the peg was made of balsa wood, which broke easily and at the right time. Unfortunately, the Eskimos couldn't get balsa wood from the local store, so when they repacked and reloaded their unused bombs from the previous year, they substituted wooden matchsticks for balsa. Unlike the balsa, however, the wooden matchsticks were too strong. They often didn't break when the bomb hit the whale, and when they didn't break, the bomb didn't explode.

How tragically bizarre, I first thought, that bowheads might be lost for lack of balsa-wood pegs. It seemed terribly sad that the springs were too weak, the primers too hard, the cartridge rims too thin. Something must be done to help the Eskimos, to save the whale. I thought they needed a mechanic, and apparently the federal government thought so, too, since that very spring it had initiated a program to improve the Eskimos' weapons.

To anyone who asked, the hunters would give expert instruction on the mechanics of misfires and malfunctions. I found it curious, however, that my instructors included hunters whose guns so persistently failed. In their homes I saw the best technical handbooks on gun repairs, maintenance, and loading. I watched them pack their own ammunition and heard countless conversations about guns. They knew how they worked and they knew what went wrong.

But if they knew what went wrong with the guns, I started to wonder later on—and still to myself—why the hell didn't they fix them? What would it have taken to make a matchstick as weak as balsa? They could have shaved it down. If the springs were too weak, why didn't they replace them or fashion their own? And if the rims were too thin, why didn't they build them up? These were people who faced and solved problems with rifle cartridges all the time. They were resourceful and clever. So why didn't they make the adjustments?

Yet, at the time, I continued to commiserate with those whose guns had failed. I still wanted to blame the gun. The gun

GAMBELL: THE HUNT, CONTINUED

didn't smile, didn't laugh and ask me to tea, or tell me about its ways and the nature of the land and the sea. But it was because I wanted to blame the gun that I started asking questions more openly, like an interrogator.

It was Leonard Apangalook who set me off on the right track. He was repairing his outboard engine one day in the spring of 1978 when he tipped me off. Leonard was an analytical man—I could see that by the assembly of parts and tools on his living room floor. He was talking about the importance of bomb care, which he said he had learned from his father and his Army munitions instructors.

The black gunpowder in their bombs and cartridges posed a big potential for trouble, Leonard told me. It soaked up moisture, and when it was wet, it was worthless. Unfortunately, the Arctic climate created all too many opportunities in which that could happen. Perched in the boats or lying on the ice, gun barrels could collect moisture from condensation or saltwater spray, and whenever objects were brought out of the cold and into warm houses or tents, they began to sweat with condensation.

There were ways, though, to minimize the powder's troublesome character. To prevent moisture from collecting in the gun barrel, for instance, hunters could seal it off by regularly plastering naphtha soap around the end of the barrel and the bomb. They could also keep their bombs and cartridges well wrapped in a dry, protected box, and at the very least they could change the powder each year, because like fluctuating temperatures, time also took its toll. Leonard said his crew did these things as their father had told them. Then he matter-of-factly stated that 90 percent of the problems having to do with the darting gun occurred because hunters hadn't repacked their unused bombs or checked their equipment before going whaling.

I was dazed by Leonard's revelation. At first I couldn't believe it. I was afraid of its implications, afraid of the effect such a conclusion might have when reported Outside, and I was afraid too about the effect such open criticism would have on my relationship with people in Gambell. It took another year and a visit to another village for me to accept it, but I finally realized that the problem was with the hunters, not their guns.

The debate within myself stopped only after I had talked

to an old whaling captain in Barrow: David Brower. David reckoned that his crews had caught thirty to thirty-five whales over the course of six decades. In all that time, he said, he knew of only one bomb that had ever failed him.

He worked on each one personally, to make sure the fuse, the percussion cap, and the powder were replaced each spring. Even when he was too old to go out whaling anymore, he tested all the bombs before sending his crew onto the ice. From a height of four feet, he'd drop each one, *minus its powder*, to the floor to make sure the plunger in the bomb's head would hit the percussion cap upon impact. If they went "Bang!" (like rounds of a kid's cap gun) he knew each one was right.

"Some hunters don't take the trouble to check," he would say quietly, stating an observation rather than a rebuke. "My dad, he told me and taught me: 'Take care of your bombs.' I've followed my father's instructions."

Success spoke by example, and in the hands of those who took care of them, the guns seldom failed. Occasionally, perhaps, a misfire or a malfunction could justifiably be attributed to forces over which the hunters had no control. But what went wrong all too often fell into the realm of phenomena that could have been avoided if Eskimos had taken care of their weapons and ammunition. The simple fact is that many of them didn't.

I had asked Gambell's hunters why their guns had failed, and they had given me mechanical answers that were both accurate but short of the primary cause, which had more to do with them than with their guns. Many of them were careless and negligent. But because Eskimos were so loath to criticize others, no one blamed the hunters whose guns failed. And like bad carpenters, the bad hunters blamed their tools.

We white men didn't have to apologize for the darting gun. It worked, and however hard the federal government might try, it was unlikely to bring about any major improvements. Nineteenth-century Yankee whalers, who knew more about killing whales than any government researchers in this century ever would, had already tried. They had tested all manner of possible improvements, from two-barreled guns that fired bombs and harpoons simultaneously to early-day bazookas that fired harpoon-carrying rockets underwater. In the course of experimentation, they refined the darting gun to near-perfection. Federal researchers might develop a more explosive powder, which would also make hunting more dangerous. But short of developing a whole new technology that might substitute cannons and ice-traveling catcher vessels for hand-thrown harpoons and skin boats, the federal government could do little else.

Especially when it wasn't the gun, but many Eskimos' connections to their guns that needed improvement. Only the Eskimos could make their guns work better.

15. The Umpire's Dilemma

We were drifting about at midday, for the wind had died and only the current carried us ever so aimlessly along. The ominous dark clouds of early morning had dissipated into a glaring, formless sky. Under its white light, I wondered if we were waiting for whales or for the call to come home. Having struck and lost the second of two whales, the hunters had reached their quota. I couldn't believe the hunt would come to such a sudden and empty conclusion. Perhaps the hunters couldn't either, because no one had taken a decisive tack for shore yet. In the stillness they must have wondered when the announcement would come from the beach.

This second loss seemed to be just the situation the enforcement agents had dreaded; who could blame them if they didn't relish the prospect of calling the hunters home before Gambell got its whale? Like the Sheriff of Nottingham, they were assigned to guard the king's animals from poachers, a job that was no more endearing here than it had been in Sherwood Forest. As Andy and Bill sat on the beach, among disappointed old men like Oovi and Irrigoo and other villagers so easy to like, the action they might take must have weighed heavily on their consciences. Afterward, big burly Bill asserted softly, "We're taking away their buffalo just like we took it away from the Indians."

When and if it came, the call to stop hunting would be made by Andy, the lead agent, who was no more eager to make it than his assistant Bill. He resented the constellation of forces that had converged to make him judge and jury. He doubted the scientific rationale that had brought him here in the name of saving the last few bowheads from extinction. "We're telling them something that may in fact not be true, which probably isn't true," he complained in private.

He was angry at the quota, angry at the government's intervention, and angry at the gun for not working, and probably troubled like the rest of us by the carefree, almost lighthearted negligence many of the villagers displayed toward the weapons they used. But he shielded his doubts in the same manner in which we all guarded ourselves from each other and from the villagers.

Much of Andy's exasperation stemmed from the weakness of his position. Without the villagers' compliance the quota could never be enforced, so he tried to soften the image of his mission. He succeeded to the extent that some villagers separated him from his assignment. Over the course of his efforts, however, the need for their acceptance took its toll, as it did on us all. I grew tired of jokes aimed at white people. I seethed at my own compulsion to smile, to apologize, to laugh with even the most scatterbrained belligerent, like the one who roared, "You god-damn white men! Ha-ha, ha-ha-ha." The face of the Fat Man became an annoyance that gnawed at my self-respect; humoring his malice seemed as degrading as wearing a "Honkies for Huey" button back in the 1960s. But it was an indignity of the sort Andy and I both endured with the idea of eventually gaining the Eskimos' acceptance. And what would that acceptance mean? Andy must have known that all the goodwill he cultivated would scatter like snowflakes when he began enforcing what the villagers didn't accept. I expected the same thing would happen to me if I began giving voice to the questions, doubts, and disappointments that were churning inside me.

Without the villagers' compliance the quota could never be

enforced, but without the threat of enforcement the villagers might never comply. If the villagers wanted to continue hunting, Andy couldn't stop them. Nothing short of armed confrontation could, and that, fortunately, was deemed too terrible a price for saving whales. All Andy could do was report violations for later prosecution, an action that would prove difficult at best and would fuel further hostility in any case. Andy was more PR man than cop, a guy who had been asked to sell bacon to Islam. Though he made friends, though he smiled, laughed, sympathized, and tried to protect the villagers' interests, he was a lonely man even with Bill at his side.

On the beach, tensions peaked at midday, when it became clear that the hunters I was with out on the water might not be able to abide by the quota and get their whale, too. With the loss of a second bowhead, the pregame banter between white men and villagers on the beach faded. Andy had been pushed behind the plate, an unwilling umpire, but an umpire nevertheless. Knowing that it was his job to call strikes, the crowd on the shore watched anxiously. If kids can be said to reflect their parents' mood, the air was noticeably unhappy. Although open hostilities were limited to the sting of snowballs and angry questions (an almost welcome alternative to the nightmare of violent confrontation), even these minor assaults bruised the sensitivity of white researchers and agents on the beach. Perhaps they were disturbed most by one question posed so unassertively by elders and repeated vehemently by a younger generation whose manner was quite different. Why, they all wanted to know, were white men taking the whale away from the Eskimos?

Those who asked were so deeply puzzled by our presence that those of us who had come here grew confused and uncertain. The rationale for sending enforcement agents and researchers was this: we're here to help you conserve the whales so you and your children can still hunt them in the future. If the whale were truly endangered, the white men reasoned, wouldn't the Eskimos, who had the most to lose, be the first to agree to restraints?

The Eskimos were not nearly as troubled about the population of bowheads as we white men were. "Lots of whales," they told us. On the beach, as we got off the plane, in the store, at basketball games, and over tea, they approached us as apostles

GAMBELL: THE HUNT, CONTINUED

would pagans with this good news: "We see lots of whales." Of course, this was just the gospel that might pacify white men, who were inclined to believe whales were more scarce than abundant, but even the elders said they were seeing more bowheads now than ever before.

I think the Eskimos' lack of anxiety was tied to a conviction more involved with old-time religion than science, however. Over fried bread and tea taken on the floor one day, a middle-aged woman tried to enlighten me. "The Eskimos were made by God to use the whale, walrus, seals, mukluk, and birds," she said, counting each of them out on her fingers.

The Eskimos had always believed in a being who provided and protected the bowhead. They thought the Moon was the one, until missionaries persuaded them that there was a single, all-powerful God. "And God created great whales," spoke the missionaries, convincing the Eskimos that this God surely blessed them with bowheads. And if the God of Abraham watched over the whales, they didn't need the federal government to look out for them.

For the moment, Andy did not have to force a confrontation. He had been delivered from making a decision, and for this he could thank the temporal authority of Washington as well as the hunters of Savoonga. Gambell's neighbors had had the same quota of two struck-and-lost whales or one landed, but they had captured their bowhead on the first attempt. According to federal regulations that made the infield fly rule seem simple, this meant Savoonga had an additional "unused" strike that could be reassigned, upon its request, to another village by the federal government. Past noontime, Silook's uncle Roger called shore to ask Andy if Gambell could have Savoonga's extra strike.

"Okay, Roger," Andy radioed back, relaying the word that federal officials had no objections.* "Keep going and good luck." He'd been talking to headquarters in Juneau from the village's only phone, linked to the outside world by a satellite communications system that skipped, echoed, and obliterated conversation

---

*Juneau headquarters said it saw no reason why Gambell could not have the extra strike as long as the Alaskan Eskimo Whaling Commission (AEWC) consented. Gambell's hunters officially requested and got permission from the AEWC headquarters in Barrow the next day.

THE UMPIRE'S DILEMMA

as if to say, "You can install a phone here just like you can install a quota, but that doesn't mean it's going to work like you expect it to."

In Washington, they must have thought that allowing such transfers was magnanimous, but it only aggrandized the government's pretense as ultimate dispenser of whales. So they gave Gambell another chance. Three strikes and you're out. They were making it a real ball game now.

Continuing the hunt, the villagers came upon a large bowhead basking like a beach bum in the noontime sun. As Benjamin's crew sailed closer, they noticed how the skin of its hump had dried under the hot rays of sunshine. By Arctic standards, the day seemed balmy, and the hunters had pulled back their fur hoods, but it would have seemed like the Ice Age to Benjamin's neighbors in California's Bay Area. He had lived there seven years, working as a carpenter, a migrant in the federal government's great attempt to relocate, train, and absorb Natives into the mainstream of American society. But Benjamin and other island emigrants awoke one day wondering why they were there, so far from the island. Soon after, Benjamin had returned to Gambell and had bought himself the gear to become a whaling captain.

The whale's sunbaked island of a back would have made a good landing area and allowed a more accurate and deeper strike. But Benjamin and his striker didn't think they could get any closer. Both the whale and the boat were drifting in the same direction. Without waiting any longer, and hoping to get lucky, his striker hurled the darting gun from afar.

This time we heard the yell as an electrical signal drifting across still water from the radio in another angyaq. "We have struck a whale!" the radio sparked. Once more, our crew soared with anticipation. Silook had that same look of wild, boyish excitement that seemed to express itself in even the most grave-faced Eskimo at the sound of that phrase.

Aghvengukuut! Do you hear that, everyone? We've struck a whale. And when we catch it, we'll bring him home. We'll cut strips of mungtuk from his skin and blubber. We'll eat it raw right there on the beach. We'll bite and crunch and chew with our big jaw muscles that got strong this way when we were children. We'll load up our sleds with it and bring it home and share it with friends and elders, who love it so much. We'll eat it frozen and we'll eat it boiled, plain, or dipped in salt or Worcestershire or seal oil or Accent. We'll cut it with our uluks and chew until the warm, rich oil trickles down our throats and dribbles down our chins. Then we'll let the rest of it get old down in our cellars or in covered boxes or under rocks like our ancestors used to do, until it gets real tasty and teases our tongues like a can of soda pop and makes us tired when we eat lots of it. Mungtuk makes our stomachs glad to be Eskimos.

The Apangalooks were thrown into a frenzy. Years later I can still hear them shouting the news, so happily and unselfishly glad for those who had struck Aghvook and were about to bring glory to themselves. I can still feel the sail falling down as it had before so that we could furl it and mount our engine and lower our mast and race after the harpooned whale.

Yet once more, it was all done needlessly, because the whale was soon gone.

Benjamin's floats had snagged in the mast stay as someone tried to throw them overboard. Like a running dog at the end of its chain, the darting gun jerked back out of the whale—and Benjamin and his crew were actually lucky that it did. If the harpoon had stayed in, the diving whale might have dragged the entangled floats, the angyaq, and its crewmen underwater. Afterward, Benjamin called what had happened a "one in a thousand" thing. (I realized it hadn't been just a case of bad luck a year or two later, when, berating his crew for just this sort of negligence with harpoon lines and floats, my captain at Barrow shouted: "Murderers! That's what you are if you do things that way! You'll kill us all.")

As disappointed as the hunters may have been at their losses, Andy must have been distraught because their failures were forcing him to make a decision. Out in the boat, I and the others awaited his announcement.

Almost everyone on the beach seemed to know about this third strike. The villagers were talking about it, the whale researcher knew, and the old men who interpreted the radio conversations for the enforcement agents knew. But somehow Andy didn't know, to judge from his account. He said later that in the confusion and because the Eskimos were speaking Yupik, he could not be sure if another whale had been struck and lost. Yet it appears he never asked those on the beach or, more importantly, the Eskimo reporting officer, Roger Silook.* (In the spirit of cooperation and because it could do nothing else, the government paid him and other Eskimos to assist enforcement agents in maintaining lines of communication with the villagers.) Without the hunters' own reports, the enforcement agents had no legal grounds for stopping this hunt. They were on the beach, they never saw any strikes themselves, and they didn't have any bodies to prove that too many whales had been struck and lost. Actually, Gambell's whalers were remarkably cooperative and forthright compared to whalers off the island. Unlike Barrow, where many more whales were struck and lost and never reported, Gambell reported all its major strikes.

In fact, the third whale had probably been only superficially wounded in its blubber, since the darting gun had pulled out before the firing mechanism could be triggered. "The harpoon didn't go in six inches," Benjamin said later. "I'm glad I didn't wound it." Apparently Roger, Benjamin, and the other hunters didn't think of it as a real strike, and, indeed, it was more like a ball than a strike. But the umpire could only call strikes, and for that reason, I later suspected that Andy had judiciously let it pass without taking notice.

The fourth whale was lost that afternoon when it escaped into the ice with one harpoon and a single float dragging behind it. The other one, a plastic fishing float, sprang loose from the line somehow and was found later that summer by Diomede Islanders a couple of hundred miles north of Saint Lawrence. No one ever found the whale. The hunters hit it with a bomb, but the bomb didn't explode.

*In his report to headquarters, Andy wrote: "There was possibly another strike attempt; however, not much information was ever available or could be found out about the incident." The report does not state whether or not he questioned either the reporting officer or the captain in question.

16. In the Thrall of the Shamans

The escape of whales was history and prehistory. And although we white men tend to romanticize ancient hunters, ancient Eskimos were even less successful than modern ones in stopping Aghvook from reaching the ice.

The ancient hunter truly must have been a brave and resourceful man. His skill in using what weapons he had was sometimes awesome, and what he had to kill large animals with was very little. As a result, he often hunted without the precision we white men retrospectively attribute to him. In his quest for food and warmth, he killed or injured many animals that he either couldn't capture or didn't use.

The Indians' hunt for buffalo, which forms our most popular image of American Native life before the coming of white men, is a good example. Many of us think of Indian buffalo hunters as bow-and-arrow-wielding horse riders, but in fact the horse was a new "technology" adopted from the Europeans. In earlier times, Indians hunted buffalo with clubs, pits, snares, spears, and an imaginative pretechnological method called the buffalo jump. To orchestrate the jump, hunters stampeded herds of grazing buffalo toward a cliff. Since the animals had poor eyesight, they didn't see the edge until it was too late and charged headlong over the brink. From the carnage below, the Indians took what they could use in their nomadic travels, then moved on. Behind them they left many hides because they needed only a few, and they left many carcasses because they could eat only so much. They left what they might have dried, because they preferred fresh, fatty meat to jerky. Though it was an effective, resourceful means of killing, the buffalo jump hardly fits our modern image of ancient hunters living in harmony with Nature.

Using their wits to make up for the shortcomings of their weapons, ancient Eskimos hunted as resourcefully as Indian buffalo hunters. Armed only with ivory- and slate-tipped harpoons and lances, early Eskimos couldn't kill the bowhead quickly, but they could bleed it to death over a course of hours. So they used floats to slow its escape, and they chased after it each time it surfaced in order to harpoon it again and drag it down with still more floats in the hope that Aghvook would exhaust itself before reaching the ice. Like the Indian buffalo hunters, the Eskimos hunted without precision: they aimed at many whales. While the buffalo jumpers captured many animals they couldn't use, Eskimo whale hunters harpooned many that they couldn't capture—just as today's hunters lost animals when their guns didn't work.

Of course, one reason the bowhead was surrounded by more taboos and ceremonies than any other Arctic animal was that it was so hard to capture. Yet even the old method of hunting was an improvement over the way they were hunted a thousand years earlier, before the adoption of floats and lines, a technological breakthrough in its own right. Like the Aleuts of southwestern Alaska and the Eskimos of Kodiak Island, northern Eskimos of that earlier era may have tried to capture whales by throwing poisoned spears in hope that one from the lot of their victims, after growing sick and dying, would wash onto shore rather than away from it.

Indians and Eskimos have never comported themselves like the sportsmen we have wanted them to be. Our values of sportsmanship derive from European aristocracy. After all, the defining image of a true sportsman is the gentleman who returns

GAMBELL: THE HUNT, CONTINUED

his fish to the stream after playing it out on a rod and reel. Even more significant is the noun we still use to refer to the animals that Natives hunt for food. We insist on calling them "game." A sportsman must play fair, after all, and a sportsman must give his opponent or his prey a sporting chance.

According to such values, Eskimos and Indians have been most unsporting. For, after all, they have been playing for keeps. If their methods have been sometimes indiscriminate, they have also been frightfully effective, for what has mattered most is finding meat. Both the Indians' choice of buffalo jumps and then horses and the Eskimos' choice of spears and then harpoons and sealskin floats were dictated by one consideration: whatever worked best.

Whether the Indians and the Eskimos lived in harmony with the buffalo and the bowhead before the coming of white men seems less clear than a more important, biological truth. For all their buffalo jumps, bows and arrows, clubs, snares and pits, a hundred thousand Plains Indians had little if any effect on some 75 million buffalo. Nor was it any different for the harpoon-wielding hunters of bowheads. And perhaps in the end, the relationship we white men have worshipped as harmonious was no more than Native powerlessness over the world they lived in.

To be able to live with such powerlessness, the Eskimos developed a cosmology as rational to them as Christianity was to Western men.

To both ancient and modern-day Eskimos there was a plan and a purpose for the whales. The purpose was clearer perhaps when the whale gave itself up to them. Whether it had been sent by the Moon or by the God of Abraham, the Eskimos had always believed its capture was a blessing; after their triumphs they gave praise and thanks, and before the next hunt began, earlier generations of Eskimos offered a sacrifice to Him whose gifts they sought. But if God gave them whales, He also took some away, as the Eskimos saw in sometimes spectacular events. There was the time in Barrow, just several years ago, when four bowheads came to the rescue of an injured whale that Horace Ahsogeak's crew had shot and probably killed. After one of the animals flipped the stricken whale into the air, they carried it off underwater and away from the hunters. Surely this was a sign, they said, that the whale was not meant to be captured.

Why God would ordain the whale's escape seemed more of a mystery than why He would ordain its capture. In the old culture, however, Eskimos found a reason for it, although they might have to consult with their shaman and he with the spirit world before they determined exactly what it was. In those days a fearsome array of taboos had governed their behavior while hunting, and invariably it would be found that someone had done something wrong to offend the whale or Him who had sent it. Perhaps someone had worn old skin clothes or perhaps a menstruating woman had gone out on the ice; the whale was repelled by uncleanliness. Had someone brought cooked food out in the skin boat? Had someone pointed at it, or had a crew continued hunting after the snowbirds began laying eggs? It may have been something someone said or thought, because like the Christians who came later, Eskimos could sin by thought and word as well as by deed. That's why talk of quotas and threats of breaking them alarmed elders in Barrow. One must never talk about how many whales he will catch, they warned. One must respect the whale and show reverence to the spirit in which it comes. At Point Hope, for instance, hunters still returned the skulls of butchered whales to the sea as their ancesters had done before them, in order to appease the spirit that resided in Aghvook.

There was a telepathic connection, Eskimos believed, by which the whale could understand them. So it was that hunters once sang songs calling the harpooned whale back to them with promises of kind treatment after they had killed it. Each crew's song was both secret and sacred, and some cast a magical spell.

"My brother Okhtokiyuk was a singer man, a spirit man," Irrigoo once told me. "He could talk to animals.

"There was a man, Aningayou. He was the first Christian here. He lost a whale way out there among the ice, near Siberia, one April. He had killed it too far out to tow it home. My brother said to him: 'If you believe in me, I will let you get a whale. I will hold that bowhead until summer so we can find it near the village.' And my brother talked to the animals to hold the whale back.

"That summer, someone came to me and said, 'Your brother says to tell you that Aningayou's whale has drifted on shore somewhere on the island.'

"I didn't believe it. 'That whale is too far out on the horizon, maybe way up north of Diomede Island,' I said to him. Then, after a while, someone came from Savoonga and said that they had found Aningayou's whale on the other side of the mountain [at Northwest Cape]. It just drifted ashore not far from here."

There were other stories too of Okhtokiyuk, the singer man and shaman. Irrigoo had seen him make whales roll onto their backs and lay motionless. He had extraordinary powers, as did others who talked with animals, and both he and they knew there was a reason why whales escaped. What was left of the old culture attested to its concern that the hunters be worthy of the greatest gift the Moon could send.

With the ascendance of Christianity and Western technology in the early twentieth century, Eskimos began attributing the whales' escape to more mysterious causes. Most of the taboos faded or were stamped out, and the shamans who upheld them were discredited. Missionaries used modern medicine to cure sickness where shamans couldn't, and the metal thunder of Yankee technology wielded more force than those who consulted with the spirit world. What happened to Okhtokiyuk is a good example of how the Eskimos' attitudes changed.

"Our crew struck a whale one time. We used up all our bombs. And we couldn't stop the whale. So the captain says to my brother, 'Will you try to do something?'

" 'All right,' he says. When the whale came up again, my brother spit on the water. The bowhead turned over dead. Then it came alive again. My brother spit on the water, whale roll over dead. No bombs. Three times it happened, but after the whale came alive the third time, my uncle says, 'Too bad when he spits, Okhtokiyuk can't sound like a bomb too.' " Irrigoo wheezed with laughter. "Then another boat came, strike it with a bomb and killed that whale."

Increasingly the singer men and shamans must have seemed to be children of a lesser God. Against the machinery of science, the missionaries of Christian civilization, and the onslaught of Western education, the shamans' influence faded like the melting ice. So too did moon worship and sacred whaling rituals, because as villagers became enlightened, they were urged or commanded to abandon the past. "When we learn what the ministers said, we changed," Oovi told me one day. "We tried to get away from the bad things. Keep Moses' law, what the Bible says: put away the old things and take the new way, and you will become the new Christians."

The Eskimos were reborn, and yet they were being torn from the spiritual womb that connected them to the whale like a child to its mother. Gone were the sacred songs to the whale: the singer men stopped singing. Okhtokiyuk became a Christian, and he took his songs with him to the afterworld. Gone too were the idols they had rubbed and the secret charm bags—Irrigoo threw his brother's overboard to return the once-prized objects to their place in the sea when his brother was baptized. In place of rituals and taboos came the cold enlightenment of a world that no longer talked with whales.

Yet though the shamans were gone, the reasons given to explain why whales escaped were often no more rational than the ones given before. When shamans still held power, Eskimos believed that personal behavior was culpable for the loss of whales, even if the hunters didn't know what the reasons were until after they consulted the shamans. Today, however, instead of blaming their failures on something someone had done, many Eskimos blamed their guns or talked of the mysterious ways in which God worked. With the help of technology, Christianity had taken the shamans out of society. Now it was as if technology had put them into the gun, to judge from the way many hunters acted. Among those Eskimos, the sense of personal accountability seemed to have faded like the shamans themselves. All that was left was the mystery of *why* the whales had escaped.

If God did ordain the escape of injured whales, it was better for them, I thought, when neither the gun nor the bombs worked; better when only the harpoon stuck in their bodies and the floats dragged behind like anchors. Logs kept by Yankee whaling captains commonly reported old harpoons being found in freshly killed bowheads. Apparently, floats and lines could be abraded and shorn off by the ice, and the harpoons might come to a negotiated settlement with the body like shrapnel in an old Army veteran.

Bombs were a different matter. If they exploded, the whale's escape might be short-lived at best; and even if they didn't, they could shatter a vital organ as they shot into the body. For the same reason darting guns were more effective than traditional weapons, the whale's escape had become more costly now, to the bowhead and the Eskimo alike. Yankee logs never mention old bomb fragments being found in a whale, and when Gambell's hunters did find some several years ago it was the first time anyone could remember.

Bombs and harpoons aside, my hope was that there were many more bowheads than the scientists thought.

But what did scientists know about Aghvook?

They had not been able to pinpoint either its wintering grounds or its summering grounds, but scientists claimed to know the route the herd of whales followed when the ice began to thaw in springtime. Scientists said the whales started out on their migration from somewhere in the South Bering Sea, from amid the loose ice along the southern edge of the ice front where they spent the winter. From there, the bowheads began following the edge of the retreating ice pack northward toward Saint Lawrence Island. After coming to the island, most of the whales swam slightly westward, the scientists thought, then northward through the channel between the island and the coast of Siberia.

The scientists knew (or thought they knew) that the whales followed "leads" of open water running through the pack ice like game trails through the brush. Sometimes, off the west coast of Saint Lawrence Island, for example, the trails were more like corridors or giant lakes littered with broken ice. But a few hundred miles north, after the whales passed through the Bering Strait and into the Chukchi Sea, the ice got thicker and extended in an unbroken sheet except for some fissures that ran like fault lines along the coast of Alaska and split the pack ice from the shore-fast ice. These leads might be a half-mile to thirty miles wide, depending upon the winds and currents that pushed and pulled, opening and closing lanes like a freeway at rush hour. When and where they opened determined when and where the number of migrating whales would peak off each whaling village.

Most of the leads were oriented in a southwest-northeast direction and carried whales northeastward as predictably as ship lanes from one year to the next. Narrowing as they approached the Alaskan mainland about two hundred miles north of the Bering Strait, the leads usually converged into a single major lane that brought more and more whales within range of Inupiat Eskimo villages that jutted into the sea, such as Point Hope, a major ancient and modern-day whaling village.

Fifty miles north of Point Hope, at Cape Lisburne, the lead generally took a more northeastward tack, paralleling the shore ice and passing the village of Wainwright. Farther along and ever narrowing, the lead turned eastward, funneling some, most, or perhaps all of the whales close to the shore of Alaska's northernmost point and into the Beaufort Sea.

Here at Point Barrow, some 750 miles north of Saint Lawrence Island, the federal government put a team of young scientists on the shore-fast ice and in the vicinity of Barrow hunters to count the migrating bowheads. After passing the last set of Eskimo whalers and whale researchers, the whales followed the leads eastward, far off the coast of northern Alaska and toward an uncertain destination in the eastern Beaufort Sea of the Canadian Arctic that scientists said was their summer feeding grounds. In early fall, the whales returned westward, skirting the northern coast of Alaska where they were hunted in open water by the villagers of Kaktovik, Nuiqsut, and Barrow before heading out to sea, first westward toward Siberia and then southward through the Bering Strait, along the Siberian coast and back to an uncertain destination in the South Bering Sea.

But was the route that the scientists plotted, from somewhere in the Bering Sea, past Point Barrow—where the counters were—to somewhere in the eastern Beaufort, the only route of the bowhead's spring migration? And was the Canadian Arctic the destination for the entire population?

The Eskimos of Saint Lawrence Island and of northern Alaska both said no. They claimed that part of the herd migrated along other paths and to other destinations. North of the Bering Sea, they said, were three main lead systems: a near-shore lead that brought whalers close to the Alaskan shore and past Point Barrow; a middle, offshore lead system that headed whales due north; and a far-distant lead system that pointed bowheads westward to Siberia. So, according to this long-held belief, the whales traveling through the latter two lead systems would never swim close to or even in the direction of Point Barrow. Supporting evidence for this theory came from earlier accounts of some Yankee whalemen who had noted that a great many whales swung west at Point Barrow instead of going eastward in springtime. If the Eskimos were right, the scientists were counting whales past a fork in the road.

To find out if the Eskimos were right about bowheads following other paths, or perhaps to prove they were wrong, the federal government sent teams of researchers out in planes, icebreakers, and other ships from the spring of 1976 onward. From the sky, they could see farther than the counters camped on ice, but like the others they could see whales only when they came to the surface of their world and to the edge of ours. And because the flying counters were traveling so fast, in the end they were able to see far fewer than the counters below.

Even so, the scientists said that what they didn't see was more important than what they did. After four years of aerial surveys, they said, they had not spotted a single whale in the western Chukchi or in the far-offshore leads. Furthermore, they said that vessel and aerial surveys indicated few if any bowheads remained south of Barrow after the counting camps were closed. Thus, the federal scientists concluded what they already believed: that essentially all the bowheads passed through the nearshore lead off Barrow almost as if they were patrons passing through a turnstile. And since the scientists were confident they could count most of the whales from there, they also believed that they could come up with an accurate estimate of the actual population. Were they right? More important, they countered, was the risk of thinking them wrong.

At the ice camps off Point Barrow, the scientists were posted like sentries standing atop a rock—indeed, they had chosen a perch atop a towering, grounded iceberg—but their task was not simple. They counted whales when they surfaced in the open lead within range of sight. But they didn't see whales that swam under broken ice, through a wall of fog, or far out to sea.

"If you want to count whales, you have to learn to travel like a whale and swim in its own environment," I was told by an Eskimo in Barrow. Perhaps the shamans had once traveled that way, under the pack ice, to consult with the spirit world that sent Aghvook. No one else had, certainly not the scientists who came bearing the tenets of scientific rationalism. Ours was a powerful system of knowledge, as could be seen in the planes that enabled them to search from the sky and in the ships that broke through the ice to search from the sea. Yet when our scientists tried to describe the dynamics of Aghvook's world, they were reduced to counting whales from above the ice and from the perimeter of the ocean the animals swam in. Their methods were not nearly so precise as their instruments and machines.

In the cold and wind, the counters watched for whales as best they could throughout the day and the night that no longer grew dark. They used binoculars, walkie-talkies, stopwatches, compasses, and surveyor's instruments to determine exactly where a whale was when they saw it and how fast it traveled and whether it was the same whale surfacing twice or one of two whales surfacing in the same vicinity. They never really knew for sure because they had only one perspective. Sometimes they even radioed back their sightings to a computer in order to figure out the probabilities that would help them decide if they were seeing one whale or two; they were playing the odds, a game at which Western science excels. They were inventive and bright researchers. They counted as best they could—and after a while they were probably able to spot whales as well as the Eskimos—until the rock they camped on thawed, split, toppled into the sea, and drifted away. Then, when they couldn't count Aghvook any longer for fear of their own safety, they retreated from the edge of the whale's world into the heart of their own.

Afterward, their already uncertain data would be offered up to the computers, and our machines would send down statistics that would be heralded as answers. Somehow the data would be corrected for whales believed to have been undercounted and whales believed to have been overcounted, for whales that passed by when the counters were unable to watch, and for whales that may have swum to Siberia or other far-flung spots outside the counters' range. *This* was shamanism too, and the programmers who conferred with the computers were our own magicians. Most of us didn't understand what they had done or how they had done it. The programmers followed mystical rites, and the machines bestowed them with "statistically significant probabilities" that they in turn handed up to the chief scientists as proof of the scientists' hypotheses. An aura of objectivity surrounded them both; a kingdom of economic prosperity seemed to attest to their claim, the claim of the rightness of Western science.

Were the federal scientists right that the bowheads were in danger of becoming extinct, as their "census" seemed to indicate? I didn't know. I did not understand the statistics, so accepting was a question of faith. This made me angry, especially when the scientists insisted their science was completely objective, as if they had made their computer models of the whale's migration and analyzed their data without any bias, expectation, or design. In the end, however, doubting the scientists' claims less than I doubted the Eskimos', I found myself on the scientists'—and what seemed to be the white men's—side of the great divide. If these scientists were playing the odds, I thought, the stakes of betting against them were too high. I hoped there were more whales than they estimated but reluctantly agreed there probably weren't; the bowhead was in danger and this hunt was dangerous. I was still a white man and, like it or not, still in the thrall of my own shamans.

17. Friday's Blessing

Again I waited to hear Andy's voice come over the radio to announce that the hunt was legally over. Apparently some of the captains were waiting too, for they seemed ready to sail ashore now that they had used up the quota they had agreed to abide by. I wondered why Andy didn't call, just as I wondered what it was I wanted him to do. It was nearly impossible for him not to know what had happened, even if Roger had not yet informed him. He knew from the voices, the talk, the open excitement and disappointment of those on the beach. By the book the season was over.

But the book was illegitimate and dictatorial. Asking, indeed telling, Gambell's villagers to stop hunting before they got a whale and while a wave of whales was swimming past the island ran counter to need and instinct. Trying to stop the hunt or trying to prosecute the hunters would only jeopardize the chances of future cooperation, Andy explained later. All the government could hope for, he added, was that the hunters would stay close to the quota. If the government could get the Eskimos to comply with the quotas within the next four years, it would have done a tremendous job. He said these things to me after Friday midnight, and he said them angrily, out of frustration at the day's turmoil.

It was as if we had switched positions. I had come to see a storybook hunt and to defend it from those who wanted to stop it. But the hunters' failures plunged me into an unpleasant reality. Angry and frustrated by what I had seen, I was contemptuous of Andy for not being more decisive. On Friday afternoon I wanted him to be a hard-line enforcement agent, reserving for myself the prerogative of extending sympathy to the hunters. But if I could afford to vacillate, Andy couldn't. The day's events forced him into making a decision.

One choice was harder to make than the other. To declare an end to the hunt, he needed confirmation from the hunters themselves that they had actually struck and lost this latest whale. And to get it he would have to call over the CB and ask them directly. Otherwise, and without an affirmative answer, he would have no legal grounds for acting (unless the hunters called in the report themselves). But even if he got the evidence he needed to act that afternoon, calling off the hunt seemed tantamount, as Andy's assistant said, to taking away the Eskimos' buffalo. Andy didn't do it.

"Lookit, Davit. Lookit." In the distance Aghvook lunged free of the sea for a brief moment, then fell, sending an explosion of water upward and a rumble of thunder across the broken ice. Silook and the others were excited, even though it was very far away. Silook passed me the binoculars as once again the whale leaped skyward like a salmon skipping in a mountain stream.

"Lookit, lookit!" Preston urged, and Silook, who was anxiously waiting to get the glasses back, said with a titter, "He's lookiting, he's lookiting." Six or seven times the whale breached free and fell. I thought of a trout I had once lost and how it danced upon the water to its freedom.

I had wanted them to capture the whale. Indeed, I had come to see them make their kill. But as Friday passed I was confused, disheartened, and embarrassed, no longer sure I wanted to be involved any longer. It was too late to bail out, though, too late to wish myself into an up-tempo version of Eskimoland.

FRIDAY'S BLESSING

"Lookit, Davit. Lookit." I saw the same whale that my crewmen did, but I didn't share in their delight. I could have accepted the loss of one or two whales, yet the thought that every village struck and lost four or more for every one it captured made me fear the bowhead was not long for this world. I had hoped the crews would return to shore, to wait until next year before resuming their hunt. Yet fearing now that they would go on harpooning whales until they captured one, I desperately wanted them to succeed. The song to Aghvook was gone, but my crewmates prayed, and so did I, that it would give itself up to us. Come, Aghvook. Come swim here, to us, so we can kill you well, so we can save the others.

We sailed listlessly along, waiting and searching for an unsuspecting swimmer that never came. To the south of us, however, Solomon Morgan's crew had begun to stalk their prey as afternoon passed into evening. It was a half-mile away when they spotted it floating like a dead man on water. One of them raised a black flag and waved it slowly to signal other crews within range, but at the time, the whale's capture was no more than a distant possibility. Their sail was empty of wind and the angyaq floated as restfully as the semisubmerged whale. In the stillness, they watched patiently.

For a half-hour, the whale lay motionless save for one sleepy emergence of its blowhole to exhale carbon dioxide and suck in oxygen. The sound of that percussive snort was unforgettable. When villagers asked why I had come here, I told them I had been a commercial fisherman before and now I wanted to catch the biggest fish of them all. They never laughed. Not once did they even smile. Instead, they would make the same serious and emphatic reply: "We don't fish for whales: we *hunt* for them." Yes, of course. If there was ever a question of the whale's biology, I had only to hear the sound of its breathing to know this was certainly no fish. When it flared its nostrils out there amid the ice, it sounded like a dozen agitated horses.

They watched it for a long time, while one of the crewmen paddled them gently ahead. After a second whale joined the first, the idea of capturing one of them seemed to take hold more firmly. Several crewmen dipped their paddles through the sur-

GAMBELL: THE HUNT, CONTINUED

face and dug forward. Ever so gradually, they narrowed the distance between them and their prey, until they came to a patch of broken young ice that was twenty feet across. They were close now, close enough so that the slightest bump of wood or ice could resonate an alert down into the water. As the angyaq drifted through, the whales bobbed up and down beside each other, apparently undisturbed.

They were only a hundred feet away now, in open water as still as a pond. In the other angyaqs, on the beach, and in their homes, villagers huddled over the radio like Depression-era fight fans, though the suspense, except for the prey's loud breathing, was noiseless. Solomon wanted the big one, the one that had turned on its back. The angyaq's bow was pointing directly at its head, so Solomon steered to port in order to swing the angyaq in a wide arc that would intersect the whale in its middle. But when they were fifty feet away, the big one started splashing water on its dry underbelly. Switching places with it, the smaller whale began a sudden and fateful swim toward the hunters.

In the bow, Solomon's striker—a man called Junior—stood up as the whale approached. He took the safety off and balanced the darting gun in his right hand. With his left, he held the coiled line that ran to the floats. "My heart was beating like it was going out of gear," he told me later. "I had to take a deep breath because I didn't want to get too excited."

The whale kept coming toward a boat it didn't and couldn't see because its line of vision was limited to either side. Then, twenty feet from the bow, it began turning broadside. Junior checked his balance. He looked down into the water and saw the whale's eye looking up at him from ten feet away. Now it too seemed to know. But too late, for it had shown its side to the hunter. With a grunt, Solomon's striker thrust his harpoon straight and deep into its flank.

It seemed to happen all at once. Junior saw the whale shudder, heard the percussion cap go off, saw its smoke and smelt its gunpowder as the recoiling gun shot backwards over his head and thirty feet behind the boat. In the periphery of his vision, he saw the floats going overboard. He watched the whale arch its back, kick, and disappear below.

Down went the first float as the line uncoiled behind a running forty-ton anchor. A moment later, the second one followed the first. Then, *"Whump!"* Metal thunder followed metal lightning and the bomb inside Aghvook blew up like a depth charge. The crewmen felt the wooden boat frame shake beneath their feet. Blood and oil lay like a slick on the water's surface.

Screaming with joy, Solomon was already jumping up and down in the stern when Junior, stunned and nearly speechless, turned and, not knowing what to say, said the obvious: "You've got a whale."

"Aghvengukuut!" The news was hollered over the radio, across the water, onto the beach, and throughout the village. "Aghvengukuut!" They worked quickly now to strike the sail and hoist an orange poke up the mast to signal the others who would be racing in from wherever they were to help cut the whale off before it reached the ice. It had already come up once, just three hundred yards away, apparently hungry for air because it hadn't been able to fill its lungs before diving. When it came up again, they must try to harpoon it a second time, then a third, until its hope of escape was exhausted. Converging at the slick of oil, fifteen crews searched for a pair of pink plastic floats whose emergence would signal the whale's desperate return to the surface.

To the southeast of us, two floats burst forth twenty minutes later and the fleet roared off in high-pitched, gas-fumed pursuit. They were closing in on a wounded mammoth, and it did not matter that they were using steel instead of stone and motors instead of walrus-skin sails. The chase stirred the same emotions in them as in their Stone Age ancestors. The whale rose, blowing out strong, tall columns of diesel-colored exhaust. Junior knew now that he had pierced the whale's lungs. It was injured badly, but before the boats could reach it, the whale dove among the ice. Worrying that it would escape, Junior puffed on another cigarette and talked to himself. This time, however, the ice was different from when the other whales were struck. It was thin and scattered, so the boats charged forward, dodging ice cakes like a halfback running downfield.

Only ten minutes passed before the whale rose once more, so tired this time that its exhaust was short and shapeless. It lay panting like a big black dog in the summer's heat. Short of air, it was unable to avoid Marvin Walunga's crew when they came alongside and thrust their harpoon forward, below its flippers.

Again there was the sound of a loud cap gun, the sight of the darting gun flying backwards without its bomb, and, a few seconds after the whale disappeared with another set of floats, the *whump!* of an explosion that made me shudder. Its lungs pierced, its internals shattered, Aghvook beat on. But its dive was still shorter this time; the hunters measured with their watches.

Two more angyaqs caught up with the floats and then the whale that followed them upward. No longer needing harpoons, the strikers threw just the bomb-tipped shaft of the darting gun as their boats came alongside. Aghvook's blow turned to a bloody spray—a sight that had prompted Yankee whalemen to cheer, "The chimney's on fire!" Aghvook sank below the surface, weak, dying, unable to dive, yet still swimming toward the ice that was too far away.

The village's fleet converged on the floats—they dragged along like beacons directing bombers to their target. Ready for the kill, the hunters motored closely behind; then, as the whale ascended for the last time, they gunned their engines and raced at it, one by one, in a triumphant frenzy of gunfire, explosions, and blood. Only half the bombs worked, but as it was it didn't matter: the hunters shot more than they needed. The high-nozzle spray of blood from the whale turned to a trickle.

As the cherry bomb- and firecrackerlike sound of the gunfire subsided, a ring of angyaqs surrounded the whale. Fifty minutes and nine bombs after it had first been struck, we lay beside it. From the boat it looked formless, a giant black hulk lying in black, fathomless water, with no bottom or head or depth to distinguish it. We watched in silence as its fluke turned into the air like the fin of a shark. Lazily, a flipper lifted, too. All involuntary reflex. Rolling onto its back, the whale showed its white chin to the sky and died.

Taking possession of its body, cheering hunters swarmed to its sides. Even while some secured it with extra floats, others climbed onto its stomach and eagerly began cutting out strips of skin and blubber. It seemed they couldn't work fast enough. Pushing their blades into the thick, rubbery skin, they drew heavy squares of mungtuk, then punctured a corner of each slab with a finger hole so they could lift the treasure out. It was as if they were cutting into a monster watermelon. Underneath the rind was a pink inner layer of soft, glistening blubber; it was oily and thick, but when they cut into it, it gushed like a watermelon too. Its juices formed a sheen on the water.

Floating above the whale's chin, I watched from our end of this huddled fleet, looking down the forty-five-foot-length of its body that was lined with boats and men leaning out of boats and men working atop the whale like diggers in a field. We were eight miles from shore, which was no different from being in the middle of this ocean. Gambell was invisible and seemed far away from us, but we could see Mount Seevookak, a low hump pushing through dark clouds.

With knives between their teeth, hunters leaned over the rail to pass along the heavy slabs of mungtuk. Silook lifted one into our angyaq and my crewmen excitedly went to work on it. Slicing off thin pieces, they shoveled the black and white mungtuk into their mouths. It had a fresh taste of hazelnuts, the skin was crunchy, and the blubber ran with juice as thick as mineral oil. I chewed and chewed like a boy masticating wax. They beamed when I asked for more.

"Now the International Whaling Commission has a whale," Roger pronounced after surveying the scene. The others laughed gleefully when someone else replied, "They'll probably give us half of one next year."

Pointing to his watch, an old-timer urged, "Let's hurry. They're having a carnival back in Gambell by now and I don't want to miss the dancing. He-hee he-hee-hee." Soon afterward, Junior cut the flukes from the whale and they started homeward: a long chain of walrus-skin boats with Evinrude engines towing a forty-ton whale to the shores of Seevookak.

Part Four: Stranded

18. Saturday's Spoils

On the night of their blessing, the hunters returned to Gambell in a long, motorized procession of victors and vanquished: huddled crews and their eighteen boats linked like a chain and leashed to a forty-five-foot-long, forty-ton whale. Though their prize was submerged in black water and otherwise obscured by nightfall, they could feel its enormous presence weighing them down as fumes of gas and the high-pitched cry of straining engines choked the air. Ever so slowly, they dragged Aghvook through the night, around ice, and up along the coast where flares were being touched off. Arriving in front of their village, they beached a gift that seemed as big as the Trojan horse. For me, this whale would provide as many surprises.

An exuberant commotion started after midnight, when the fleet came ashore like a wave of amphibious invaders. The beach suddenly throbbed with villagers and skin boats, sleds and snow-goes that flowed and buzzed about like fireflies in the dark. Converging on their crews, families hauled the angyaqs over a ledge of shore ice. They pushed and pulled through soft snow, until they reached hard ground. Then they cinched the angyaqs up to their treaded snowgoes with a towline and ran full tilt beside the boats, holding onto the rails, as the snowgoes raced full speed to the boat racks. There the villagers unloaded gear, overturned the angyaqs, and began ferrying equipment back to the village. Under the beam of snowgoes' headlights the crews brought out the mungtuk, cut from Aghvook's stomach just after it died. They divided the boat shares among the crewmen and sent the food homeward atop sleds and plastic toboggans.

Meanwhile, shortly after midnight, a chain of lights skirted the southwest flank of Seevookak and whirred into town like a surge of freeway traffic. The people of Savoonga were coming from across the mountains to share Gambell's victory. Industry burst into the night, filling it with noise, smell, and intent movement. The air seemed to quiver with anticipation: What would happen next?

Nothing I saw in Gambell ever exhilarated me more than the scene that night. The day before had been afflicted by dark, brooding emotions, but in the first hours of a new day there was bright promise. If the hunters' success had been attended by too many failures, I now would find atonement for their losses. I would see them share this whale until it disappeared in a virtuous display of Native use.

After the villagers landed all the boats and stowed the hunting gear, they collected near the shore where the whale was. It had been a long, cold, and difficult day, so after standing around in the dark for a while, Silook and some other villagers assumed the plan was for everyone to go home, to change clothes, eat, and warm up first. Then work on the whale would begin, they figured, although no one actually knew for sure. They could not start until Solomon took charge—by tradition the whale belonged to him because his crew had struck it first—but Solomon was out of sight. He had disappeared, probably into his house and maybe into bed, too, for it had been a long, cold, and exhausting day and the whale wasn't going anywhere.

After walking back home, Silook and I entered a house filled with the steamy smells of coffee, boiling mungtuk, and fried doughnuts. In buoyant spirits, some neighbors and relatives from Savoonga had come to celebrate the day's success. Joking

and telling stories, we sat around the table and ate to content-
ment. Sook smiled as I dipped the sashimilike slices of raw whale
meat into some Accent she'd poured onto the serving tray, and
popped them into my mouth. "Hey, Aap', you really must like
that," she laughed. "Have more."

Everyone seemed excited about the day's events. The
hunters had seen many whales, and several crews had come close
to capturing one before Solomon got his. "I like it best when we
see lots of whales out there and no one knows who'll strike one
first," Clement said. "It's just like horse racing."

After an hour or so, Silook went back down to the beach.
According to all that I knew before coming here, the villagers
would work feverishly around the clock until the whale was
divided up and dispensed like communion wafers. I didn't want to
miss the beginning, so I hurried out a few minutes later, intent on
seeing the action. What I found instead was a dwindling number
of villagers and two whale researchers who hoped to make
measurements and collect specimens once the animal was hauled
onto land—they had been waiting there since the hunters returned to shore just after midnight. But nothing happened
without Captain Solomon, and he was apparently asleep. And
though they seemed willing to work, the villagers gradually
wandered off, spontaneous souls sailing into the night. Apparently, work on the whale would begin when it began, all in due
course.

After Silook and I returned home, a couple of us in the
kitchen played at an impromptu game of basketball with a
miniature styrofoam ball and a small basket Silook put six feet up
on the wall. A little bit later, exhausted from the day's exertion, I
pulled my sleeping bag out and fell asleep on the floor, at the feet
of my host and his guests.

Two hours later, I awoke to the clanging bell of an alarm
clock. Dawn had broken; it was a little past four and the others
were gone, so I dressed quickly and went out into the cold,
anxious to see the villagers pull Aghvook out of the water.

I walked down to the shoreline where the hunters had left
the whale. It was still there, barely buoyed up by four plastic
fishing floats. I was all alone, standing a few feet away from it
and staring vacantly. Here lay the whale: an idol of devotion, a
symbol of white men's yearnings, and the object of our tor-

mented intervention into Gambell and eight other Eskimo villages. I was as close as I had ever come to a whale. Though it was as dead as a dinosaur, I stood there as if I were waiting for it to say something. I drew a blank instead. If I thought it could understand me, I would have asked, "Say, have you seen Solomon?" Feeling more stupid than reverent, I trudged home to go to sleep and dream of what would come. But first, I wound the clock once more and set its alarm. How silly, I thought, to rely on such a mechanism amid such spontaneity. Not wanting to miss a step of what was happening, I set the clock to wake me in another two hours, but my mistake lay in the belief that life in Gambell followed clocks and schedules.

After breakfast, I went down to the beach again, and this time I found Solomon, along with an assembly of villagers as well as the two enforcement agents and the two researchers. We white men stood on the periphery waiting for the villagers to begin hauling and butchering the whale. I was too self-conscious and too much aware of my being an outsider to ask the villagers questions, especially when they were grouped together. Seeking to unravel what was going on, I gravitated toward the whale researchers, Ken and Eric. They were easygoing fellows about the same age as I was, and although they were wary of reporters, I got along with them better than with any of the other whites. Talking with them, I found out that during the night they, too, had made repeated trips to the beach. So concerned had they been about missing the Eskimos pull up the whale that they slept in shifts, scrambling out of their outpost each time a few snowgoes appeared on the beach. Like me, they were baffled by the villagers' inaction.

We watched and waited for the villagers to begin work, but Solomon was conferring with some elders and other captains. This delayed the start for another hour or so. Finally, by some signal or movement, at about nine o'clock Solomon set work in motion. I didn't know what he was doing for sure, but his actions became more purposeful. He started pointing and talking more forcefully and some of the villagers began following his lead. A few of them launched a boat and paddled it out to the whale to attach a line.

Most of the villagers were unengaged; they stood about or sat like spectators at a sporting event, enjoying the sunshine and

158   GAMBELL: STRANDED

the scene at center stage, while the handful that were working occupied themselves in desultory action, holding a line perhaps or checking a cable or debating how this thing or that should be done. I attributed my uncertainty about what they were doing to the novelty of the experience. I had a front-row seat for a foreign film with no subtitles, performed in Yupik and orchestrated in cryptic code.

I wondered when the villagers would queue up to haul Aghvook out of the water. Before coming here, I had seen pictures of long chains of Eskimos in a tug-of-war with a tethered carcass. I imagined this whale emerging onto land the same way: manpower, heavy manila lines, and a big block and tackle. Things were done differently in Gambell, however, or at least they were on this day. They didn't have a block and tackle in the village, and, according to measurements of old jawbones lying about the village, this whale was much larger than most of those they had captured in the past.

Had I known ahead of time that there was no block and tackle or that the whale was too big for one anyway, perhaps I would have been less surprised by what came next: the clanking approach of two diesel-driven bulldozers. Here was the straight-ahead, go-get-'im approach of Modern Men at work. It was as American as apple pie: If you want to pull a whale out of the ocean, why mess around? Bring out the heavy metal and let 'er rip. Out of their stalls up in the village, a big D-4 Caterpillar and a John Deere 350 chugged, snorted, and charged their way down to water's edge, as if they were about to yank a car out of a ditch.

The bowlegged captain waddled over—he seemed an inspired man at this point—directed a couple of men in a boat to tie a cable around the stem of Aghvook's tail, and then signaled a driver to open up on the throttle. Going one on one with the whale, the bull rattled its exhaust stack, snorted a dark shot of diesel smoke, and tore into its leash. The cable snapped like cheap string under strain. They wrapped the cable back on the whale a second time: same thing. Then a third time, and again and again until finally the cable held and the machine surged forward, groaning and grabbing up ground as if it were really going to muscle its opponent onto land. But after conceding a few yards, the whale caught hold of gravel bottom and dug in.

Perhaps it would have been easier if a smooth shelf of ice

were clinging to the beach and had greased the way for Aghvook to skid into drydock. But the shelf had been shorn away by ocean swells and in its place at the water's edge slumped nothing more than soft gravel. The D-4 was the first machine to bog down, I think. Fighting for a foothold, it churned up snow and gravel until it dug its own ditch and settled in up to its treads, looking like a big yellow toy in a sandbox. The villagers abandoned it for its smaller companion, lighter on its feet but overmatched by the bulk of its adversary—hardly a car in a ditch or a stump in a field, after all. Without a block and tackle, the job was a fitful jerk-and-yank affair that sank both the Eskimos' hopes and their second bulldozer into the gravel. Conceding a stalemate, the captain withdrew to consider another course of action. They had no choice but to butcher Aghvook where it lay, dug in and half covered with water, some twenty feet from the beach.

Later in the morning, after a long, involved discussion among a crowd of captains, elders, and assorted bystanders, work began on a new tack. A crew of men set out in a metal skiff to cut off the back end of Aghvook's body so the bulldozer could haul the whale up one piece at a time. Manning three, maybe four ice chisels and cutting tools—including one that was no more than a kitchen knife lashed to a pole—this handful of villagers awkwardly thrust and hacked away at the thick trunk of skin, blubber, bone, and muscle. It took them at least a couple of hours before finally, from the sheer persistence of their labor, the tail section fell away for the bulldozer awaiting it. Compared to their ancestors, who had used flints that were as big as a man's hand and as sharp as any steel, they suddenly seemed like modern primitives. Kitchen knives and Caterpillars. Which of the two was the real anachronism?

I think it was the John Deere that pulled the D-4 out of its ditch, allowing it in turn to tug the whale's first installment out of crimson-stained water and onto high ground. The severed tail end of the whale looked like a giant log in cross section: the dark red, almost magenta-colored flesh encircled by a foot-and-a-half layer of white glistening blubber. It was as tall in diameter as the man who marched beside it, his knife held up in the air like a torch. This, the narrowest part of the whale, took nearly an afternoon to be carved up into meat and mungtuk.

With the landing of the tail section, Solomon seemed to

GAMBELL: STRANDED

run out of ideas. Where the morning had seen a futile clash of titans, the afternoon and much of the evening would be used up hacking away at the whale in the water.

It was, in retrospect, a pathetic scene. The few men in the bobbing skiff were hopelessly outmatched, especially given the tools they were using. If only they had been able to get Aghvook up on the beach! Then an army of villagers might have compensated, in manpower, for the primitive nature of their tools. And then the whale might have been picked clean. But in the water Aghvook posed a more formidable challenge.

Why so few people were involved in the effort puzzled me greatly. No more than six men were ever at work alongside the whale (the same six, throughout the day), while on shore, one man held a line to the single skiff and some two hundred others sat or walked aimlessly about water's edge like onlookers at an accident. Unsatisfied by the lack of any apparent explanation, I grew angry. Surely some boats and cutting crews could have gone along either side of the whale—it was forty-five feet long, after all. But this was Solomon's whale and Solomon was in charge, even if he wasn't using all the workers he had at his disposal. For the lack of coordination and leadership, he turned most of the villagers into an audience. Yet the inefficiency and wasted time did not appear to bother them. The atmosphere seemed as pleasant as a picnic's.

Looking back now, I know how much better things could have been that day. But at the time and for much of the next two years, I could not understand what had happened or why. I would not understand until I found out how whales were butchered elsewhere.

If you want to learn about bird-feeders, call the Audubon Society; if you want to know about butchering whales, talk to the Japanese whalers. Though they are the most despised whalers of all in the eyes of international conservationists, they're masters at what they do, even if it isn't very nice. Yet if one could forgive them for a moment the vice of their excessive killing, it is possible to stand back and admire their virtuousity in carving up a whale. They work their knives like surgeons, and they approach their catch in a diligent, well-orchestrated effort of cutting, sawing, peeling, and mincing up the whale without ever wasting time or any of the product. As butchers they are a credit to their profession.

Although bowheads aren't found as far south as Japan, Japanese villagers hunt whales that are just as big; and had they been in Gambell that day, they would have handled Aghvook much differently than the Eskimos did. After pulling the whale as close to the beach as they could, they would have held onto its tail stem tightly instead of cutting it off as the villagers had done. They could have used a bulldozer to keep the line taut, and men with long, sharp knives and spades could climb over the animal. At its far end, behind the head, they would have made an incision across its body, pried back the skin and blubber, bored a hole through the flap, and attached cables or lines. Then everyone on shore would have pulled the strips of skin and blubber backward, end over end, as if they were peeling a giant banana. An impressive thing to see.

After removing its coat of skin and blubber, the Japanese would have tied a line around Aghvook's back muscle and stripped it in the same manner. They'd have pulled from the beach once more, and off would come its dark red flesh, peeling back from the thorax and abdomen until half the whale was gone, like a fish that had been filleted on one side.

Before they could strip the whale's bottom side, they would have had to turn Aghvook over. The Japanese have a system for this too. Grabbing hold of the whale's flippers, they attach a line and run it through a block and tackle—at Gambell, they could have anchored it around a large iceberg that was grounded close to the whale. By hauling on the line (at Gambell they could have used a second bulldozer for this), the Japanese can roll the whale from one side to the other; and when they are done flensing, they haul Aghvook out of the water as one would drag the skeleton of a breakfast trout off one's plate. The whale's head would still be intact, just like the trout's, but it would weigh perhaps ten tons, a weight Gambell's bulldozers might have pulled, instead of forty.

This was the way Japanese villagers butchered whales on the northern coast of Japan. The method could have worked as surely in Gambell if only the villagers had known about it. But apparently they didn't, because once they failed at pulling the whale out whole, they set about cutting off every handle they could have used to grasp onto. What was left was nothing more than a huge cylinder rolling in the tide. I realized only much later that in those first few steps they had taken—cutting off the tail— they had made the rest of an already difficult job impossible.

After landing the whale's tail end on the beach, a handful of workers turned next to its head. It lay on its side, facing us, its jaws spread apart so that the mouth looked like the beak of a giant, gaping raven. Behind the corner where the lower lip met the upper, a large round eye stared skyward from within a circle of white. Aghvook's head is as stout as any that can be found among whales. Built like a battering ram, it takes up a third of the body's length. The way the villagers were doing things, it couldn't be beached until they dissected it where it lay. So three or four men began jousting with its lower jaw, pushing and thrusting long poles along the bone like knights bearing lances. Their steed was a Starcraft skiff of green and white metal that bobbed on greasy crimson water as they did their surgery.

I had never hunted mammals before coming here; I had only butchered fish, and seeing them dead and disemboweled by the deckload when it was my job to catch them seemed a most natural state of affairs. I had wondered how I would react seeing the Eskimos slaughter a whale, but once Aghvook was dead, I reacted as if it were no more than a big fish. In death Aghvook held no horror for me. It was too big, too remote for that. It was more spectacle than pathos, and I watched the villagers butcher it with the clinical interest of a doctor looking down on someone else's surgery.

They hacked off Aghvook's head from its body, and one of the bulldozers hauled its lower jawbone and then its heavy, gelatinous slab of tongue up on the beach. It was late in the afternoon, eighteen hours after the villagers landed the whale, and apart from a flurry of activity when the tail end and now this new installment were dragged out of the water, the day had been sluggish and spiritless. It had none of the fire, animation, or joy of the day before. Up on the beach, some people busied themselves cutting up slabs of meat and mungtuk, and people's comings and goings often made the icescape look busy. But most of the villagers were remarkably and unfathomably uninvolved in the job of getting Aghvook out of the water. When the cutting tools they were using got dull, for instance, the handful of men who were struggling to hack through the whale had to sharpen their blades themselves, even though a couple of hundred idle villagers were close at hand. I couldn't understand why no one came forward or was directed to keep individual cutters supplied with sharp tools or to replace the men when they got tired.

Amid the sheer tedium of it all, my interest in the details of Solomon's operation dissipated. I didn't like sitting still; I wanted to do something, to help cut and saw and peel the whale, yet this was hardly the participatory ritual I had expected. I became annoyed, a sentiment I discovered was shared by the two whale researchers, Ken and Eric. By mid-afternoon, Ken, an experienced observer of whales and whalers elsewhere, had seen enough to make up his mind. "These people don't know how to catch a whale or how to butcher one either," he muttered.

By evening, the Eskimos had dragged the upper jawbone, the most important part of the head, out of the water. Hanging down from it was a long row of tall, black, and flexible mouth-plates—baleen—arranged like slats of a venetian blind hung sideways. There were six hundred or so plates, some as long as six feet, with strands of hair fringing the outer edges and blowing like corn silk in a breeze. Functionally, baleen serves to strain passively floating or weakly swimming crustaceans from the water that Aghvook takes into its mouth and pushes out through the sides. As flexible as fiberglass, it was once used to make sleds, lines, nets, and containers, but now it is used to make jewelry and carvings or as a commodity in itself to be sold to white men who want a piece of the whale from Eskimoland. In short, baleen is worth money, so when the jaw came up, axe-wielding villagers collected around the clattering slats to hack them off at the gumline.

Tradition called for the villagers to share all the baleen and everything else they took from the whale. Yet so far, no one had taken anything, because by tradition, the shares were not dispensed until all the work was done. Otherwise, Leonard explained, people might not stay around to help after they got their individual shares. Of course, most of the villagers still did not

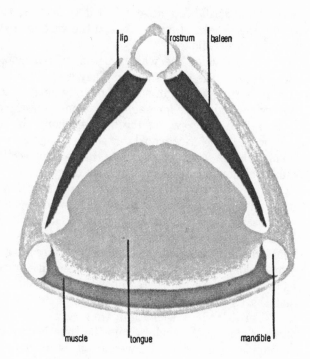

A single plate of baleen, and a cross-section showing position of baleen in whale's mouth.

help. But that didn't matter when it came time to divide the baleen, the chunks of mungtuk, and the yard-long steaks sliced from the whale's flukes.

They divided the whale in front of Solomon, whom the villagers recognized as its owner. They waited for him to supervise. According to one of several definite rules that seemed to have originated in the long-ago past, along with the other traditions, he and his crew got the biggest share; the next largest share went to the crew who'd thrust the second harpoon into the fleeing whale. Then came the others—supposedly to share equally, although this wasn't quite the case.

Crowding around the site where the shares were laid out on the snow, many villagers now moved with a vitality that had been missing earlier. Some of them hovered close to the biggest shares and positioned their feet or gaff hooks so as to stake their claim. In effect, the division of shares was already accomplished before Solomon ever ordained it. Like losers in a game of musical chairs, those who hadn't acted quickly enough ahead of time got small shares, or in some cases even less.

The islanders who came from Savoonga also collected shares of Solomon's whale. From the time Natives of Gambell had founded the village of Savoonga early in this century until the 1970s, Savoongans had joined their relatives in Gambell each spring to hunt bowheads—because the whale doesn't usually pass along the shore of their own village. With the adoption of snowgoes, however, the Savoongans had formed their own whaling crews who traveled to Southwest Cape to hunt, a journey that would have been too long to accomplish in the days of dogsleds. There were two whaling villages rather than one now. They still shared their whales, though the division did not always proceed smoothly.

A week earlier, when the Savoongans had captured their allotment of one bowhead, some crews from Gambell had not received their shares. Whether other Gambell crews had taken too much or the Savoongans had been stingy was still a matter of debate. But now that the Savoongans had come for their share of this whale, they got a cool reception from those who had not received a piece of Savoonga's. When a few Savoongans made too eager a move toward the shares of baleen, they created a pretext or a provocation for an aggrieved whaling captain to launch into a tirade in front of Aghvook's jawbone. The picnic mood that may have existed earlier faded in the chill of the evening.

Afterward, Leonard asked me if I had noticed how some of the villagers had behaved that day. It was he who pointed out how men had rushed to claim their shares and then stood guard over them; I saw it later on when my photographs were developed. He disapproved of what they had done, disapproved in a typically quiet, unaccusing manner, saying simply that it made him sad to see "good, honest people turn greedy."

To my surprise, Leonard blamed white men for the villagers' behavior. Responsibility didn't belong to Eskimos, he said, because had they been allowed to land more whales, they wouldn't have acted this way. As it was, they had been made greedy by this solitary catch because it would be the only one.

I wondered. For years before a quota was ever levied, Gambell had landed an average of less than one whale a year. And a scarcity of whales, if that's what this was, was still a scarcity whether it was imposed by white men or by nature and circumstance. Some people were just greedy, that's all. In any case, other villagers had behaved quite differently. I had seen Silook, for example, quietly walk away from the beach even though he hadn't received a share of baleen. Rather than complain or bicker over property rights, he had disengaged himself from the proceedings.

Yet Leonard's concerns about how people had behaved when the shares were dispensed impressed me far more than the behavior itself. If I was surprised by some of the bickering and the grabbing for shares, it was because I came to Gambell expecting a Communist utopia. But I didn't react nearly as adversely to what I had seen as Leonard and others had because that behavior did not seem unusual in the world I lived in. Leonard's and others' disapproval of it only underlined what I already knew: that, though imperfect, there was more sharing in Gambell than anywhere I'd ever been before.

By nightfall, most of the Savoongans had packed their shares and left for home across the mountains. They left, it seemed to me, almost the same way they arrived: without a sign of emotion or a clue to what they were thinking. Surprised by their departure, I wondered why they weren't staying to share the rest of the whale, too.

SATURDAY'S SPOILS

Twenty-eight hours after Gambell's crews had delivered their death blow, Aghvook still lay a few feet from shore, stripped of its skin and without a head or a tail, but for the most part unbutchered and awaiting a new day. The villagers were giving it up to the night, a vaporous dusk that enshrouded the beach, its veil hung with lightly falling snow. They could reclaim Aghvook in the morning. It would be there tomorrow, but today came only once, and the villagers had gone home to enjoy what it provided.

19. Toward a Change of Tide and a New Beginning

I have a history of chasing fantasies, like a cat that chases mice. Only the mice I chase are more elusive; the farther they are from my grasp, the harder I chase.

My first yearning to live and hunt with Eskimos germinated in a Seattle movie theater. I was watching *The White Dawn*, an early 1970s film version of James Houston's novel about the poignant encounter of three shipwrecked nineteenth-century whalers with a band of Canadian Eskimos. I was captivated by the joy and mystery of Native life that it celebrated. No matter that the life depicted on screen belonged to another century or that the movie ended with the Outsiders murdered for the troubles they'd brought with them. When unleashed, my romanticism swims upstream. I'm incorrigible, I suppose, but, after all, how many reformed romantics do you know?

A few years after seeing *The White Dawn*, I was in a small plane flying through snow and clouds over the Bering Sea toward my own fantasy island. My dream was within reach, and as I came closer, higher soared my expectations of the people who were hidden so far from my world. After I landed, I began to understand just how elusive my dream really was. Two days after the villagers captured Aghvook, I plunged into a black hole of doubt and depression.

Sunday began as a day of rest. Nothing really happened until noontime, when two men began removing one of Aghvook's stubby black flippers, vestigial arms of a creature that had roamed the land some 60 million years ago. They used a kitchen knife and the Caterpillar to take it off, and afterward, they turned to the opposite flipper, struggling with that one for a few hours more before someone brought them a real flensing knife to do the job right. By cutting this second flipper off, they also removed their last handle and their last chance for maneuvering the whale.

Where the day before there had been a couple of hundred people, I now stood with a score or two. The beach, nearly deserted, looked like the abandoned site of a slaughter. Around us were patches of blood and oil-stained snow, trimmings of blubber, scraps of meat, that stark slab of a tongue that had been left pretty much intact, and the long arched bow of an upper jawbone stripped of its flesh and baleen. What lay on the land was unwanted, but what of that which lay in the water? And why weren't the other villagers here to work or even just to wait to take their shares from what was still to come?

In the late afternoon, the last participants divided what meat the few workers had cut from the whale that day. I saw Oovi walk over to a thick two-foot-square slab. He and a group of other elders had been sitting quietly for several hours waiting to get a share. Wielding his knife, he bent over to cut into it, but to my surprise he stood up again before he ever started and walked home without taking any.

Wondering why, I walked over to the meat—it still lay unclaimed where he left it—and as I bent over I caught the sting of soured fish. The unpleasantness of it hit me at once. The whale was rotting! And how could it have been otherwise, I asked myself later, for the body had lain dead and encased in blubber for over forty hours without anyone cutting so much as a hole in it to cool the fire that smoldered inside.

No sooner had Aghvook been dead than its internal chemistry had short-circuited. Though its skin was enveloped in the

GAMBELL: STRANDED

coldest of water, it grew hot inside and began to digest itself. The same thing happens in all dead mammals, except that the whale is insulated in a thick layer of fat, so the reaction occurs even faster. And while the insides burned, the returning hunters slept or, when they did turn to the task, were outmatched. By Sunday, the meat was rotting.

I felt as if I'd uncovered a corpse in a closet. Staggered, but imagining that all eyes were on me, I tried to shield my grisly discovery from the villagers—a discovery I must have been the last to make, since it was all too evident. Still incredulous, I walked to the water's edge as nonchalantly as I could. There, a few feet away from shore, a violent hissing flatulence escaped from a small hole in the bloody stump of Aghvook's chest. It was a whine, a hiss, a gurgling that blew bubbles of gas from the decay within. Inflated by the by-products of its own consumption, Aghvook floated higher in the water than it had the day before.

I was in shock. Where were the workers? Time was critical if they were going to get the meat. How could they be so passive, unorganized, apparently unconcerned?

Desperate to understand what was happening, but suddenly afraid of my questions, I looked for the whale researchers. Ken, who had understood what was happening long before I did, gingerly broached the subject with Solomon. He asked if perhaps the villagers should take the meat off before it spoiled. Cheerful to the end, Solomon dismissed his worries. "You see," he said, "we like our meat a little peppery."

Greatly disturbed by what I had seen, I went to visit Oovi, wanting answers without having to ask the dread questions inside me. And so I asked indirectly, sneakily, embarrassed and not wanting to sound like a detective.

Yet each of my questions presumed there was something wrong, someone responsible. If that's what Oovi thought, he never said so; I could detect no disapproval of what had happened. I wanted him to reassure me that this rotting whale was an aberration, so that I could continue to believe what I had come here to believe in. I did believe in Oovi himself, but I was too caught up in the whale to appreciate that as I pumped him for information. He couldn't and didn't give the answers I wanted, so I left to return to the beach.

TOWARD A CHANGE OF TIDE

When I got there, in the early evening, I noticed that the whale was no longer tethered to land. Apparently Gambell had done as much butchering as it was going to do. The villagers were giving Aghvook back to the sea. All they needed to convey their present was an east wind and a change of tide.

I couldn't believe it. For the second time in two days, I felt stupid in front of this whale. For the past ten months I had heard Eskimos making the same claims: "Every bit of the whale is used"; "We waste nothing"; "Without the whale, we would go hungry." Everywhere I went, the words were repeated. Newsmen, like the AP reporter here for three days, had written them down as facts, which had the effect of perpetuating them as facts. We didn't question them, and the villagers didn't either. Eskimos beheld our image of their virtue as if it were their own reflection, though it was often just the brush strokes of our painting.

"See. See how we use all the whale." In front of this bloated hulk, the words were Kafkaesque. Yes, I saw. It had no head, no tail, and the mungtuk was gone—they'd gotten that much—but the biggest part of Aghvook's body, a tapering cylinder seventeen feet long and eleven feet across at one end, was whistling in the wind. According to the researchers' estimate, it weighed forty-five thousand pounds, more than half the whale's total. The corpse gave the lie to popular truths.

Cold with anger, I turned within. So this was the result of their hunt? They'd struck, lost, and perhaps killed three whales before they finally captured one. And one was not enough, they had said. No, they needed two or three—it was a matter of hunger. Couldn't white men see this?

I cautiously asked for explanations, and since I was looking, the villagers offered them readily. Gambell hadn't been able to get Aghvook onto land because the ice shelf had gone and the bulldozers bogged down in gravel; or because the block and tackle the village had ordered from the mainland didn't arrive until three days after the whale was abandoned. It was too bad, the villagers said, but that was why they couldn't butcher all the whale: they couldn't get it out of the water. With a sense perhaps of the poignancy that white men wanted, one of them added: "We were sorry we were not able to cut the whole whale up."

What villagers offered as explanations, however, only explained why they didn't get Aghvook out of the water. To

172

accept them as explanations of why the whale was abandoned with most of its meat was to accept that, after its first setback, Gambell had been helpless to do anything more, which was not at all the case. To be sure, there had been obstacles to getting this whale up on the beach and problems with butchering it in the water. But the obstacles and problems were inadequate explanations of why so few people had involved themselves, and why those who had had put out such a sluggish and inefficient effort. One white man was so amazed by what he had seen that he suggested the villagers had consciously acted to embarrass or punish Solomon, because they resented his monopoly of business with white men who came here to look for birds and walrus. The theory's implausibility was an indication of how far afield some of us went to avoid the two explanations that seemed most straightforward, if least comforting. The first was that Gambell's whale hunters, or at least those who butchered Aghvook, were quite unskilled; the second was that mungtuk and baleen were all that the villagers had ever really wanted.

If only I could have found an interpretation that both explained and excused what I saw! If only I could have believed that some natural force, something like the ice over which they had no control, had been responsible! Then I could have accepted the loss as unfortunate. But what I had seen forced me into a far more uncomfortable reality.

What I'd seen, or thought I'd seen, did anything but enhance the whalers' image and was not likely to impress the International Whaling Commission either. Of course, the political implications of what they had done never occupied villagers' minds as they did mine. Anticipating such Outside reaction, I grew afraid and even more embarrassed to question the villagers openly.

Feeling terribly alone, I gravitated toward other white men, those from whom I had tried to set myself apart earlier while vying for the villagers' acceptance. But with the exception of the two whale researchers, the others responded hostilely to my questions and observations. They seemed to have seen something quite different.

"There is no waste," Dean Hickox, the local Presbyterian minister, snapped, indignant that I would suggest such a thing. Having overheard my conversation with another Outsider, he heatedly interrupted. "For God's sake, don't write those things," he said, and began accusing me of sensationalism.

He had been an Arctic missionary for a long time, first in Barrow and now in Gambell. As the pastor of the church started by V. C. Gambell in 1894, he and his wife, the high school principal, had lived in Gambell longer than any of the other few whites there. Because of his position, and especially because the combined church and rectory where he lived offered the only public accommodations, Dean had become the unofficial contact point for white bureaucrats, travelers, and journalists who came to town. The AP reporter, for instance, had come looking for Dean, had stayed with him, interviewed him, and asked Dean to help him get permission to go out whaling with some of the hunters (Silook and Leonard). As the man-to-see-in-Gambell, Dean had the status of village chieftain. He enjoyed the visits he was paid by Outsiders wanting to learn about Eskimos. He liked showing them his collection of carved ivory, once described as one of the best collections west of the American Museum of Natural History, and he obviously liked talking about his congregation. He spoke of them in two voices: one, of a sociologist coldly and critically describing the effects of acculturation, much like a preacher talking about sin; the other, of a father trying to protect the children he loved from the threat of the outside world. I first met him when he interrupted me that day to give me a stern lecture.

"You can't impose a New Yorker's idea of waste on these people. This isn't the Fulton Fish Market. Every time they go out to get food, they're risking their lives.

"These people are not able to leave this island and establish productive ways of life. They are so tied to the Eskimo way of life that if the ties are denied them, there will be a rapid extinction.

"I've watched them take whales apart. They were working on a rotting ice shelf and they got what they could. I loaded hundreds of pounds of meat onto the plane to go to people in Nome."

The minister may very well have loaded that much onto the plane. But hundreds of pounds of meat would have filled just a few sleds; and it was a minor fraction of the thousands of pounds that weren't taken. And if more than a few sledloads of

174   GAMBELL: STRANDED

meat were carried from the beach, neither I nor the researchers ever saw them. I was served lots of mungtuk in the homes I visited that week (and hundreds of pounds of mungtuk probably were flown to Nome), but only twice did I have whale meat, and even that may have been from Savoonga's whale. As far as I could see, there just was no evidence that Gambell had recovered much meat.

What I saw was, I thought, obvious. There was the rotting, hissing hulk of a whale. But what did it prove? Nothing, said the missionary: the villagers had taken what they could; the ice was to blame; they wasted nothing. And what was the evidence of a crime? Even the proportions of the abandoned carcass were challenged. Andy, the enforcement agent, denied the estimate of its weight made by the researchers. He questioned Ken and Eric's scientific authority, scoffing that they hadn't even been able to tell if the whale was male or female.

Of course, determining the sex of a whale lying belly-down in the gravel was a difficult proposition, to say the least. When the tail section had been pulled up on the beach on Saturday, Ken, the chief researcher, recognized a loop of the penis and pronounced the animal a male. Several villagers insisted it was a female, however. Only females had gray-streaked mouthplates (baleen), they said, and when the researcher saw what looked like a genital slit the next day, he became unsure of himself. Had the Eskimos butchered all the whale, he would have had an easy time of it, but now he'd have to climb into its belly to get to the bottom of things, a pickle the Eskimos enjoyed immensely.

Seizing on the researchers' uncertainty, Andy claimed they didn't know what they were talking about. He discounted the size and weight of the abandoned carcass and reported back to headquarters: "The center portion of that whale was not completely salvaged because they could not pull it up on the beach." It was as simple as that, Andy told me. And if I tried to make anything more of it, I'd be doing nothing less than witch-hunting.

I felt much the same way Ken must have felt when he climbed into the belly of the whale on Sunday afternoon. There he stood in a roughly cut trench, up to his crotch in guts, his boots filled with blood and the stink of rot in his nostrils while he groped around for Aghvook's sex glands so he might determine

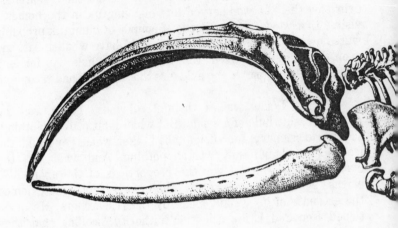

bowheads landed by Eskimos that spring, the federal government told the International Whaling Commission:

> There is no evidence that any part of the whale which could be utilized in any manner was wasted or improperly utilized.

So the villagers didn't use the whole whale. It was a shocking discovery, but later, in saner moments of reflection, I wondered what it proved. That reality didn't play up to its advance billing? I've made greater discoveries than that in my lifetime. In the end, what I'd seen proved little more than this: that the Eskimos didn't belong to the Clean Plate Club, after all. My discovery was hardly a cudgel I could carry in good conscience.

"How can people down in the Lower Forty-Eight talk about waste?" asked the missionary. The answer, of course, is that we can't, at least not in the self-righteous tones I had voiced. It was easy to get carried away, to moralize in front of a bloated carcass when my own and other white people's wastefulness was out of view a thousand miles behind me. Waste ran through the

GAMBELL: STRANDED

Skeleton of bowhead.

its gender. All in the cause of science. For two days the whale had been dead. Ken stood there up to his waist in its juices, his lower half being slowly cooked while his head and his slimy and bloodied arms—when he raised them—were frozen by the Arctic wind. It was a messy, miserable affair and dangerous, too, for the whale was floating freely in the current as Ken groped amidst its bowels for an answer. All of us white men were like Ken that afternoon, it seemed to me. We had run amok in the Eskimos' whale, which in this case, by the way, was a male, just as Ken had first thought.

I regarded the enforcement agents and missionary with contempt and let my anger over unfulfilled expectations devolve onto them. I wasn't opposed to the Eskimos' hunt. I was opposed to the apologies offered for their failures. The apologies—that the guns didn't work when they struck and lost whales, that the whale had been cut adrift because the ice was bad—implied that the villagers were almost totally helpless. Yet how could the hunters be both helpless and as skillful as they were popularly portrayed as being?

The apologies and myths went on. In its report about

soul of our society like salt sown in a field, a truth that didn't for a moment justify it in Gambell, but that should have taken the wind out of my sails a little sooner. In front of the bloodied hulk, however, I lost perspective.

I was aware even then of the distance I was putting between myself and the villagers. I had come here wanting their acceptance. I had sought it while taking their pictures and asking questions, and the amazing thing is that I had received as much of it as I did. They had invited me into their homes, shared their food and clothing with me, brought me along in their angyaqs, provided knowledge, and some of them had even taken me into their confidence. Yet taking all of that for granted, I brooded about not gaining still more acceptance. For all that I wanted from them, I was the one who was unaccepting, for when the hunt was over, I found myself judging the villagers at arm's length with a disappointment that they weren't the people I had expected to find.

That Sunday evening, I spent anguished hours on the beach, depressed, confused, and angry at the Eskimos and the white men. Embarrassed by my reactions, I avoided going home to Silook and Sook. I felt apart from my hosts and all those around me, adrift like the offshore ice. I had expected to leave Gambell convinced that the Eskimos were fabulously gifted hunters of whales and their survival depended upon the food success brought them. But in front of the whale, I was sure of nothing except that the absolutes existed no longer. Befogged and malcontent, I trudged several miles southward, putting still more distance between myself and Gambell until I could neither hear nor see it and its hunters had become an abstraction.

Too tired to walk any farther in the softening pack of snow, I climbed down an eight-foot-high bank of ice that lined the shore and tucked myself between a couple of icebergs on the narrow shelf of uncovered beach to keep out of the wind. Listening to waves washing the gravel a few feet away, I stared seaward into the falling snow. In such desolation, I speculated about what I had seen, heard, and smelled back in the village. Did it mean that Eskimo whaling culture was dead? If so, who were these people and how were they different from us? What

GAMBELL: STRANDED

did the whale really mean to them, and why should we sanction their hunt?

After a while, when the cold sank in and I began worrying about getting lost in a blinding whiteout of thick, driving snow, I ended my deliberations and headed for Gambell. Homeward to villagers whom only distance and safety could abstract, because as long as I was cold and hungry and amid the ice, they stood between me and death. They were no longer just the stuff of a story, no longer objects to be rubbed against an ancestral touchstone to see if they proved to be Genuine Eskimo. They were friends, hosts, fellow crewmen; they were heroes, rogues, stars, misfits, or, as was most often the case, just average human beings. The closer I got to them, the more they faded as abstractions and became people once again. They were life itself, which "you see . . . is never as good or as bad as one thinks."[12]

That wisdom was a long way ahead of me as I approached Gambell, but I *had* begun to deliberate upon my own involvement. Why had I come here anyway? It was an adventure, a quest, a story, and a way, I hoped, to make a living. I had been aroused by something unique and ancient the Eskimos had that I didn't. My motives were not simple or clear.

When I became aware of my own judgmental high-handedness, I felt painfully guilty, especially among those I was assessing. What were my responsibilities to them and, above all others, to Sook and Silook, whose lives were before me in poignantly full view?

They had taken me into their home, where nothing they did or said was beyond the range of my senses; they even spoke English in front of me so as not to be impolite. I scanned them for consistencies and contradictions, for the similarities and differences between us, and for the symptoms of a culture in crisis. They had opened themselves up to me, and I often wondered if they realized how much they trusted me. More to the point, I wondered how much I deserved their trust. They were my friends and my family, but they were also my subjects, and I was stalking them for a story.

What good will you do here? I was asked by the enforcement agents. Questions had turned on the one who asked questions. After inquiring the same of them, now I was up for the dance.

What good will you do here? they asked, and with unaffected simplicity, I had once had no trouble answering. My story was going to show how virtuous the Eskimos' hunt really was: the ice was to blame for their losses and they couldn't do anything about nature. But now I had no answer. I felt exploitative and even traitorous to have come here and taken their hospitality for anything less than to "do good."

What good would my story do if I portrayed the truth of what I'd seen? And what was the truth anyway? I had seen one spring's hunt of one whale by one village. Was this lost whale an accident of fate, the hunt gone haywire and the world temporarily turned upside down? Or was it business as usual? I'd been here one week, a short time indeed to be announcing the results of my inquiry or to be pronouncing truths about Eskimos that were based on what happened to half a whale.

What good will you do here? I could not fully answer the question, and the others couldn't either. The agents had come to secure compliance with a quota that had no scientific basis and questionable moral authority as well. The researchers had come to make measurements and counts of whales that would be processed, anointed, and consecrated as answers by those who made their own determinations of what answers were, then accepted by still others as objective scientific truth to decide if Eskimos should be allowed to continue hunting whales. And me? I had come to get a story, a cause, an adventure, and friends among the Natives, but after seeing them kill their first whale, I was ready to write an obituary on Eskimo culture.

Two years passed before I was able to resolve what had happened to the whale that spring and why. For months I tried to understand, reliving what I had experienced like someone who'd been at the scene of an accident. I was confused and depressed, and beyond my uncertainty, I did not want to accept the one interpretation that seemed most accurate: it was too unpleasant and threatening. When I returned south that first spring, I ended my newspaper feature story with the villagers' capture of the whale. With time and experience, however, my resistance softened like a worn piece of leather. I let go of my grip on denial, because I knew that my first interpretation of what had happened two years earlier had been right, after all.

Mungtuk and baleen were what Gambell's hunters had wanted most: the meat was secondary. When they talked of bowheads, mungtuk was first and foremost on their minds: there was nothing else quite like it in texture and taste. Meat? They could get that from walrus, seals, and mukluks (bearded seals). They could get it from the store, too, and, no doubt, some of them would have taken more from the whale that day if they could have. But Gambell wasn't skilled in beaching or butchering whales in the water. And because of that, or perhaps because there were other foods to choose from, Gambell was not, as had been supposed, accustomed to eating the rest of the whale. Did they eat the heart, kidneys, liver, and brains? "Never tasted them," Oovi once told me. Only Irrigoo, I suppose, had shared in more whales. "I tasted intestines once," he added, wanting to provide me with more of his knowledge. "They were big and thick."

His answer drew me back into the past, beyond the changes of more recent vintage, such as the final coming of a cash economy and the quickening pace of modernization, which we white men tended to blame for the aspects of this hunt we called "problems." His answer drew me back to a place that lay beyond the memory of present-day hunters to Oovi and Irrigoo's early years, where we would have seen some of the same things we saw over a half-century later. In the late 1920s, for instance, an anthropologist living in Gambell noted that almost every time he hunted with the Eskimos, their guns misfired.[13] And such was the degree of failure in Barrow in those same years that another white man, who had lived there since the mid-1880s, commented: "It was as if they had forgotten how to whale . . . Whales were plentiful close among the ice. Many were struck and bombed, but only two small ones were taken."[14]

Somewhere further back in time, in the dimness of Oovi and Irrigoo's childhood and beyond the reach of their memory, something had happened that had reduced the effectiveness of both whaling guns and whalers. Having seen the superior killing power of white men's technology, most of their fathers' generation had adopted the guns without ever learning how to use or handle them properly. As a result, they struck and lost many whales. Yet using the gun, they still captured more than they might have using their old weapons, so they had no reason to go back to the old way. Those who mastered the gun achieved great success, especially when they combined it with the traditional skill of going alongside or atop the whale before striking it. But having abandoned the old weapons in favor of the guns, most Eskimos abandoned the traditional techniques as well. They did not teach them to their sons, and, falling into disuse, the old art of whaling was forgotten. Instead, the sons' generation inherited an unmastered and deficient technology—with the result that two white men in different villages already in the late 1920s could remark on the striking degree of failure that they saw.

Perhaps Gambell had forgotten, too, how to butcher the whale, just as other villages had forgotten how to hunt whales. It would have explained why even Oovi and Irrigoo wouldn't or didn't recognize anything different about the way Aghvook was hunted or butchered the first spring I was there.

Two years passed from the time I saw the first whale butchered until I accepted the accuracy of my observation. When I finally accepted it, I felt none of the emotional or mental frenzy that had beset me that first time. Unskilled butchering, incomplete consumption of whales, and the loss of injured and killed animals were all truths, but they did not form a complete picture. There were other truths as well.

What good I will do by writing what I have here, I don't know. And though you never asked me, it is my thought of you, Silook, and my thought of Sook, too, that makes me agonize over having no ready answer. You've been my brother and Sook my sister, and all that you've meant to me over many months fills me with anxiety about the public moment of your unveiling. I worry that I've stripped away the privacy of your lives while trying to capture who you are. You've never tried to define yourselves: here we are, you told me; the answer was kinetic, but I worry that I've caged you with my definitions.

Who would have stayed so long, asked so many questions, and written such things as I have? Indeed, who would have tried to "capture" you? Not an Eskimo. According to ancient code, one would never do what I am doing. Analyzing you as I have done is like breaking dead men's bones in search of their souls. And by voicing my doubts, my dissatisfaction, and my criticism of your hunt, I have passed judgment on the people among whom I lived, judgment that an Eskimo would express, if at all, through means far more subtle than these bold words that point from a page beyond your reach. In writing about Gambell, I have transgressed a decorum of reserve, when I should have been weeding my own garden to make it a better example. A proper Eskimo would not have done what I have, and in this way, Silook, you and I are very different.

My relations to people were like your relations to animals, I think. As you hunted them, so too did I hunt you and the others of Gambell, studying your every movement, your habits and customs. I was not nearly as patient or as even-tempered as you were, and you were no doubt closer to your prey than I was to mine. But having stalked what we were after, our instincts were the same. We both raised our sights. We both took aim, though I loved you like a brother; and we both fired as we were conditioned to do, you the hunter and me the writer. You hunted for food. Hunting alongside you was the nourishment I sought.

My story and your ivory have much in common. Both are a medium for expression, and like a carver breathing life into his forms, I was bedazzled by my own narrative. In the end, however, both your ivory and my story were commodities for a cash economy. Although I was too preoccupied with presumptions of artistic purity to recognize it, I too was trying to make money. The difference was that you and the rest of Gambell were my raw material, as Leonard saw so well: he was more attuned to such things than you were, because in some ways he was more like me than like you.

It was when I returned to Gambell the second spring, full of renewed hope and expectations, that I ran up against him. After my first whaling season, I had flattered myself into thinking I was a member of his crew, a role I had wanted most of all. Maybe I could have been one, too, had it not been for the expensive new outfit of cameras and lenses I brought along with me. If I could have done it over again, I suppose I would have brought secondhand equipment instead. Or when asked about their value—it seemed that villagers always wanted to know the cost of white men's possessions—I suppose I would have answered, "I don't know, they were a present." Because when Leonard saw my cameras and heard of my reply, he was convinced I had cashed in on last year's pictures, cashed in on the uniqueness Gambell and he had shown me. That it wasn't true did not really matter.

Before coming here, I had anticipated that Gambell's resistance would stem from the fear I would not write a fair story. I realized afterward how mistaken I had been, for no one seemed able to imagine how I could see any other side of the story than Gambell's. The resistance, which was as entrenched as ever, came from somewhere else. In Leonard's case it was fairly elemental: he thought I was making money at his expense. I think most of the villagers thought the same.

I remember our encounter well. The night before we started hunting, you brought home a message that Leonard wanted to see me. He was down at the store doing after-hours paperwork, dressed as he usually was, in a clean, pressed, button-down shirt. He was a shy, gentle man, and smiling softly, he invited me to sit down. When it came time to do business, however, he was as hard and persistent as winter ice. He wanted to charge me to go out in his boat. His boat, because after your father died the summer before, Leonard had become owner and captain alike.

Talking in terms of "man-hours" and "capital investment," he explained that hunting whales cost him a lot of money. The message: I would either have to pay him or stay ashore when his crew hunted whales. I think I explained that I hadn't yet sold a picture or a story; I'm sure I made a naïve appeal to his public-spiritedness, something to the effect that mine was a story that could help the Outside world understand the importance of his people's hunt; I probably even enumerated all the sharing I had done here, for suddenly I felt defensive, as if being accused of colonialism. I suspect I succeeded to the extent that he considered my case the prelude of a counteroffer. He set a price and I countered by offering him a percentage of my commissions from published photographs. He asked for verification of my assignment and we settled instead on a handshake, a fee for each boat trip, a percentage of future commissions, and a contribution of "man-hours" to defray the cost of my coming aboard, whatever in the world the cost might have been.

When we shook hands that night, it was as buinessmen and nothing more.

Wanting to be accepted into your crew, I was hurt and angered by Leonard's rejection. I accepted the fairness, indeed, the duty of sharing with you and Sook, who had given me so much and asked for nothing, and with Leonard, too, because he had so graciously taken me into his boat the year before. But his preconditions for going out that second spring ended all illusions of my ever being part of this hunt. I was an Outsider, and though Leonard might think of me as more than a customer, I was still a customer and money seemed the only nexus between him and me.

Of course, it was presumptuous for me to think of this as tragedy, and I was too self-conscious to whip myself into third-degree rage. His wanting a piece of the action was more of a nuisance than a tragedy. I could have refused him out of principle (though I was never sure which). If I didn't pay him, however, I wouldn't go out, and if I didn't go out, I couldn't do the magazine assignment I'd just gotten. "I am a businessman," Leonard told me. "I am a man of the cash economy." And so was I, although I didn't want to admit it. So I saved my tears and took lots of pictures, and my sense of obligation to Leonard ended two digits right of the decimal point.

Having cut my deal with your brother, I went out hunting with his crew until I couldn't afford the price. But my presence in Leonard's angyaq was never again the same as it had been before. You, Silook, were embarrassed at what Leonard had done, and I was resentful. There was nothing you could do because it was your duty to follow your captain's command. As it turned out, there was nothing I could do either.

Hoping to become part of another crew, I joined a captain who was shorthanded. He was grateful for my help and wanted me back the next day. But when it came time to sail off again, he made an embarrassed shuffle of excuses, apologizing that he couldn't take me any longer. There were voices he had heard. I inferred the message: either go with Leonard or don't go at all.

I had hoped it would be different the third year I came, for this time the whale hunt was already over. I hoped that now I could go hunting with you, Silook, just the two of us, or maybe with one of your other brothers, too, while Leonard was running the store. But whether you went out to hunt walrus or to catch fish or even to collect driftwood, I was never invited to come along. And I knew without ever asking that, like the boat and all of the gear, the decision belonged to your captain, and that his decision was final.

I was more sad than angry, for I was resigned to what had happened and what might continue to happen as long as I came here. After two years, I had come to terms with Gambell.

It had been foolish to come here wanting to be accepted by a whole village like The Man Who Would Be King. For two years that ambition blinded me to what I had gained. Each time I left Saint Lawrence Island, for all of my disappointments, I carried away one thing with me if I carried nothing else. And that, Silook, was your friendship. It rose above the resistance I met from others, outlasted my free falls into depression. And greatest of all, it transcended the barriers that normally divided my culture from yours. I hope that it will survive my story as well.

You would not have done what I have by writing this. But I hope you won't consider it a betrayal. Perhaps my story is like your relationship to Aghvook. Knowing its habits allows you to capture it, and to capture the whale is to give it honor. To the extent that I have captured you here, may I give you as much honor.

On Monday morning in that spring of 1978, the ice was far from land and a wide arc of sea was smoothed like a pond by the oil that seeped from Aghvook's body. The whale still clung to Gambell's shore, unattended save for a few visits by passing hunters, a class of schoolkids, and a couple of white men. In the water's stillness was a clear image of its pink blubber and crimson-splashed hulk, but I suppose we all saw something different in its reflection.

Solomon and Silook's uncle Roger were characteristically carefree and cheerful. Asked about that great tongue and the scraps of meat and blubber that lay scattered about the beach, they said nothing would go to waste. All of it would be used for fox bait. Asked about the carcass in the water, they were equally upbeat. It, too, would serve a purpose.

"It's part of the life cycle," explained Dean, the missionary. "There are animals who'll eat the spoiled meat.

"Why, you should see killer whales. They kill bowheads for nothing more than their tongues. But there are other animals that eat the rest of it. It's all part of the life cycle."

Looking at the bloated hulk, I thought I'd rather leave nature to its own devices, instead of fertilizing its waters with whale meat to feed fish and crabs and things that go bump in the bottom of the ocean. Yet I also knew that this half a whale wasn't doing any of us any good where it was. Its purpose had been served. So I hoped for an east wind, because when this half a whale had drifted away and out of our sight, I could begin to look forward, like the poeple around me, to next spring, to the joy of hunting Aghvook once more and to the precious gift of its mungtuk.

BARROW

20. Uptown at the Top of the World

The Apangalooks and the rest of Gambell's hunters were await-ing whales when I came back the following year. But as in spring 1978, hunting whales in 1979 would also prove difficult. This year the pack ice had never descended from the Arctic Ocean. Usually it came in late fall, and its expanse of thick, tireless, old, and sometimes ancient ice floes packed around the island and the Bering Sea, holding back the bowheads until spring's thaw. But because the pack had never reached the island, the ice surround-ing Saint Lawrence this spring was local: young and relatively thin ice formed in the Bering Sea. Unlike the pack, it couldn't impede the whales, who began migrating past the island as early as February. And by the time April came, they often went by unnoticed, swimming through fog and fields of thin, congested floe ice that provided enough in-between space for whales to surface, breathe, and rest in, but generally too little for boats to penetrate.

This was a year when the old Arctic authority prevailed. Gambell would catch no whales in 1979. It was a gloomy place in early May, when I decided to leave for Barrow, the northernmost point of Alaska, where bowheads that had passed Gambell were approaching another group of hunters.

At no other point along its migration did the herd come closer to land than it did at Barrow. No village caught more bowheads from year to year, and no village was angrier about the International Whaling Commission's quotas. Between 1970 and 1977, Barrow had captured an average of sixteen whales a year. Then the IWC stepped in, and in 1978, Barrow was allotted a quota of three whales. Thinking that the IWC would go away once it saw how many bowheads there really were, the hunters agreed to go along with the quota that year. And indeed, the first scientific bowhead census estimated there were two or maybe three times more whales (between 1,783 and 2,865) than the IWC had assumed when it had intervened. The IWC, however, did not go away. Instead, it continued to impose quotas, limiting Alaskan Eskimos to a catch of eighteen whales in 1979. That meant Barrow's village quota would be increased only to five, far short of what the villagers said they needed. The hunters had vowed that this year they would ignore the quota and follow their own law.

Drawn to the potential confrontation and impelled by the need to find out if what I had seen the previous year was typical of other whaling villages, I anxiously awaited a plane. When we heard the sound of one descending through the clouds one morning and circling the village, Silook and I raced his snowgo to the runway, where we embraced good-bye.

I took the six-seater to Nome, then grabbed a jet to Fairbanks, and then another jet bound for Barrow, the largest Eskimo village in Alaska. Two hundred miles north of Fairbanks we flew over the Brooks Range, a wild chain of rock, forests, and rivers that walled off the North Slope from the rest of Alaska. On the other side of it stretched a territory bigger than Minnesota— our twelfth largest state—and bordered by the Chukchi Sea, the Arctic Ocean, and the top of the world.

Nearly everything I had read and heard about Barrow was bad news. Whether they'd been there or just heard the same stories, the white people who talked to me about it or wrote what I read didn't like the place. Even fellow Alaskans, who tend to be a fearless lot, were afraid of Barrow. They had all manner of horror stories to tell about wild drinking binges and the dizzyingly violent aftermath, stories of suicides, rapes, murders; a sometimes open hatred of Outsiders and people out to "get Whitey." I was told I'd be taunted in the streets. "The place is so bad," a friend of mine claimed, "that they call black people honkies." When two white backpackers were shot to death in their tent back in 1977, the AP reporter (whom I later met in Gambell) had flown in and created a statewide sensation with his story of fear and loathing at the edge of the world.

"There are people up there just spoiling for a fight," a federal official warned me. "You'd think they were a different race from the Eskimos you've known in Gambell."

In *Going to Extremes*, Joe McGinniss called Barrow "life in the caboose of the world." At a press conference held in New York to announce the results of a study commissioned in Barrow, a sociological researcher pronounced it "a society of alcoholics." And in a piece published by *Harper's* magazine in September 1977, Barry Holstun Lopez portrayed the people of Barrow as soulless hunters who were trashing their environment and being trashed in turn by Western culture and money; titled "An Alaskan Tragedy," the story relied upon the views of non-Native, outside officials and bureaucrats. Lopez paraphrased one state planner and environmentalist, for instance, as saying Eskimos "should be moved out simply to save what is left of the Western Arctic caribou herd and other local wildlife," and he quoted a State Fish and Game officer as warning, "We are going to pay dearly for this kindness to Eskimos."

Barrow was seen as the focal point of Eskimos' adjustment to the modern world: the crossroads of contact with big money, Western culture, and industrialization. Eskimos in Barrow were seen as object lessons. They were portrayed as the fallen descendants of once-happy hunters pulled out of paradise and thrown into a jungle of modern civilization. They had become trading-post Indians, and on the walls of their trading post, in this case a modern two-story grocery market and department store, they were writing *Fuck Honkies* in Day-glo, for now they'd turned on us. The people in southern Alaska, where I lived, warned me not to go there. They said I was asking for trouble; I was heading into a ghetto on ice.

I was scared.

I got off the jet and through the airport without incident,

yet what I saw, after having lived in a village like Gambell, was a profound shock. For the first time in weeks, I was walking down a street, a street that was lined with telephone poles and traveled by cars and pickup trucks driven by Eskimos. On both sides of me was a busy clutter of houses and shacks like those I'd seen in Gambell, but there were also long two-story apartment buildings that rose above the flat tundra. The streets even crossed at right angles. I gaped like a farm boy coming into the city. I imagined that this might be what Gambell would look like in the year 2000.

To walk down these streets, even when deserted, was to see an inventory of how people lived their lives, for there in the front yards of Barrow lay all the material things of this world. There were Fords and Chevys, Datsuns and Hondas, snowmobiles, motorcycles, sleds, bicycles, fancy fiberglass outboards, skin boats, and house trailers. There were the carcasses of broken-down vehicles, haunches of darkened meat atop sheds, here the hulk of a washing machine and there a couple of caribou hides or a polar-bear skin hanging like sheets on a clothesline.

Here was the modern equivalent of the heaps of bones discarded by ancient hunters and so avidly pursued by archaeologists, the kitchen middens of today: a litter of lumber, whale ribs, plastics, packing crates, kitchen sinks, and caribou heads amid the burned-out bodies from a world on wheels. And that was only the junk on top of the snow! Still waiting to emerge from its white shell was a whole other stratum of Native bric-a-brac and consumer items cast aside in the ancient tradition of a use-and-drop culture or resourcefully stored for a rainy day like spare parts in a white man's basement; I was never sure which was closer to the truth. I was truly amazed, not by the litter—for this was true Bush Alaska—but by the quality of the junk.

In two different years, I came to Barrow from two quite different directions: first from the Bush and then from a big city down south. My reactions could not have been more different. Coming as they had from the Lower Forty-Eight, most white men saw Barrow without ever seeing the villages. Without the reference point of village life, they saw Barrow at its most unappealing. I too tended to see it that way when I came from the "real thing" in the Lower Forty-Eight. But one's sense of beauty is relative, and coming to Barrow from the Bush, I delighted in flowers among the trash. After witnessing Gambell's desperate search for money, I felt as if I were walking down the rainbow road of economic prosperity. Black plastic trash bags that squatted along my path seemed the fatted calves of affluence.

From the center of all this rose an impressive three-story Native-owned office building, the tallest structure ever made by man or nature for as far as the eye could see. It was fed—as were all the houses, shacks, and even live-in shipping crates—by a metal pipe that individually connected it to a branch of a branch of a main pipe, in the manner of a water system down south. But since this pipe could not be buried—for the ground was frozen to a depth of a thousand feet—the pipes crisscrossed town in a ubiquitous grid, running atop rusty sawed-off oil barrels and timber beams that spanned street crossings like lonely arches. At a leaking juncture or two of pipe near an intersection, I could smell natural gas being carried from a nearby field. It was cheap energy in a land where heat was always dear. But gas was only a minor treasure compared to the other commodity that lay beneath this industrial version of God's good earth and which had sprouted Eskimo corporations and cash.

Walking toward the corporation building, I passed a group of Eskimo women in front of the general store. They were dressed in bright flower-print snow dresses like those worn in Gambell, and were surrounded by little boys in big parkas and little girls dressed like their mothers. Atop the women's backs and tucked inside their parkas were babies they carried like papooses while they held their bags and boxes full of groceries. While I was watching them, a big new white and blue Mercedes bus pulled up in front of us. They all climbed aboard. PAGLA- GIVSI, the sign read: "Welcome Aboard."

Ten years earlier, a villager once told me, he had often walked through Barrow without seeing a car, a truck, or more than a few white men. In those days only bush planes flew in, not jets, and the bulk of Barrow's supplies arrived by barge once a year when the ice opened. But that was before white men had struck oil and the Eskimos had formed the North Slope Borough to charge them rent. Those were also the days before Congress had traded 5.5 million acres of land and $52 million to North Slope Eskimos as part of a bigger deal in which all of Alaska's Native people gave up their claims, based on aboriginal use and occupation, to 90 percent of the state, including Prudhoe Bay. As a result of the Alaska Native Land Claims Settlement Act, the land and money had been channeled into a regional Native corporation designed to manage the assets and to make Eskimos partners with white men in the economic development of Alaska.

Oil yanked the string and the Top of the World spun in a whirlwind of development. Almost every one of Barrow's twenty-seven hundred residents was getting a piece of the action. Half its households now owned a car or a truck—and to afford one you not only had to have the purchase price, but an extra $2,000 or more to fly it in from the world down below and the wherewithal to pay two bucks a gallon for gas once you got it here. But despite price tags as high as $14,000, cars and trucks kept coming, along with snowgoes, refrigerators, freezers, and a windfall of other goods and services.

Pumped up with jobs and cash, Barrow had raced from subsistence village to what seemed like city over the short course of the 1970s, swallowing up Western objects and culture like an engine sucking air. The transformation of life-styles was nothing short of mind-boggling. A music store opened by a company called Eskimo Inc., for instance, had sold $100,000 worth of stereo equipment in the last three months, and its two white managers expected sales of half a million dollars at Christmas. "Eskimos," they smiled, "are our biggest customers." At Stuaqpak, the biggest and best general store I had ever seen in rural Alaska, the aisles were busy with Native shoppers and the shelves laden with what seemed an extraordinary variety of foods—at least compared to the meager stock of mostly canned goods on hand at Gambell's Native store. Stuaqpak had a big-moving supply of frozen foods, fresh produce, and dairy products. Its top-selling items included frozen pizzas and Banquet Fried Chicken. TV dinners were popular too—and no wonder. At home, Eskimos could watch eleven channels of satellite television, which was ten more than Gambell watched and more than most households even in New York City. At my captain's house, I could watch Cubs' home games live from Wrigley Field in Chicago, the *Dialing for Dollars Movie* out of San Francisco, and *Donahue* on network.

White men's food filled the shopping carts of those who hunted whales, but shopping wasn't the only way they got *tannik* (white man's) food, for they could order burgers and fries from a fast-food outfit called Benson's Arctic Kitchen—it delivered, too. Down on the beach one summer day, a family was butchering a big walrus. With bowie knives and traditional crescent-shaped *ulus*, they labored to cut through two thousand pounds of blubber, muscle, and bone. Blood dyed their hands and forearms as they performed a timeless act of harvesting food. Suddenly, they stopped in the middle of their work: the fast-food truck was pulling up to bring them hamburgers, french fries, and cans of soda pop.

Walking farther westward to the end of Agviq (Bowhead) Street and the edge of the Arctic Ocean, I came upon the Top of the World, a modular two-story hotel assembled from units shipped up from the Lower Forty-Eight and put together atop pilings driven into the permafrost. In the lobby a stuffed polar bear stared down at me from inside a glass case; it had been shot near Point Barrow, north of the beach that started a few yards from the hotel. For all of Barrow's changes, it was still a place "on the edge." At the front desk, I flinched when the desk clerk told me rooms were $85 a night.

Here I stayed, between countless excursions through the streets of Barrow and back and forth to office buildings, trying to make contact with the people of the whale. I felt like a captive. How different it was from Gambell, where I had not been able to step off the plane without drawing attention to myself. Here I could walk through downtown streets without arousing more than a glance. Just another white man.

About five hundred white men (around a fifth of the resident population) lived here, and many more came through town in a steady stream of tourists, businessmen, and bureaucrats. On behalf of their Native employers, white men in Barrow ran the hotel, the general store, the schools, the bureaucracy, and corporate affairs. White men picked up the garbage, delivered water, and emptied honey buckets full of human waste. The cops were white. So were family health counselors, legal-service lawyers, missionaries, and doctors at the hospital. So too were the entrepreneurs who started businesses geared toward people who were ready to be consumers and could suddenly spend as they could never spend before.

Inside Eskimo office buildings, I was just another in a long line of reporters who had come during the last five years, all of them looking for the same people, the ones who were the voice of Eskimos. Those we came to see were contact points between the Outside world and their fellow villagers, and when they could be found they were most often seen here, in the Western world of government and business. They were more accessible to us this way, wearing the masks of administrators, board members, and elected officials. But they also saw themselves as hunters, and so their sense of schedule escaped us. In the two springs I spent in Barrow, I made countless trips back and forth to offices that were empty of the people I was looking for or supposed to meet. Word had come of whales and they had dropped their masks on the desk, next to their nameplates, and disappeared along with the people they spoke for. Though Barrow had a fleet of taxicabs, for example, I had to walk the mile or so into town that spring of 1979; all cabs were out of service because their cabbies were out on the ice hunting bowheads.

After unsuccessful missions into streets and offices, I would return to my hotel room and sit dispiritedly by the window. I was a stranger in a city, searching to make contact with people who were more elusive than those I had left in Gambell. Listlessly I watched cars drive by and kids play baseball in the street below. My pulse quickened to see the caravans of snowgoes, sleds, and skin boats that rasped and rattled over gravel roadbeds. They passed through downtown crossings below my window and faded from view into the seemingly endless tract of shore-fast ice that separated Barrow from open water. From my window the icescape looked like an immense furrowed plain, swollen by heavings of earth, eroded by wind, a surface that erupted here and there with glistening blue and white boulders. Though hardly flat, the icescape seemed flattened by the immensity of sky. Only on its horizon did the surface seem irregular, there where it had been thrust upward by the pressure of colliding ice fronts.

Traveling across this plain to the water's edge, the hunters made camp to await the whale. Though the men were miles beyond my range of vision, I could tell where they were by the dark clouds that hung above them in an otherwise bleached-out ceiling. Wherever the ice opened in springtime, the uncovered sea reflected upward in a dark "water sky" like this one. How I squirmed in anticipation, knowing that whales were swimming by while I was trapped in Barrow, alone and tantalized.

I wanted to know the hunters on the ice, not in their offices. Out there, Eskimos were in another world that seemed more distant than the one I'd known in Gambell. Instead of sailing off for a day, Barrow's hunters would go away for weeks on end. To get invited to live so intimately with them for so long a time was much more difficult than going on a day excursion, as I had in Gambell. And the Eskimos themselves were more distant. In Gambell, I'd been invited to tea almost everywhere. But this was a custom apparently more common in villages, where life was simpler and white men were less commonplace than in Barrow. Though Eskimos lived among the office buildings that I and other white men walked to so often, they lived in a world unto themselves, behind the walls of city life. I needed an entranceway into this complex society. Without one, I was confined to my room, to the streets, to gazing at objects and exteriors while waiting to be let in the entrance.

After a week or so, I struck up a friendship with a white man who worked for the North Slope Corporation, and he invited me to move from the hotel (where my bill was running par to the rent on Boardwalk) to his apartment in a brand-new building near the airport. Through him, I eventually met Sarah, his next-door neighbor and one of the few Eskimo women I ever came to know. She had high, finely sculpted cheekbones, a round face, almond-shaped eyes, and a high forehead, features she acquired from ancestors who had come to America from two different directions: Asia and Europe. Her grandmother, a Native woman, had married a commercial whale man who'd come to make his fortune hunting bowheads. By white men's standards, her great-grandfather had belonged to an old American family. But his family were newcomers compared to the other lines of ancestry that had crossed from Siberia several thousand years earlier.

By blood, Sarah was Eskimo far more than white, but in terms of life-style she seemed not much different from many other twenty-five-year-olds in the Lower Forty-Eight. Although she had been married once, she was single now, and, being popular, she and the younger sister who lived with her had many friends. She decorated her apartment with hanging plants, posters, and photographs, and she had a rack of record albums and tapes of the Eagles, Emmy Lou Harris, Willie Nelson, and Waylon Jennings, to name a few. She smoked marijuana (not illegal in Alaska if possessed for personal use and smoked in private), snorted cocaine, occasionally popped pills, and drank till she felt good. Because Barrow had no bars, she did her partying at friends' houses and out at the DEW Line station at the northern end of the road, where radar technicians drank at a private social club when they weren't watching their screens for Soviet bombers coming in from over the Pole. And whether she was employed or not—for she liked to hold a job only for a stretch at a time—she often played by night and slept through the mornings.

I liked her very much. She was affable, outgoing, and sufficiently well traveled to remind me of one or two cowgirls I knew in eastern Washington. In fact, she'd spent some time in Montana, where she had gone to college for a couple of years before dropping out. While there, she had picked up a western drawl; she liked the sound of it and had adopted it for effect. Invited over to socialize, to watch television and listen to the stereo, I spent a lot of time in her apartment. Wistfully she talked to me of moving to "sunny" southern California, an ambition she shared with many young women elsewhere. She'd loved it while visiting there with a white boyfriend she had been living with in Montana. But after breaking up with him, she had returned to Barrow the year before. Unhappy in her hometown, Sarah hoped he would move here, where there was lots of work, so they could get back together. In the meantime, she partied as hard as any cowgirl. And after her buzz wore off and the lush life turned inward on itself in the early hours of another day, I would awake on the other side of the wall, in the next apartment, to hear her crying. We were both immersed in total darkness created by thick sheets of black plastic that may have kept the midnight sun out of our rooms, but also made the night too long.

In the boredom and isolation of this lonely little world that isolated me and perhaps many in Barrow from Barrow itself, I spent my time considering the ways in which Sarah and other Eskimos here were different from me and other white people. I had asked myself the same thing in Gambell and had come to an answer. But here, amid such dramatic contrasts, the question persisted. In the offices I went to and the public hearings I attended, Barrow's Eskimos were asserting their cultural identity as passionately as black Americans had in the 1960s. While fighting against Outside efforts to limit their hunting and to drill oil in their hunting grounds, Eskimos insisted, "We're *different* from white men!" Yet to all appearances, Barrow's residents were the most assimilated Eskimos in Alaska.

I wondered these things in the aisles of Stuaqpak and while walking past cedar homes with Subarus and Saint Bernards. Out in a suburban section of the city named Browerville, after Charles Brower, the most important white man in North Slope history, I meditated about the differences while gazing at rows of "twelve-plex" apartment buildings or watching kids on swings at a nearby playground. Did the essence of being Eskimo lie in the heart, in the mind, or in actions? Did it reside in the language? Many Eskimos no longer spoke it. Was it in what they did? Many no longer lived in the Arctic, and others no longer hunted. Was it in the blood? Most of them had at least some white ancestry, and some had more white blood than Eskimo. I pondered such questions while eating tortillas and tostadas at Pepe's-North-of-the-Border, a crowded restaurant whose emblem was a Mexican in a sombrero outside an igloo.

A path out onto the ice and into Eskimos' private lives finally opened up for me in a fortuitous way. I met a kindly old whaling captain named David Brower, a son of the famous Charles Brower. Impatient to go out with a whaling crew, I followed the lesson I had learned from the AP reporter in Gambell: I didn't wait to be invited; I asked. Sure, David said, I would be welcome as long as I was willing to pull my own weight, but I would have to find my own way to camp. He himself didn't hunt anymore, all his crew were out on the ice somewhere, and he didn't know when any of them was coming into town for supplies.

If I was going to get out to David's camp, I'd have to find a snowmobile ride and then the route. Luckily I then met a traveling Eskimo repairman of Xerox machines and typewriters. He had come to town from Fairbanks for business and to join his relatives out on the ice for the weekend. Their camp happened to be located next to the camp of David Brower's crew, and he agreed to give me a lift.

The next morning, as the daily jet flew overhead, I rode out of Barrow like a dogmusher, standing at the back of a wooden sled. The snowgo we were hitched to pulled us fifteen miles southward, below a high bluff of land parallel to the beach. Then we turned westward, and suddenly the plain of ice no longer seemed as flat as it had looked from my hotel window. Over a twisting trail we made our way into an Arctic badlands of sharp-edged boulders, spires, and giant slabs of limpid blue ice that had buckled skyward like an upheaval of stratified rock. After climbing or pushing up ridgetops and slag heaps, we'd plunge down the backside in a roller-coaster ride of sleds and snowgoes. We often overturned, yet over the next ridge the ice might be as smooth and flat as a frozen lake; there we'd race onward until we reached another ridge.

Close to land, the icescape had been dingy and streaked with soil blown from the tundra. But farther seaward, it turned into an all-encompassing white brilliance that glowed here and there with crystalline-blue remnants of glaciers. The sheer sweep of its empty whiteness was breathtaking and, in the spring sun, blinding. Nothing was behind us, and in front of us there lay nothing but more pressure ridges, until bouncing over yet another we saw tents along the dark edge where the icescape ended.

21. "The Men Preeminently"

A few yards in front of us, the shore-fast ice ended and the sea lay uncovered, its dark waters sparkling with the play of sunlight. To my right and to my left, the ice edge ran in a jagged line along a southwest-northeast heading. Looking outward, I felt as if I were standing on the edge of a wide, flat-banked, and desolate canal. Open water extended a half-mile or so seaward until it reached a parallel line of ice that faced us from the opposite side. That other side was the offshore pack ice.

Every winter, pack ice came from the north and connected to shore-fast ice that grew seaward from the land. But in springtime, the pack ice tore away, and when the two split apart, they created a lane of open water in between them—this was what whalers called the lead—through which the whales swam on their northeastward migration. The landward side of the lead was attached to the shore—that's why it was called shore-fast ice. But on the opposite side of the lead, the pack ice floated free, in whichever direction winds and currents pushed it, so that the width of the lead might change at any moment. From day to day or hour to hour, it might grow from a one-lane road to an eight-lane highway to a corridor several miles wide or, conversely, contract like a fissure of earth closing up. Wherever it ran, the lead made its presence known in the sky overhead. Reflecting what lay below it, the sky turned dark above open water and pale white above the sea ice. A water-sky told hunters where to look for the migrating bowheads.

We headed north toward a large rectangular tent—white to blend with the surroundings and nestled among some low blocks and slabs of ice close to the water's edge. A minute or two later, we pulled up to the back side of the tent. Some of the crewmen came around to greet us and help unload supplies that my newfound friend from Fairbanks and his relatives and friends had brought from Barrow. I stood back from the others, smiling and waiting to be invited into camp. Though puzzled by my presence and somewhat reserved, the men at camp welcomed me as a companion of the visitors they were glad to see. They brought out coffee and crackers, and as we stood about, quietly watching for whales to surface in the lead, some of the crewmen smiled at me affably.

Their camp consisted of a skin boat, an array of whaling gear, a couple of sledges, and the white canvas ten-by-twelve-foot wall tent. Wondering how they staked the tent down, I noticed that in a number of spots the men had chiseled two shallow holes into the ice side by side and connected them at the bottom to create a small handle around which the tent lines could be tied. The front of the tent faced the sea so that the men could quickly move to their skin boat—called an *umiak*—that was perched over the water's edge. Smaller than the angyaqs used in Gambell and without a sail, the umiak resembled a broad canoe. While scanning the sea, the men would stand behind the boat or sit beside the tent, in front of a windbreak they had made by turning one of the sledges on its side and putting it behind the other sledge, then tying a sheet of canvas behind it.

I was intending to find and join David Brower's crew, camped a hundred yards away, but they weren't there—they had motored northward to find a spot where the lead was narrower, thus better for intercepting whales. After an hour or so, the hunters I was visiting decided to do the same thing. They loaded a spare tent, a camping stove, their whaling gear, and some supplies into the umiak and started climbing aboard. Mindful of my manners, I stood back and smiled as everyone else got in: I guessed I would have to wait alone until either they or David Brower's crew returned.

"Aren't you coming?" one of the crewmen who was ready to push off asked with a quizzical look. Surprised and delighted, I climbed over the gunwales and in atop some gear. We launched into the lead.

As the ten of us motored northward, I glanced repeatedly at one man who was at the helm. When I think of Eskimo hunters, my first image will always be of him: Johnny O. He was taller and leaner than most Eskimos. He was young, in some ways adolescent. But Johnny projected a skill and an intensity of purpose that filled me with awe. I saw him as the essence of ancient hunters.

His eyes were staring coals set in a narrow, olive face. Curly wisps of whiskers sprouted from under his chin, a mustache dropped from the corners of his mouth, and jet-black hair hung down past his ears almost modishly. His teeth were rotten with black cavities, but Johnny was ruggedly handsome. He reminded me of Charles Bronson, and was just as intimidating.

He wore the same kind of parka as the others. Its fur was turned inside out, and over it he wore a light-colored cotton snow shirt; all the hunters did. Like them, he too had a hood that was trimmed with fur (in his case, wolverine, best of all because it was warmest). When he pulled up his hood, part of the ruff dangled alongside his face like a pom-pom: it was the wolverine's paw, its claws still intact.

From that very first glance, I knew Johnny was unlike me and other whites. In some ways he was also unlike the Yupik hunters of Gambell, for he and the other Eskimos in northern Alaska spoke a different language (*Inupiaq*) and called themselves *Inupiat* (variously translated as "Real People," "The People," or "The Men Preeminently"). Inupiat people had inherited some different traditions and also a different way of hunting the whale—which they called not Aghvook but *Agviq* (*ahg-vik*, pronouncing the *g* as if they were gargling without water).

Off Gambell, hunters sailed through mazes and fields and giant lakes of water that were variously strewn, scattered, or interspersed with ice floes in April. In such waters, whales were distributed almost as randomly as they might be in summer seas. But off Barrow, where a frozen mantle still covered most of the ocean in May, the ice opened up in well-defined, often very narrow leads and the whales swam a much more predictable course, like ships through a channel or canal. So instead of sailing after them, the hunters waited in ambush along the lead. And since the edge of shore-fast ice lay beyond easy reach from town, the crews camped there for weeks on end. Sheltered in white tents and dressed in white snow shirts, they camouflaged themselves so the whale wouldn't see them. In front of their camp, they erected tombstones of ice for the same reason. "Whale has small eyes but can see far, small ears but can hear much," Johnny later explained. Instead of stalking their prey, they waited for it to come to them. They were like Zen warriors that way: waiting, vigilant, and merging into oneness with a world of white ice, white noise.

In the evening of my first day with Johnny and his crew, the whales began to come. Seven miles north of the camp we had left earlier, we were setting up the spare tent when three bowheads surfaced nearby. I did not see them at first but sensed they were present when the crewmen suddenly froze in silence. I turned to see one of the hunters crossing his arms in a signal that we should come quickly. Six men stole, half bent, to the umiak, launched it into the lead, and dug in unison with tapered paddles through the still waters that reflected their image.

Coming to a promontory of piled-up ice, they stopped and poised their umiak for the ambush. Like figures in a still life, the crewmen held their paddles motionless across the gunwales. In the bow, Johnny sat trancelike by his darting gun as long, bending wavelengths of light turned the icescape orange. On the opposite side of the lead, a couple of hundred yards from where we waited, was the pack ice. They often called it the "mother ice." Because of its thickness, the pack ice absorbed and flattened out the sea swells and waves before they reached the lead. And while the mother ice calmed the sea's motion into a smooth surface, the cold air kept it as still as black glass—except for the occasional ripples that radiated outward when whales came up to breathe.

When the whales emerged again, they were too far off for the crew to reach. Somewhere along the lead to the north of us, perhaps, they would come closer to another camp. As the bowheads showed their flukes to the sky, the crewmen returned to camp to watch for others that would follow from the south.

It might be a matter of minutes, hours, or even days before another whale surfaced in front of camp; one never knew.

The hunters slept with their boots on. Someone was outside scanning the sea twenty-four hours a day. Meanwhile the others slept, sat staring in front of the Coleman stove, and played laughing games of cribbage or, as they called it, Fifteen-Tooo.

When ducks and seals came close and whales were thought to be out of hearing range, the Eskimos hunted them, too. Millions of ducks flew north along the lead in springtime. Coming into view on the southwest horizon, each flock looked at first like a long train streaking across the distant plain. As it traveled farther up the lead and toward us, the flock rose off the horizon in a long diagonal formation, approaching like planes coming down a runway. Soon we could hear the cry of ducks and the rush of air from countless beating wings. The sound drove my crewmates wild with excitement.

"Oh, my goodness!" Patrick cried as a dark swarm of eiders flew in fast and low off the water one day. "Duck soup! Lookit, Davit. Duckkh soup!" It was always *duckkh* with a long, exploding *ka*-boom on the tag end.

David and Fred dashed for their shotguns, giggling as they scrambled for cover and called the streaking flock closer. "Quack quack quackquackquackquack," a whoosh of air, then *ba-doom, ba-doom, ba-doom*, and the duck express swerved off course minus a half-dozen eiders, which the hunters handed upside down to Patrick a few minutes later.

"Oh, my goodness," he marveled as if he'd never seen such creatures before. "Look at the duckkhs." They all laughed deliriously. Announcing with comical formality that "we must have duckkh soup," our cook took the dead birds, threw them into a pot, and boiled them with rice and onions while the others smacked their lips.

Following a couple of crewmen one day, I too grabbed a shotgun and ran for cover in the shore-fast ice behind the tent. As the flock swooped down close to the block of ice I happened to be hiding behind, I stood and fired. "How could I have missed?" I wondered when at first nothing fell. Then I saw not one but six ducks drop downward of me. Incredulous at the idea of having killed all six myself—for I had never hunted ducks until that spring—I called out to the two crewmen, who were fifty yards away from me, "Are these your ducks?" They thought that was pretty funny. When I walked back into camp holding the birds upside down in one hand and my shotgun in the other, the crew gave me an enthusiastic reception. Patrick said it all when he proclaimed: "Duckkh soup!" It never tasted better than it did that night amidst such zany camaraderie.

I cherished such moments all the more because they relieved the strain I had begun to feel after a few days in camp. At times, while standing watch over uneventful hours with the wind in my face and a chill in my marrow, the wait for whales seemed interminable. But worse than the wait alone was a twisting tension between me and some of the young crewmen, a tension caused, I knew, by my presence among them.

When the time came for the Xerox repairman and the other visitors to return to Barrow, I stayed, much to the surprise of those I was with. At first I had intended to find and join David Brower's crew. But after a pleasant day or two with Johnny's crew, I wanted to stay with them instead. David Brower was back in Barrow, and now that I was finally out on the ice and the whales were coming, I didn't want to take the chance of leaving one crew and trying to join another I didn't know. I did not relish the prospect of walking into Brower's camp to announce that their captain had invited me to stay with them—I wasn't even sure if he had told them. And if they didn't want me there, I knew I would have to go back to Barrow. Instead I imposed myself on Johnny and his crewmates.

As the time approached for the Xerox repairman and the others to leave, I asked Johnny if it would be all right for me to stay. He replied, in about as many words, that yes, it would be okay. But though he had consented, some of his crewmen grew resentful of my presence and their actions told me I was un-welcome. What I had mistaken for rapport that first day or two when I was in camp with the other visitors had dissolved over the next few days. Some of the crewmen and I might share a provisional camaraderie whenever ducks were flying and whales were swimming past our tent, but afterward, the tension be-tween us gradually returned. At times, in the crowded confines of a ten-by-twelve tent shared with crewmen who were distant, aloof, and sometimes hostile, the wait for whales was agony.

Yet my fascination with Johnny made my often unpleasant relations with the others worth enduring. Within a day of meet-ing him, I grew to have total confidence in his judgment and

208

ability. When the outboard engine broke down and the umiak was bobbing miles away from the nearest crew, it was Johnny who got it running again. When my gloved hands were numb, Johnny worked bare-handed with a screwdriver and a wrench to jerry-rig the engine. On thin ice that undulated with ocean swells, he could walk when others might have fallen through. Before the ice I always felt incapable, but Johnny was as adept as any man I've ever seen.

For hours at a time he stared seaward, searching from behind a pair of aviator sunglasses. On a skin of caribou atop a slab of ice, he'd lay prone like a seal, a pair of binoculars at his side. Or he'd climb to a perch atop a nearby pressure ridge or sit in front of the windscreen. Pulling his arms up the sleeves of his parka, he would fold them across his stomach and sit tucked up on his haunches to keep warm in the frigid cold.

In any stance he seemed statuesque, but it was this one— with empty, dangling sleeves that reminded me of an abandoned marionette—that struck me most. Save for darting eyes that scanned for signs of whales, he floated in a state of suspended animation as if concentrating on some moving form in the vastness of space. Even inside the tent, he might enter the same trance, fixing his eyes on the flame of a Coleman stove that provided our only heat. Sitting beside him, I wondered whether what occupied him was an intensity of contemplation or a transcendental vacancy of thought.

He said little. Indeed, I imagined he had become the ice itself, so alone did I feel in his presence. Apart from saying I could stay, he did not speak to me once until two days after I appeared. I was on a limb, unsure of myself and wanting reassurance that I was welcome. I was alone inside the tent with Johnny, and feeling desperate.

Suddenly Johnny opened up. "Joey over there, he's a good boy. He learns well. Me? I'm thirty-four."

I had never been so elated by such a short conversation. Suddenly the air seemed fresh with acceptance.

As intimidating as he might appear, Johnny was a gentle and easygoing man. He made life in camp more pleasant for everyone. Whenever the hazing I was getting from a couple of crewmen became intense, for instance, he interposed. Though generally quiet, he was hilariously comical: he could turn from statuesque hunter to class clown in a moment. Paging through a skin magazine one night while the walls of our tent shook from a bitter storm, Johnny stopped at the centerfold with wide-eyed exclamation over a swooning woman. "Lady, you sure must be getting chilly out here," he said. We all howled with laughter while he mugged like one of the boys at the back of the bus. To pull someone's leg, he would often tell wild tales with feigned seriousness. The others would tense for the punchline, which was always the same: "I jokes, ha-ha, ha-ha, ha-ha. I jokes." And they all laughed just as hard as if they hadn't known what was coming. Around Johnny, life became more upbeat. I liked him immensely, and when racial and cultural tensions between me and some of the others twisted tighter, Johnny alone was my reason for staying.

The ice also drew attention away from personal conflicts, since its edge continually cracked, split, and tore off where we were camped, forcing us to move almost as often as the ice changed. Sometimes we had to move at a moment's notice, regardless of everything else. In the middle of the night, for instance, when I awoke to a thunderclap or groan of ice like the mast of a wooden ship creaking, I knew without Johnny having to tell me that it was time to collapse the tent, pack all our gear, and retreat as fast as we could before the ice underneath us gave way. At other times, however, the fissures started silently and just widened like cracks across a pane of glass. The crew watched for such things, and when they saw them, we moved before the fissure snapped open and sent us drifting seaward into the jaws of grinding floe ice.

We also moved whenever the lead closed. Sometimes it happened when shifting winds and currents pushed floe ice up or down the lead and clogged the open water. Sometimes it happened more dramatically, as when mother ice came toward us from the other side. Indefatigably it would advance, in an eerie silence, narrowing the lead until open water disappeared altogether and mother ice overran the shore where we were camped. A cold night would close the lead most subtly of all. Slowly, like a spider spinning its web, it would fill the sea with crystals that blossomed like molds of white fungus; still, black water became slush, and slush became the skin of new ice that soon grew too hard to paddle through.

Johnny was the man to follow whenever we had to move. Despite helicopters and other technology, men still died on the ice. It was always easy to die: by being sent adrift, by falling into a crack or off the edge and being swept under the ice, or just by falling into the sea—two minutes of exposure and you were gone. Around Johnny, however, I had a serene sense of well-being.

He was magnificent to watch. Once on a blue Arctic night, when the lead had frozen over in front of our camp, he strode off like a general, his hands behind his back, to scout the surrounding icescape. Disappearing behind blocks and slabs of ice, he reappeared again high atop a pressure ridge that looked as if it had been made out of giant building blocks. From there, he surveyed the terrain, then climbed down out of view. From our own perch, we saw him once more; he was a tiny figure by then and soon he faded from sight altogether. An hour later, he returned to camp with the same purposeful stride, his hands still behind his back. He had walked a mile or two—there were never any straight lines to measure. He had moved in the direction of black clouds, until he came to the water-sky. Under it, he had chosen a safe place where he thought the whales would surface. He had also chosen a trail for us to get there, and with few words he set us into motion.

Armed with pickaxes and ice chisels, we became road builders, chopping our way through a hell of ice so we could move our snowgoes, umiak, and gear to the edge of water again. It took hours of hard work to break trail and flatten it, but the men were exhilarated by the challenge.

"Lotsa work," smiled a hunter from another crew that had joined us to help blaze the path. He and the others were taking a rest while Johnny went up ahead to have another look at the terrain. "Here, have something to eat: you're going to get skinny," he urged. Over coffee, cigarettes, and marijuana, he and his crewmates told us about a whale they'd almost gotten two nights before. Suddenly I felt a sense of that elusive camaraderie I had sought. "All this for meat and the taste of whale," someone said cheerfully, and taking up a pickax, he attacked another boulder in the path we followed behind the man with a wolverine paw dangling from his hood. I felt a thrill of admiration, for it seemed at moments like this that I was truly among the men of legend, "the men preeminently."

22. Keepers of the Flame

Although he was in charge of the crew, Johnny wasn't a captain. He had the skill to be, had he wanted to, but he didn't have the money. It took about $9,000 to buy the guns, bombs, umiak, and other gear needed to put a crew out on the ice, and to keep them there might take $500 a week extra in food and fuel. And Johnny did not have a job.

Not that he couldn't have gotten one if he had wanted to. There were plenty of jobs in Barrow. It was just that Johnny, and many other young men here, were not interested in working full-time. Instead, they lived within extended families that pooled the earnings of those who worked with the catch of those who hunted. This continued the age-old tradition of sharing, and no one became upset about who contributed what or how productively someone spent his time; quotas and work ethics were exotic species from the temperate zone that did not grow well in the land of the Inupiat.

I think Johnny had held a job once, but he never said anything about it to me. I knew him only in the present tense. About all that he ever told me or apparently considered important about his life, apart from hunting, was that he was thirty-four and came from Wainwright, a village a hundred miles to the southwest. From others, I learned of his reputation as a skilled striker. The year before, for instance, he and his captain's crew in Wainwright had captured a fifty-three-foot bowhead, the second whale he had to his credit. Talking about his life as a hunter, however, Johnny did tell me that before he ever became a striker, he had taught himself the art of where to thrust his harpoon by examining carcasses that were butchered on the beach.

The actual captain of the crew was a short great barrel of a man named Ralph. He had a pudgy nose, eyes that were set inside baggy pockets of flesh, and big cheeks that pushed out against his glasses. He worked full-time as a plumber in the hospital, where he earned $16 an hour "and lots more for over-time, holidays, and weekends," he once told me proudly. Every May, which was when bowheads usually passed Barrow, he took a month's vacation to go whaling, but this year he had broken his ankle, so he had asked his cousin Johnny to take command of his dozen or so crewmen. Most of the men were in their early twenties; they came to camp at various times, often depending on their jobs. His crew included a janitor, a construction foreman, an expediter or two, a commercial fisherman, two common laborers, and the Xerox repairman who had come back, like many emigrants to Anchorage and Fairbanks, for a few days' reunion with his relatives and roots before returning south of the Slope. Four or five men formed the core of the crew, and the others came at night or on their days off, especially on weekends or when the action heated up.

Without a doubt, spring was the most exciting season of their lives. It combined challenge, drama, and the immense joy of shooting and chasing the whale. After a dark winter's confine-ment in the small, cagelike houses of an overcrowded city, the hunt was freedom. It was spiritual renewal from the frenzy of Western materialism. In their pilgrimage on the ice they got as far away as they could from the world of white men's culture and white men's values. Back in Barrow they had jobs, but the jobs only gave them money. What they did on the ice gave them their identity. "To be an Eskimo," some Native high schoolers once wrote, "is to know the ice and the wind and the movement of walrus and whales."

KEEPERS OF THE FLAME

Out on the ice, they could live the nomadic ways of their ancestors, coming as close as they ever would to those who had not needed a definition. But as residents, perhaps prisoners, of the present, they brought part of contemporary Barrow with them.

"Hey, Eskimo Boy, you got your ears on?"

"Roger, roger. This is Eskimo Boy, c'mon."

We were listening to the citizens' band radio network which connected every crew to its home back in Barrow and to more than thirty fellow crews, camped along the lead for some fifteen miles. All of them had "handles"—Eskimo Boy, ABC Crew, and Red Fox, to name just a few—truckers on the bowhead highway. After establishing contact with each other, they would switch over to Inupiaq wavelengths save for intermittent code words of American.

"Red Fox base, this is Red Fox crew."

"Go ahead, Red Fox crew."

"Yeah, we need some batteries, *misigaaq* (seal oil), gas, Coca Cola, Sailor Boys (crackers), sandwich meat, and Spreadables." Red Fox was calling an order to the captain's house in town so that a crewmen could bring out new supplies when he came to camp that night. Listening to this shopping list of a conversation, Johnny looked at the CB set we were monitoring and said, to the delight of his crewmates, "You forgot the napkins."

The CB radios and white men's grub were not of themselves incompatible with a Native hunt (though it did seem strange to hear Johnny tell the crew to turn down the radio lest the sound of *Casey Kasem's American Top Forty* scare off the ice whales). But there was other baggage that affected the hunt more deeply: the baggage of social and economic change that made many of them seem not much different at times from a bunch of Pittsburgh steelworkers who had gone deer hunting for the weekend. Although some showed themselves to be the very best of hunters, others proved to be among the worst.

One night, for instance, when grease ice was filling the lead, we saw the tall blows of distant whales surfacing to the southwest of us; their warm, vaporous exhaust hung in the cold air like gunsmoke. Two other crews, camped around the same bay we were, saw them too. They signaled us by crossing their arms. Someone hurried into each crew's tent to kick the feet of sleeping crewmen, waking them noiselessly so the whale wouldn't hear. From a sound sleep huddled together on caribou skins, we awoke with a start. Up went the tent flap and out we scrambled, low to the ice and totally focused on the moment.

Because the lead was hardening, it would be difficult to paddle, so Johnny climbed into the bow and had his crew stand along the gunwales; if the whale came close enough, the crew was going to hurl the umiak and its single, harpoon-wielding occupant right at his target; instead of throwing the harpoon, Johnny would brace it as if it were a lance and the force of the boat's movement would drive it shaft-deep into the whale. We waited by the umiak while another crew lay poised in the middle of the bay, where they had earlier broken a channel through brittle ice. There they silently waited, hoping the whales would surface close by.

Twenty minutes later, two bowheads emerged off the point. They moved slowly along the contours of the bay, seemingly undisturbed and eerily unaware of our ambush. Except for the sound of their lungs exhaling, the air was still.

If the whales followed the contour of the lead, they would pass in front of Johnny; and if they turned out toward the middle, they would come close to the crew in the umiak. But first they came to a bend in the bay, just south of us, where the third crew was camped.

Too far away to throw a darting gun that would harpoon either whale, two men on shore picked up what looked like brass shotguns, each with a sixteen-inch shell sticking out the end of it. The weapons were called shoulder guns, but they had big eight-gauge barrels, weighed at least twenty pounds, and gave such a terrific kick when they recoiled that many men held them against the hip instead of the shoulder before pulling the trigger. Unlike the darting gun, which both harpooned the whale and shot a bomb into it at the same instant, the shoulder gun was armed only with a bomb and it was fired like a rifle, not thrown. Yankee whalemen used it in place of a lance to blow the life out of an injured and thrashing whale from up close. It worked best that way: from up close, after the whale had already been harpooned with the darting gun and the floats prevented it from sinking. In Gambell, the hunters didn't use shoulder guns, but in Barrow most crews had at least one in the boat and another they left on the ice in front of camp just in case. On the principle that two bombs were deadlier than one, Barrow and other North Slope Eskimos fired the shoulder guns at the same time their strikers threw the darting guns. Used together, the weapons could work quite effectively; but when used alone, the shoulder gun was a long shot in a desperate game. One shot probably would not kill the whale outright unless it struck the neck and was fired from less than twenty-five feet away. And if the bomb didn't instantly kill the whale, it would probably escape.

Shoulder gun and bomb.

One of the men was standing and the other was down on one knee when they lifted their guns. They shot from sixty feet. I saw the smoke rise first, heard the crack of fire; then, moments after the whales dived, my feet twinged from a vibration of ice that shuddered as the bomb exploded underwater. They'd blown a hole in the whale, all right, but that's all. After standing about for a while to see if the whale would come up again, they went back into their tent and the crew that might have harpooned Agviq paddled their umiak back to shore.

When I thought it was safe to do so, I asked Johnny why the other crew had fired the shoulder gun. "Maybe they were afraid to harpoon the whale," he answered and, after a long silence, added: "It is so important to put floats into the whale [by harpooning it with the darting gun], because without floats, it just disappears."

The next day, when the ice across the lead had hardened, another whale surfaced in front of the same crew. It broke through ice along the edge, and this time someone on shore threw a darting gun at it. But even though the whale was dragging a float when the bomb blew, the crew couldn't go after it because the ice was too thick to launch a boat. Up through a hole where the whale was last seen floated oil and chunks of blubber, leftovers of an animal they would never again see.

Barrow's hunters struck and lost at least eight more whales that spring. One crew fired its darting gun and shoulder gun simultaneously, but from too far away, so the line ran out before the harpoon reached the whale and only the bomb from the shoulder gun hit it. Another crew chasing another whale came close enough but lost their prey—hit by nothing more than a shot from their shoulder gun—when the darting gun came apart in mid-flight; the bomb-wounded animal swam off to an uncertain fate. And then there was the whale that escaped with harpoon and floats even after the bomb from the darting gun had exploded. For four hours the crew chased it, until a hole punched into their umiak's hull by sharp-edged young ice forced them to give up and return to shore. Catching the whale is truly hard, and even if the guns never had failed, some whales would still have gotten away. But far fewer whales would have escaped if the hunters had cared for and used their weapons properly. Even this crew might have gotten their whale if they had been able to fire a second bomb into it when they harpooned it. Though they had the shoulder gun to do that, its trigger spring had rusted, so it didn't fire.

At season's end Barrow's unofficial record was two and a half wins and at least nine and a half losses (the hunters had found one whale, appropriately called a "stinker," floating dead on the surface days after it had escaped its killers, but they were only able to salvage its muktuk; the meat was rotten). Barrow's hunters had not captured anywhere near the number of whales they wanted to. They had not even been able to break the village's catch limit as they vowed to do when the IWC had set 1979's quota the year before. On the other hand, they did violate their village's allotment of strikes, according to the estimate of federal enforcement agents. But since they never reported their losses and the enforcement agents hadn't seen and couldn't prove anything, the hunters were officially in compliance.

The picture, familiar from Gambell, was more ominous here, where so many more whales came close to so many more, and better-equipped, hunters. In a year when ice conditions were optimum and open waters narrowed, the lead could resemble a shooting gallery, with whales running the gauntlet. In 1977, for instance, Barrow captured nineteen whales and, in the process, allegedly struck and lost at least fifty-eight more. And as much as the hunters disputed the accuracy of enforcement agents' reports, even half as many losses would have been outrageous. (Although I considered the agents' reports credible.)

The IWC must have had Barrow in mind when it first took action to limit the Eskimos' hunt. Barrow caught more than half the bowheads landed in Alaska. It had more crews than ever before, its catch had doubled in a decade, and nowhere were the whalers' losses or their excesses greater.

Yet no other village opposed Outside intervention as effectively. By temperament and training, Gambell was more inclined to go along with the feds, in the hope of being rewarded with a bigger quota the next year. But Barrow had been the first Eskimo village to stand up to white men—during the 1961 Barrow Duck-In—and it wasn't backing down now. A new generation of activists was telling white men, "You're not going to treat us like you treated the Indians."

There were people in Barrow who knew how to fight *tannik* (white) government, and they led the battle on behalf of all Alaska's whaling villages. Barrow people organized and orchestrated the Eskimo Whaling Commission. Barrow people led the Eskimo delegation to the IWC meeting in 1978. And when "Eskimo hunters" went to federal court to challenge the IWC's authority, "they" were none other than the legendary Eben Hopson and the machinery of the world's first home rule government of, for, and by Eskimos, a government whose headquarters and birthplace both lay in Barrow.

Only bad ice conditions kept Barrow hunters from killing enough whales to break their catch quota in 1979. Had the ice proved more favorable, federal agents could not have stopped the hunters. Paradoxically, although the IWC had largely intervened in reaction to the excessive killing at Barrow, it was at Barrow where the federal government was least able to enforce the IWC's quota. The enforcement agents proved more effective in Gambell, where the hunt hardly mattered in comparison.

"Eskimo society *is* the bowhead whale and what we do with it," Charlie Edwardsen, better known as Etok, had told his biographer.[15] By the looks of the hunt in the late 1970s, the old society was crashing down around them.

It had once been a pretty hard club to get into. In a society with no chiefs or social class save theirs, whaling captains had held the highest position of status. As businessmen, hunters, and priests, they had led a communal hunt through which their villagers found food and well-being. Among a people of the whale, no one could achieve more prestige.

In the old culture, becoming a whaling captain, an *umealit*, might take a lifetime; even then it was beyond most men's means. Outfitting a crew and supporting them in the off-season took great wealth in a land where surplus property was difficult to accumulate. One of the most common routes lay through inheritance, but since there was never enough wealth to sustain an unsuccessful captain, a man also had to have skill. If a man was skilled as both hunter and leader, he could win the collective backing of his kin and the loyalty of a crew without having wealth beforehand. Skill captured bowheads, and bowheads generated property with which he could pay everyone back. But a man had to prove himself first, and that required him to rise through the ranks of apprenticeship by his own merit.

That's the way it had once been. It was different now, because the coming of Western prosperity and cash had created a different sort of wealth than the kind that grew from the hunt itself. Outfitting a crew was no longer beyond the means of most men, for a man with a good job could afford to buy what whole kin groups had once struggled to accumulate. And by accumulating bombs, guns, boats, and all the rest of the gear, a man could buy his way into the club without having to prove his abilities or to learn very much either.

Most of the new umealits were young men, back from outside schooling or career training, employed in high-paying jobs, and reawakened to ethnic identity. Because they were generally inexperienced, they tended to shoot more bombs. Eager to catch the whale, but not knowing where best to strike it and intimidated perhaps by an immense tail that could demolish their boat, they often fired the shoulder gun from a distance, instead of harpooning first. They lost a high percentage of whales, but young captains could afford to buy bombs. What they couldn't buy was experience.

Back in Barrow once again, I visited seventy-two-year-old

umealit David Brower, hoping to learn more about the past and how the hunt had changed. He was a small, gentle man with dignity of bearing and an economy of motion. His face was furrowed and crosshatched with lines of age and weather that softly accented a quiet authority as he spoke to me from behind an office desk. Reminiscing about six decades of whaling in which he had captured thirty to thirty-five whales, he talked about the training he had received from his Eskimo relatives and his white father.

"When I was a young man, the old-timers made model whales out of snow and taught the younger crewmen where to strike the whale and where to shoot the bombs," he said.

"The old-timers never struck a whale unless they were right on top of it. But this younger group disregards the old people's custom. They think that just by shooting it from a distance with a bomb they can claim the honor. But they don't know how to hit whales in their vital spot. My father used to say a hunter might as well stay at home if he doesn't put a line and float on the whale first."

Charles Brower should have known, because he himself shot quite a few bombs in his day, in just the manner he later condemned to his son. Indeed, Brower and other white men had brought the incentives that first encouraged the excessive and wasteful use of shoulder guns.

Young Charles Brower, born in New York City and raised in New Jersey, came to Barrow in 1886 as an employee of the Pacific Steam Whaling Company. In an attempt to increase their sagging catch of bowheads, his company and others had decided to establish land-based whaling stations at Point Hope and Barrow. That way, they figured, crews of commercial whalers could hunt from shore-fast ice during the bowheads' spring migration, when the herd was funneled through the leads, three months before whaling ships could penetrate that far north. Brower built a station in Barrow, hired Eskimos to man his crews, and set up a trading post where Natives could trade baleen, furs, and their wages for staples, guns, and manufactured goods.

The first white man to settle in northwest Alaska, Brower stayed for a lifetime. He took a Native wife, learned the language and ways of the Inupiat, and fathered sons and daughters who were absorbed into Native society. But as a dynamo of industry and change, "King Brower," as he came to be called, also propelled Eskimos into the grip of Western civilization.

David Brower grew up after the commercial era ended, so he never saw how mixed crews of Eskimos and Yankees had hunted whales while working for the shore-based station his father ran during the two decades bracketing 1900. In an era when baleen from a single bowhead could fetch more than $10,000, few hunters hesitated to shoot instead of letting whales pass unharmed when they were beyond throwing reach of a darting gun but within range of a shoulder gun. Charlie Brower and other white men had come north to make money, after all, and the Eskimo recruits they armed with whaling guns had even more incentive for pulling the trigger. Not only did the Natives win a treasure chest of trade goods for pay, they also got to keep the rest of the whale for food, since only its jaws held any commercial value for Brower's company and others. And compared to the payoff when an occasional whale turned belly-up, playing a long shot at a dollar a bomb was a cheap price to pay.

When the market for baleen collapsed in 1908, the economic rationale for taking long shots died with it. Yet having never used the shoulder gun in any other way, many of the Eskimos continued to misuse it. Over the course of the preceding twenty tumultuous years of change, they had lost, forgotten, or never learned the traditional art of whaling. So they relied on the shoulder gun to make up for what they lacked in skill. Their practice of pulling the trigger was curbed only by their lack of bombs, which became hard to afford in the lean times that followed the end of the commercial eras of baleen and fox furs.

In contrast, the better hunters like Charlie Brower and some of his Eskimo crewmen realized they no longer had a reason to take long shots. Now, rather than waste their bombs on low-percentage shots, they only hunted the whales that came within range and used traditional skills to go alongside or atop the whale before striking. It was men like these, at a time when Eskimos had returned to living off the land, who taught their sons and nephews, like David Brower, the importance of discipline, care, and proper use of whaling guns. They had the greatest killing power of all.

Many of the present-day hunters, however, did not learn what David Brower was taught, and with the coming of new economic prosperity, their use of shoulder guns was no longer limited by the bombs' expense. To today's hunters the whale still meant precious food, but Agviq's importance went beyond its meat and muktuk. In a society battered by change and postmortems on Eskimo culture, catching a whale for one's people was tangible proof of being Eskimo. Here was the new rationale for shooting first and harpooning second.

And so new affluence and social crisis nourished the impulse to shoot. A bomb only cost $40, just a few hours' wages, a small price compared to the cost of maintaining a crew on the ice for six weeks. And when a whale came upon them, beyond the reach of their striker, a flood of adrenaline often blocked out the elders' words (and the Eskimo Whaling Commission's own prohibition). "At a time of excitement, some remember what they learn," David's brother Arnold said, quite bitterly, "and some don't remember at all."

Catching bowheads had more to do with skill than with shoulder guns. The captains who captured the most bowheads probably didn't fire many bombs. They didn't have to: they had something more powerful.

Skill was a man's achievement. Like a hunter's success, it flowed from knowledge. And knowledge is as mortal as man himself, because it lives only as long as it is sustained.

If I had thought otherwise before coming here, I knew when I left that bloodlines did not make a hunter skillful. Though the accomplishments of their ancestors testified to man's adaptiveness and endurance, there was no reason to believe, as I think we and some Eskimos did, that skillfulness at hunting was an innate and inherited trait. Such thinking is only the flip side of the old tune called "all blacks have rhythm."

From time immemorial, the knowledge of Eskimo hunters had been passed from one generation to the next. Young and old alike had drawn from a fire of experiences accumulated as long as there had been Eskimos and shared like the food they hunted. In a culture with no written language, the fire was propagated by word and sustained by experience. To all those who took from it, it gave light and guidance. So bright were its flames that it must have seemed eternal.

In the old culture, the opportunities for acquiring knowledge began as soon as children could walk, and grew to infinity as they aged. Thus, the most respected of teachers were elders who, though too old to hunt, were alive with wisdom: in them the fire burned brightest. To the children they talked of proper behavior, the ways of their people, the ways of the animals they hunted. Traveling with his family by dogsled, a boy would learn landscape and ice conditions at the same age a young boy now would be attending grade school. In their slow tundra journey, his father talked to him of hunting strategy (how different it must have been, I thought, in the days before the whining pitch of snowgoes ended all chance of discourse on the trail). At whaling camp, the boy would be coached still further by his father, his captain, and fellow crewmen. He learned by listening. He learned by watching. And by accepting responsibilities for hitching the dogs or fetching snow to make water, he began to learn by doing, which was the greatest teacher of all.

Throughout his life as a hunter, he would strive for more knowledge. Camp talk, trail talk, and his discussions with other hunters in the men's gathering houses revolved around this constant theme. His life and theirs revolved around animals—animals were the only means of life—and to catch them consistently, he must learn all that he could about the movements of ice, sky, ocean, and the animals within. To the end of his life, he talked of these things and shared what he had learned.

Could a young Eskimo today become proficient in hunting if he also had a job and an education? The answer depended in part on what kind of job and what kind of education he had. Janitors would have an easier time of it than administrators. Blue-collar workers did not have to travel or attend meetings or work overtime. Although their hunting time was compressed into evenings and weekends or days when they did not show up for work, changes in the mode of transportation and the method of hunting reduced the time once needed to find and capture animals (on the other hand, they might have to travel farther from town to find wildlife). But a man would have to be both disciplined and dedicated to go out so often after work. At home he had the comforts of his family, a warm house, and a television. He didn't *have* to go out: with his wages he could get food from the store or from butchers in Fairbanks and Anchorage, who did good business sending orders of frozen meat up to Barrow by plane. And he could get Native food from a neighbor who had just come home from hunting or who had stocked up last year's catch in an underground ice cellar. He in turn would share his catch whenever he went out.

More than his work and his home life kept a man from hunting as intensively as he might have in an earlier era. Eskimos were traveling farther than they ever had before, not as nomadic hunters but as air travelers, because increasingly they had the means to fly out on business trips and weekend shopping trips or visits to their relatives in Anchorage and Fairbanks; flying farther southward, some even took vacations in California and Hawaii.

Back in Barrow, men and women were also diverted from hunting by the call of civic responsibilities. In place of a once anarchistic society there had emerged ambitious Western-style organizations. I'd never seen people more vitally engaged in political action and self-government than the people of Barrow. But the burden of involvement disrupted traditional activities.

"This must be the most meetingest city in America," sighed Mayor Nate Olemaun with a smile. By day and by night there were meetings of the Native-owned regional and village corporations, the North Slope Borough, the borough assembly, the school board, the city of Barrow, and the regional and village councils of the Inupiat tribal government; and these were meetings of Eskimos just making local policies. In addition, they had to deal with an ocean of Outside government that rolled onto their shores with policies, proposed regulations, and development plans that would affect their lives profoundly. On issues related only to Native hunting, for instance, public hearings or meetings were conducted by the Bureau of Indian Affairs, the National Marine Fisheries Service, the Alaska Department of Fish and Game, the U.S. Fish and Wildlife Service, the Bureau of Land Management, the State Division of Minerals and Energy Management, and numerous others that made up a soup of acronymed complexity that appeared more exhausting than nourishing. To defend himself and his hunting through the "democratic" process a man almost had to give up hunting.

By both circumstance and choice, Eskimos had much less time to hunt now. Walrus quotas went unfulfilled, though herds streamed by on summer ice floes close to shore, and less than half the men took part in fishing or in hunting ducks and seals, according to a 1977 survey of North Slope Eskimos by the University of Alaska. Jobs largely dictated when people hunted, the survey said. By the look of things in the late 1970s, being broke scared most people more than running out of Native food. They had two ways of getting food, after all, but only one way of making money. And losing a job could mean instant poverty in the land of boom-town prices. Yet whether men could sustain the knowledge of their ancestors by hunting less intensively was uncertain. The teaching of hunting also had to compete with a regimen of schooling that kept children away from their families for most of the day and away from camp life for most of the year. Schooling encouraged further schooling, and so did the parents, whose faith in its power was so great that they had broken apart families to send their children to boarding schools in Kansas, Oregon, and Oklahoma. The building of a local high school was one of Barrow's brightest accomplishments, for it allowed children to remain close to home while being educated and increased their opportunity to learn how to hunt. Yet despite the school's proximity to the sea and tundra, it couldn't help but compete with traditional ways of transmitting and receiving the knowledge. Normal activities like basketball and band, for instance, drew the after-hours' energy of students who might otherwise be out with the hunters.

Perhaps the most mobile of all Eskimos, students had a fabulous array of opportunities to travel and to advance into the Western world. When the basketball team, called the Barrow Whalers, played on the road, they, their cheerleaders, and some of their student fans went as far as Hawaii; and if the Barrow Whalers high school band didn't hit the road as often, they went just as far, on tour to places like Washington, DC. Even though many of them became apprentices out at whaling camp, the most promising students, the same ones who before would have become the best hunters, were encouraged to go away to college or training schools after graduation, so they could learn careers. When and if they returned, they were more likely to become Barrow's administrators than its janitors—and that would make it even harder for them to become skilled hunters.

As if the growth of modern education and opportunity did not pose enough competition, the transmission of hunting knowledge was jammed by television signals, too. At my captain's house, Ralph, his grandchildren, and I sat in front of the big screen of a Panasonic console one night. It was hard not to, for the television faced us like a monitor, crowding the passageway between the living room/kitchen and outer hall. We were all eating the crunchy, carrotlike gum scraped from the jaw of a bowhead our crew had captured just a week before. We were watching "Monsters from Space" on the Friday night *Creature Feature*. Suddenly Ralph turned glum. "Twenty years ago we taught our kids the language of Inupiats, and now they're talking about monsters," he complained.

The knowledge of hunting would die out with Ralph and the other elders, some said. Yet despite all the obstacles, many young men were eager to learn. They had committed themselves to learning and hunting as much as they could. That a man in his twenties or thirties could combine active hunting with a full-time job, the responsibilities of a family, and involvement in government was an extraordinary accomplishment; it spoke of vitality and dedication, the qualities of those who would sustain the knowledge for another generation. And perhaps some of today's high school students would also learn from the elders. Though television, school, and other social changes segregated them from elders for most of their youth, their few days together at whaling camp were a wonderful exception. There in the long hours of watching, moving, and hunting beside experienced hunters, they might still be instructed, and perhaps would not only learn but someday teach their children as well.

In the future, I thought, fewer and fewer people would have the knowledge of hunting that made their ancestors so expert. And what they did have would dim. But the hunt would endure, because though the hunters might not have enough knowledge to be proficient, they would still have enough to continue hunting whales. For many of them the knowledge had already dimmed. Their use of guns and other technology offset their loss of skill: they still caught whales, even if they lost more in the process. And when they got into trouble by misreading the ice, a rescue squad might protect them from mistakes the elders might not have made in the first place.

In 1980, about ten crews were airlifted to shore with all their gear intact after the ice they were on drifted two miles out to sea. They had camped on the wrong side of a crack an older captain thought too wide to cross. The crack had split the ice off its shelf to shore, just as he had feared. Only a decade earlier, the crews would have had to run for big ice—would have had to run for their lives—jumping from ice floe to ice floe, fighting a current that would carry them northward past Barrow and out to sea. In the spring of 1980, however, the drifting crews called in on their citizens' band radios to get support. My captain's crew was among those who were adrift.

Imagine yourself on the ice, drifting ever seaward, on your way to oblivion. Then: *Puppup-puppup-puppup-puppup-puppup-puppup* . . . louder than a hundred thousand ducks comes the eerie yet welcome sound of helicopters chopping through a water-sky.

Was the knowledge dying? Under the circumstances, the question seemed inappropriate. Such concerns would always fade before the necessity at hand: better to be alive in the new society, I thought, than dead on the way to an old one.

Whether the full knowledge of hunting survives or not, the hunt will live on. As their involvement in other forms of hunting diminishes, Eskimos are funneling their available time and energy into whaling. For them, the hunt represents tradition, and to engage in it means preserving the core of Eskimo life. There are more crews and probably a greater percentage of men engaged in whaling today than ever before. Most of the Eskimos now and in the future will be part-time hunters. They will hunt less intensively, but that will not make their hunt less important. "They don't need it for food," say white men who want to stop the hunt. Yet their attempts to abolish whaling will only harden Eskimos' resolve to continue, because white men have unwittingly made it the clear and powerful symbol of resistance to assimilation, and hence the symbol of what it means to be an Eskimo. And it is this definition that will drive the hunt on.

On a Wednesday in the middle of May that season of 1979, William Kaleak's crew suddenly tensed in surprise as a bowhead surfaced a hundred feet from their camp. Fred Okpeahgo, the gunner, dashed to the tent to get two other men, who were making coffee, and with their young, black-bearded striker, Wesley Ahmakak, they lifted the umiak off a small piece of ice placed under the hull to keep it from freezing to shore. At the moment the whale surfaced and blew once more, they slid their boat into the water, thereby muffling the noise of their movement in the sound of the whale's own breathing.

After covering the lead for two days, the young ice had now broken up into small drifting patches. The crewmen paddled along a zigzag course to intercept their prey. "I thought it would dive," Wesley said, but instead the whale casually surfaced several more times, to blow and breathe.

His heartbeat quickened as he took the safety off the darting gun. "Everyone's heart always beats faster. Maybe all the people in town's heart beats along with you," Wesley later said. Most of the whales had passed, and Barrow had not yet captured one.

From a distance of eight feet, Wesley saw Agviq start to come up again, but he waited a moment or two longer. "You have to know exactly where to strike it if you want to catch the whale," he said. "There's a lot of big solid bone in the throat and head for the bombs to bounce off of." When Agviq broke surface, Wesley let fly with his harpoon to the base of the whale's skull, right in the hollow between its domed head and the hump of its back. Turning sideways, the bowhead jerked slightly, then sank under the surface in a slow, almost paralyzed reaction.

Excited by the commotion, Fred had forgotten to take the safety off his shoulder gun, so that nothing happened when he pulled the trigger. He swiveled, pulled the trigger a second time, and the bomb shot out. It didn't matter that it bounced off bone and exploded in the water: Wesley's strike had been perfect. The bomb from the darting gun had ripped through Agviq's vitals and the line on the sealskin pokes didn't even unravel, because, just as suddenly, the whale was dead.

Working quickly, for there was no time yet for cheering, the crew threw another harpoon and some more floats into the whale to make sure it didn't sink. With the help of another crew, they towed it in to shore by motor. Then, after they secured it to the ice, Wesley and his companions knelt down to give thanks to the Lord. Inclair, who was the oldest of the four, prayed out loud for them and when he was through, they let out a cheer with all the joy that was within them. "We were all happy," Wesley said afterward. "People were hoping so much for a whale."

Unfurling his umealit's flag, crewmate Oscar Ahkinga mounted it to his snowgo and sped off toward town like the pony express to bring news of their victory. When he passed the golden arches of two tall jawbones outside Tom Brower's café, the customers inside exploded into jubilant commotion. Jumping up from their tables at the sight of his fluttering flag, the Eskimos ran to the windows, cheering and waving madly. As Oscar raced down the street to his captain's home, the news flashed through a once-gloomy city. Coming out of their houses, people could see the flag flying proudly from Captain Kaleak's rooftop, where Oscar had raised it so everyone would know and come to share in the whale.

There would be only two and a half whales this year, but their division and distribution took place the same way as always. Everyone still shared; the shares were just smaller, and due to their generosity, the captains may have gotten the smallest shares of all.

On the night Wesley and his three crewmates in Kaleak's crew captured a whale, men from other crews and people from town rushed to the scene with blocks and tackle, cutting spades, and hooks to help haul up the whale and butcher it. Sustained by fresh-cooked muktuk, they worked industriously and enthusiastically, dividing Agviq among all the crews until there was nothing left except a bloodied shelf pockmarked with holes where the whale's blood had melted its way through the ice. Then a convoy of sled-pulling snowgoes transported the butchered animal into town, where each crew's share was divided among crewmen's families before some was sent out to ice camps where the crews had stayed to wait for more whales.

Although the whale had already been divided, the umealit's duty had only just begun. A day or two later, he shared his share by giving a feast for all of Barrow. Deserting their jobs or whatever else they were doing, townspeople entered his home freely and received large helpings of meat, muktuk, and intestines boiled up in steaming caldrons and served atop paper plates.

A few weeks later, after shore-fast ice had disintegrated and the crews came home, victorious captains would sponsor the greatest ceremonial event of Barrow's year, the spring whaling festival, called Nalukatuk. Gathering down on the beach, the villagers danced, tossed each other high into the air with a blanket of walrus hides, and feasted once more at the captain's hospitality to celebrate and to show Agviq the joy it had brought them. It had been this way for at least a thousand years.

Throughout the day the captain's family served a cornucopia of foods. There was duck soup and caribou soup; canned fruit and cooked rice; fried dough; cakes galore; and, most importantly, the whale, which was served in several courses. First came cooked tongue, liver, and sausagelike sections of thick intestines. Then followed great portions of boiled meat that filled both stomachs and plastic bags that villagers brought with them. And still later, the captain presented his guests with special treats like *mikigaq*, whale meat fermented in its own juices. There on the beach, and at the church on Thanksgiving and Christmas, the umealit would give his people the gift of choicest muktuk sliced from the flippers and flukes he had saved just for these occasions. Out of respect to the whale, he and his crewmen wore white gloves when they distributed their gifts. By giving itself up to the captain, Agviq had conferred its blessing, and by sharing this whale to the fullest, the captain showed himself worthy of being an umealit. His reward, said one successful captain, was to see the smiling faces of his people as they ate and danced and came together over the gifts he had provided.

The next year, two days after my own captain had captured a whale, I sat on the floor of his house, amid two dozen other seated guests and a forest of legs moving along to the kitchen table. With ulus and pocketknives, two old men beside me sliced the meat atop their plates. The air was thick and cramped with smells of cooked meat and full of steam from boiling kettles, but they were intent on the food before them, for it had been a long time since they had last eaten whale.

"*Nikipiak*," one of them said to me after having restored his sense of well-being. "It means 'our food.' It's real food. Our stomachs crave it. We can't live just on white men's food. Nik-i-pi-ak." He said it slowly for my sake, then put another piece of meat in his mouth, happy in mind and body.

After a while, he began to converse with the old man beside him. They spoke in soft, almost whispering sounds of wind rustling leaves. I understood nothing except the magical flow of a story that passed between them in Inupiaq like water running through a brook. Tightening his fist, one of them began to move it up and down at the wrist. I knew then that his fist was Agviq's head. The slightly raised knuckle of his middle finger was its domed spout, and the joint of his wrist was the hollow between the whale's head and its back. He moved it in a slow, wavelike motion, hypnotically so that it was no longer a hand but the whale itself coming to the surface and swimming ever closer to the two of them. Building to a climax, his story became hushed, as if muffled in the unhearing forest of legs that stood about us. When Agviq came up once more, the old man beside the storyteller grew excited. Assuming the role of striker now, he tensed his wrinkled fingers as his skin boat slid into range of the whale. He cocked his right arm above his head, brought his left arm across his chest, and braced himself a moment longer. Then, when the umiak ran onto Agviq's head, he thrust his hands downward, driving an imaginary harpoon into the kitchen floor. The two of them grinned broadly.

They had reenacted a man's greatest achievement, and if it sometimes seemed as if in Barrow the rule had become every man for himself, tonight they could look about the room and find reaffirmation of their values and their collective identity. Here was not only a man's greatest achievement, but a people's as well. At the far end of the kitchen table sat Ralph in an undershirt, smoking another cigarette and quietly greeting all who came into his home. His face was bronzed by the sun and weathered like a ripe avocado, and his fleshy skin hung slack from, exhaustion of several sleepless nights, yet he was pleased by what he saw. Across from him were his gracious wife, Mary, and their daughters, busily tending to the cutting platter, the stove, and their many guests. There were his grandchildren, too, to see all this and someday, he hoped, to remember. There were the elders and poor people whom he was providing for in an act that in his mind was both Christian and Eskimo. And there were all those who had helped him and fed him and whom he would help and feed in turn, not because he felt obliged to reciprocate but because it was proper for "real people" to share and cooperate with each other.

"Hey, Tipook [White Fish]," he called to me with a jovial cock of his head. "You're living with the Eskimos now. Not hillbillies, but reeeal live Eskimos."

Over three years I had seen and would see many things that filled me with doubt. But I also saw this: the bonds of life that connected families, villagers, and the whale they hunted. To see this was to feel a thrill of the heart. The thrill echoed an ageless incantation that Ralph's ancestors and countless others used to greet the whale: "Yes, it is good you have wished to come and live with us."

"Eskimo society is the bowhead whale and what we do with it," Etok had said. Though the hunt was gravely troubled, their sharing truly showed that the core of old society did endure. What lived on was renewed through a poignant communion in Agviq, a communion in body and blood, made possible by those who hunted. If the blood flowed too freely, it was because too few hunters had the light of knowledge to see by. The communion itself was still pure in spirit.

Perhaps sharing, far more than whaling or any other act, defines what it means to be an Eskimo. Sharing, after all, is found in villages from southwest Alaska to Greenland, in places where the whale is unknown or never hunted. Sharing predates their hunt for the whale and reflects an inner spirit that need not die even when and if Eskimos stop whaling or if the whale itself dies out.

A few weeks later, on the night of Nalukatuk, men and women belonging to the families and crews of successful whaling captains danced ceremoniously before their people. One crew at a time, they reenacted the taking of Agviq, dancing to the beat of a drum made with the skin of a whale's liver. With their feet in place and their knees slightly bent, the women swayed gracefully, gently twisting their hips. To a faster beat, the men stamped their feet and thrust their arms into the air in precise yet agile gestures depicting the ritual hunt. As the musicians hit their handheld drums harder, faster, the crewmen called out, chanting in chorus to the beat.

Who were they, I wondered once more, my attention caught by a pair of Adidas on one of the dancers. Could a man or woman be Eskimo if he or she pumped gas, took dictation, ran a cash register, manned a desk, and wore Adidas? By their actions they had responded yes: Eskimos could be those things and still be Eskimo and dance just as ardently. They had already changed and they were still changing, like all Native people and all of mankind. They would have to change if they were going to survive, because the whale was no longer enough, and indeed, there were no longer enough whales. That did not mean they had to lose their inner spirit or identity, however. By reconciling the identity they chose for themselves with what they must do to survive in a Western world, they could still remain "real people" in spirit. But until then, Agviq would be the bridge that carried the weight of their transition.

23. A Barrowful of Oil

It was in 1888 that Charles Brower sent one of his harpooners off in a whaleboat to check out reports by Eskimos who said they had found multitudes of whales gathered far to the east. After traveling five hundred miles along the northern coast of Alaska and Canada, his man came upon waters that were flush with plankton. There, where the Mackenzie River carried its nutrients into the Beaufort Sea, he found the bowhead's last refuge: its summer feeding grounds.[16] The whales were "thick as bees," and when Brower's man returned to tell his tale, it drove whalemen crazy with excitement.[17] In quest of El Dorado amid an ever-growing scarcity of whales, the fleet steamed eastward, farther than it had ever gone before, and the first ships that hunted off the mouth of the Mackenzie were rewarded with wild profits.[18]

For the next twenty years, Yankee captains made the Beaufort Sea their whaling grounds. Deliberately allowing their ships to freeze into the ice of a natural harbor at Herschel Island, they would winter in each year. That way they could reach the Mackenzie's riptides the next summer in time to hunt the gathering whales. While hibernating, however, the fleet needed Natives to hunt fresh meat, trap skins, sew fur clothes, and guide their expeditions, so Herschel became a Native boom town, drawing Eskimos from all along the northern coast and from the interior as well. Lured by trade goods, they were recruited into the decimation of their own whale, and of their caribou, too.

Despite their splendid early success, the end was near for Yankee whalers. Over the course of a half-century, they had hunted bowheads in the Bering Sea and then in the Chukchi to the north. They had established land-based stations to capture whales the fleet couldn't reach in springtime, and finally they had set up shop in the bowhead's feeding grounds. Soon it too dried up. There being no other new grounds, the Yankees might have wiped the whale out altogether had it not been for the development of a cheap substitute for increasingly scarce and expensive baleen. Once the bottom fell out of the market, the last of the fleet abandoned the Arctic and tied up in California's Oakland Creek, idle. "As a business," Captain John Cook later wrote, bowhead whaling "was gone, never to return."[19]

Seventy years later, the population of bowheads had still not recovered and the federal government had designated the whale an "endangered species." Meanwhile, another industry had come to these same shores in the greatest invasion since the days of Yankee whalers: the oil industry. A century after Charles Brower sent his man out to discover the whale's last refuge, his hybrid descendants and the villagers of a city he shaped were now confronted with the consequences of his legacy. For "King Brower" was also the first white man to discover oil on the North Slope—and to try to get rich from it too.

Off the coast of northern Alaska and Canada lay what oilmen called North America's most promising unexplored reserve of oil and gas. The Canadian government's geologic survey estimated that the Beaufort Sea held more than four times as much oil and gas as the proven reserves of Alaska's North Slope, including Prudhoe Bay, and bullish drilling confirmed the prospects for a world-class discovery, an "elephant," as the industry called it. On the U.S. side of the border in December 1979, oil companies enthusiastically bid over a billion dollars for leasing rights in waters the whales swam through or close to on their fall migration westward. And that was only the first lot the feds put up for sale; in 1982, they planned to lease off a surrounding tract four times larger. In the Canadian Beaufort, off the Mackenzie River, the government of Canada had opened up the whales' feeding grounds as well. Thus, even as the outside world intervened in the name of saving bowheads from Eskimos' guns, it was pushing to extract energy from waters that were the habitat for the same whales. And as oil companies and state and federal governments pressed to begin drilling, they ran into legal opposition from another environmental group bent on saving the whales: the Eskimos themselves.

"How we gonna survive without whales, without seals, without fish and ducks?" asked my whaling captain, Ralph. His question was continually being posed to white men by nearly every Eskimo. But Eskimo leaders and officials asked another question of themselves: "How are we going to survive without oil?"

Lloyd Ahvakana, whaling captain and Director of Administration and Finance for the North Slope Borough, was an avuncular man of sixty with silvery gray hair, heavy black eyebrows, and a pleasant, reposeful smile accented by pudgy cheeks and jowls. He smoked Martínez y cia cigars, Havana blends that he bought during trips to New York, where he sold municipal bonds at the Bank of America.

Business for the borough was good in New York. The bonds Lloyd marketed were rated so highly that he readily sold $70 million worth on one trip in the fall of 1979. While municipalities across the nation were feeling hard times, Lloyd presided over a budget fattened by property taxes levied on Prudhoe Bay's oil and gas industry. For 1980–1981, he had a staggering budget of $97 million to manage for forty-five hundred residents.

Lloyd had held his current post since 1972, the year the borough was incorporated by North Slope Eskimos who wanted "to achieve the maximum amount of self-determination for the people." Never before had the need seemed so great as it did then, for the Eskimos' ancestral lands and hunting grounds were being violated by oil companies, the federal government, and the State of Alaska. Unlike Indians in the Lower Forty-Eight,

Eskimos had never been defeated in war, nor had they ever signed any treaties with either Russia or the United States, and though the federal government recognized their aboriginal rights to the land, it had never defined or resolved what they were. In 1966, the State of Alaska had leased off Prudhoe Bay without regard for Eskimos' claims to the land it was trespassing on. "Alaska is on the way to becoming one of the major oil-producing states of the Union," Governor Walter Hickel had announced, "and artificial barriers to development [that is, Alaska's Natives] must be broken down for the benefit of all." Intent on protecting the habitat of the animals they hunted, Inupiat leaders sought to consolidate their five isolated communities (Barrow, Point Hope, Wainwright, Kaktovik, and Anaktuvuk Pass) into a centralized government that would fight for their rights. If oil must come to their land, they vowed, Eskimos were going to regulate its development.

Until the borough was formed, they had been neglected wards of government and second-class citizens as well. They lived in an Arctic Appalachia, too far into the cash economy to turn back, yet not far enough in to escape a shantytown existence. Most who wanted jobs couldn't find any. Housing and social services were grossly inadequate. Barrow was the largest community in Alaska without a safe source of drinking water, the largest community without a high school. Yet of five North Slope communities, Barrow was the only one that could support any local services. Two of the others couldn't even afford a part-time constable, and Barrow itself was so strapped that the city went broke in 1976 after its citizens voted to shut down the city-owned liquor store that provided virtually all of the city's revenues.

Against such economic and political injustice, the cause of Barrow's Eskimos was heroic and their vigor in pursuing it inspiring. Since the early 1960s, they had been fighting for their lands; they had organized the Arctic Slope Native Association for that purpose, and it in turn had sparked a statewide struggle of Indians, Aleuts, and Eskimos. Out of their land-claims movement came the campaign for home rule. And though North Slope Eskimos lost Prudhoe Bay, the jewel extracted by the state and the nation in return for settling land claims with all Alaska's Natives, they won their battle to create an organized borough that included Prudhoe Bay within its borders.

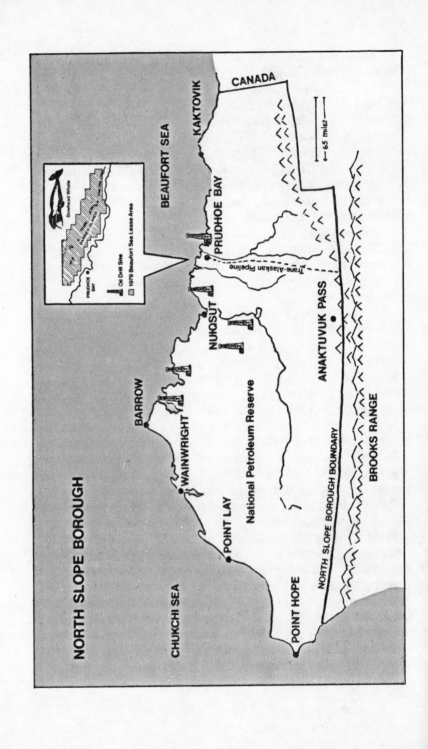

No longer divided into politically powerless communities, the Inupiat people now had a regional, Western-model government—the only Native-controlled regional government in the nation—with the power to zone and tax an area larger than all but twelve states. With North America's biggest oil field sitting in their backyard, they were intent on doing both.

Lloyd had been involved from the start, presiding over the development of a tax-assessment and administration system. "Our biggest hurdle," he said, "was getting Native people qualified to run the government." Of necessity among people with a Western education averaging less than eighth grade, the borough hired white men as consultants and administrators to show them the science of management.

If the borough employed two disparate groups, it governed two disparate groups as well: its Native citizens and its taxpayers. The latter were the oil, pipeline, and oil-field-construction-and-service companies at Prudhoe Bay. In 1979, they paid over $55 million in property taxes, or 70 percent of the borough's operating budget.* The borough's treasury had the distinct smell of oil to it.

Through the sale of bonds and with an ever-growing supply of petro-dollars, the Eskimos' government had set off to build badly needed housing, power plants, airports, roads, and schools. Wanting local control, Eskimos took over their own school system from the Bureau of Indian Affairs. A busy health and social services agency served the aged, children, adult and juvenile offenders, alcohol abusers, and "women-in-crisis." Through its programs and projects, the borough had raised its people's standard of living higher than it had ever been, to a level higher than that achieved by any other rural area of Alaska.

As a result of the same spending, the borough also brought its citizens full force into the cash economy. When asked what he thought was the biggest change of the last decade, Lloyd answered that this was it: Native people now had the opportunity to work for wages. Through a mammoth package of capital improvements, the borough had become the biggest employer of Eskimos, providing at least half the jobs they held. Barrow's

---

*If state-shared revenues are included, the figures from Prudhoe Bay production account for nearly 100 percent.

unemployment was the lowest in the state now, and a strong Native-hire program virtually guaranteed work to anyone who wanted it, although people from the villages might have to travel to Barrow first.

Without a doubt, the borough had been the best and most responsive government Eskimos had ever had. But despite and sometimes because of its success, it was faced with new social and economic problems as well as old ones that had not gone away.

For most Eskimos, the transition to a new economy had been expensive. High wages and the abundance of consumer goods only temporarily disguised the spiraling demand for more money. Buying groceries, for instance, cost two and a half times more than it did for people in the Lower Forty-Eight, and building a house cost three times more. Despite their image as Arabs of the North, most Barrow residents still lived in ramshackle housing without plumbing or running water. There was lots of money, but real wealth eluded them. What they had was spent on consumer goods and consumables, or shared with friends and relatives as if it were an animal the hunters had brought home.

"One of the first priorities of people who got money was to buy booze so they could offer it to their guests," a non-Eskimo who had lived in Barrow during the mid-1970s told me. Nobody ever got recognition for accumulating money. It was the ability to spend, to provide, that had always counted most, and throwing a good party was all part of it. "If you had booze in your house, you always had a steady supply of visitors, and providing fun for your friends was a real status symbol." In this way, traditional values became tragically entangled with binge drinking.

"I had an Eskimo roommate," the former resident told me. "After work, at six, he'd hire a cab to go about a quarter-mile, and he'd keep the cab waiting for him outside the liquor store. He'd buy a case of beer for twenty bucks and the cab would take him home: it was a real ritual. Then at ten minutes to midnight, he'd call the cab again to make another trip. If he had more people, he'd make three trips in a night, buy three cases; and when you add in cabfare, it came to ninety bucks out the window.

"A bottle of Calvert cost forty or fifty bucks, dope was one hundred dollars a lid, and cocaine cost one hundred and fifty dollars a gram. Taking two trips to Fairbanks a month, he'd blow about a thousand dollars."

The social costs were just as high. Undisciplined and unprepared for the shock of windfall and change, people grew increasingly alienated. A decade earlier, there had not been the money to buy it, but now alcohol flooded the city in springtide waves of drinking. The borough's Community Mental Health Department estimated that half the population showed signs of alcohol abuse. Families were torn apart and violent crimes increased sharply. "The first year I moved here in the early seventies all the Eskimos trusted each other," said the former resident. "Now nobody trusts anybody."

Eskimos had a word for trouble that money brought them. It was *maqu*, and it meant "torn up." From a society previously undivided by class, clear strata of economic haves and have-nots had emerged.

Lloyd seemed to have adjusted far more easily than most Eskimos to changes over the last decade. Perhaps that was because he had lived for eighteen years in Anchorage. "I can live any way I want," he said, "either the Western way or the Arctic environment—I can live that way, too." In practice, he did both. In a city where shacks predominated, Lloyd and his wife owned a $400,000 home with glass picture windows and sliding doors that faced the tundra winds in wild extravagance; it stood shahlike, shining gold at the end of a rainbow that others hoped to reach. But in springtime he often spent his weekends in a tent on the ice along with his crew, for he was a whaling captain, too.

Like other Eskimos in positions of leadership, Lloyd thought that Eskimos' well-being was tied to more education, more training, and continued high employment, not less. Despite a decade of social disruption and culture shock that had battered Barrow, he and others had not given in to the almost arrogant pessimism of so many white men. It had taken us tanniks three thousand years to make a transition from hunters to space-age moderns, they said, yet we expected Eskimos to complete the same move in a generation. Even while objecting, however, they vowed to do just that. "If we were going to try to survive from a cultural standpoint, we should have done that a hundred years ago," said Willie Hensley, an Eskimo leader from off the Slope.

"Now we have to use white men's economic tools to survive, just like we used your steel and guns."

Although the borough was inundated in oil money, its leadership worried. Most of its people had jobs only because of the work *it* created through some $400 million worth of capital improvements. More important, the revenues from Prudhoe Bay that paid for such things would disappear when the oil field went dry, as it was projected to start doing after 1987. The borough needed a diversified, self-sustaining economy to prepare for life after Prudhoe Bay. "We must develop oil, gas, coal, and any other minerals we find," said Lloyd. "Development is essential."

The oil companies would not be the first energy explorers to challenge the northern ice. Most of the barrier islands in the sixty-mile-long chain that ran through the lease area were named, at least on white men's maps, after Yankee captains or ships. During the course of their industry, over one hundred ships and many more lives were lost to the treachery of the ice they had gambled against. In a single event, thirty-two ships (almost all of that year's Arctic fleet) were caught between the ice and shore late one summer off the coast southwest of Barrow because captains ignored friendly warnings from Eskimos about the closing pack ice. They had to be abandoned altogether. Afterward, the disaster was rationalized by the industry as "one of those deviations from natural law,"[20] but five years later, another such deviation overtook thirteen more ships and crushed them into matchsticks, too, this time off Point Barrow. Hardly a year went by without a ship or two being lost. "I felt as I gazed upon the great frozen icefields stretching far down to the horizon," wrote a New Bedford shipmaster who believed in their power, "that they were barriers placed there by Him to rebuke our anxious and overweening pursuit of wealth."[21]

No one had more experience on the ice than the elders. They were the expert witnesses that other Eskimos called upon or quoted at the many public hearings held on the subject of offshore drilling. "They may not be able to explain in precise mathematical formulas or equations why nature acts in a certain way," said Nate Olemaun, "but when the elders say something will happen, it will only be a matter of time before it does."

The men who had the most experience on ice respected it more than anyone else. Testifying through translators, the elders pleaded with the panels of white hearing officers not to allow the drilling. Warning of what would happen otherwise, they often used the word *ivu*. Ivu described a sudden, extreme phenomenon of ice sheets moving in a chain reaction onto, over, and beyond beaches and cliffs. Ivu could be compared to an overloaded lumber truck running into a wall: though the truck might come to a stop, the lumber would not; it would keep on going, right over the top of the cab. Not surprisingly, the prospect of oil wells in an ocean full of lumber trucks scared the hell out of people.

Throughout their lives, Eskimos had seen the power of ice. Off the coast of Barrow each spring, hunters encountered cathedrals connected by a mountain range of pressure ridges. Some elders told of having seen pack ice surge across Barrow's shore with a western gale at its heels, climbing ever skyward and cresting within minutes into a towering, frozen wave seventy-five feet high. Writing about ivu back in the 1890s, Charles Brower marveled at its power to thrust pressure ridges sixty feet up and to grind ice into powder, tearing and "throwing pieces as large as a big house into the air."

These were only the events elders had seen from land. Offshore, beyond springtime camping grounds, lay the shear zone, a shifting, unattached battleground where rotating pack ice ground like a sandstone wheel against the edge of ice that was anchored to shore. Composed of what scientists called "multiyear ice," this pack ice was nine feet thick on the average, and because salt had drained out of it after its first summer, the ice was very hard indeed. When the pack collided into land-fast ice, the two masses buckled into pressure ridges that regularly reached thirty-five feet above eye level and one hundred feet below. And during breakup or storms and when wind and currents were moving in the right direction, the ice kept on coming, one mass sliding over the top of the other or driving into shallow water if the shore-fast ice had already melted. Dragged along by the force of mass movement, the keels of giant pressure ridges gouged deep trenches out of the ocean's bottom.

From even farther out, from beyond the shear zone that was the edge of Eskimos' experience, came derelict floes and sometimes veritable islands that broke away from the pack or drifted out of the high Arctic. Fifty miles off Canada's Mackenzie Delta, where Dome Petroleum Limited had discovered oil, winter horrors and summer ice floes made stationary platforms like those used in the North Sea unthinkable. Instead, Dome did its work from drilling ships, which, when threatened, could detach themselves from the pipe and move away. But they could only drill in the summertime, and to pump the oil out, Dome would have to operate year-round, in the worst ice seasons of all. Even in summer, icebreakers had to patrol nearby waters for predators that were as big as freighters and sometimes bigger. One floe that Dome had tracked, for instance, was seven miles long, three miles wide, and 120 feet thick. Visions of it moving south toward drilling sites seemed the sure stuff of some Hollywood disaster movie.

Yet government and oil-company officials displayed few misgivings about drilling offshore. People like Robert Crosky, the Alaska affairs manager for Atlantic Richfield (ARCO), exuded the can-do confidence characteristic of his industry. "Ivu is undocumented," Crosky said, and though he later added, "I'm not saying it doesn't happen," he assured listeners. "We're dealing with a situation we can handle." The slight drawl when he pronounced the word "Es-kee-mos" revealed his roots.

He and others pointed out, quite correctly, that conditions in the Beaufort Sea lease area sold by Alaska and the federal government were much less severe than in the Canadian Beaufort, where Dome Petroleum was drilling, and in the sea west of Barrow. Between the coast of Prudhoe Bay and the islands, the waters were no deeper than thirty-three feet, and because they were protected, they were like a lagoon, he said. Beyond the islands, he added, pack ice grounded on the ocean bottom before reaching most of the tracts. Because the waters were so shallow, the oil companies planned to drill from artificial islands that they would make out of gravel and sand dredged up from the ocean bottom or dug out of the land. Twelve such islands already existed in the Mackenzie Delta, and six had also been built close to shore in Prudhoe Bay. For all intents and purposes, Crosky said, drilling from gravel islands would be no different from drilling on the Prudhoe Bay tundra.

Making a comparison to Prudhoe Bay was important for oilmen, since they considered it a showpiece of industrial technology in the Arctic. "People thought at one time we couldn't drill in the Arctic, and here we are producing over a million and a half barrels a day," Crosky added. Ed Hillyard, the public affairs manager for Chevron, shared his sense of accomplishment. "We've been active on the North Slope for ten years now, and there's been no significant detrimental impact on the environment."

Eskimo hunters take exception to such claims. They complain about populations of fish having been wiped out because oil companies scooped spawning gravel out of rivers, blocked drainages, conducted seismic testing, and siphoned off pools of scarce water to supply the oil field in wintertime. They worry too about the continuing effect the oil field has on their caribou.

"In the early days of exploration, there were almost no regulations, and there were some disastrous impacts at Prudhoe Bay," agreed Scott Grundy, habitat protection supervisor for the Alaska Department of Fish and Game. He said that building and blasting had been conducted as if the drillers were back home in Texas. But things had changed, he added—because of regulations. Even under the regulations, however, onshore development might be causing irreparable damage.

Perhaps the borough's attitude toward Prudhoe Bay and the oil companies was best expressed by its planning coordinator. "Prudhoe Bay is *not* a beautiful operation," Shehla Anjum emphasized. "But it is probably the cleanest operation in the world, and that's because pressure was put on the industry to meet regulations they had fought against."

Although the borough still worried about the effects of onshore drilling, it had a far greater fear about the effect of offshore drilling, which, in 1979, its taxpayers were only too eager to begin. Borough officials argued that the oil companies should not venture offshore, but should remain on land until they had finished developing the oil and gas fields on the Prudhoe Bay tundra and elsewhere on the North Slope. As an inducement, borough officials even offered to relax restrictions on onshore drilling, providing capital and time for learning about ice dynamics and for designing and testing offshore environmental safeguards. The federal government, the State of Alaska, and the oil companies continued to press for the December 1979 scheduled sale of offshore leases. The borough then offered another compromise: it would not oppose drilling in the waters between the islands and the mainland, but—and here Mayor

Eben Hopson drew a line at the barrier islands, like a general arranging his forces—the borough *would sue* to prevent drilling beyond the islands (in the waters "outside"), where drilling posed the greatest dangers. When the state and federal governments went ahead with the full sale anyway, in December 1979, the borough did just that. So, too, did several North Slope villages and villagers, who, calling the Beaufort Sea "our garden, our dinner table," sued to stop *all* offshore drilling. By April 1980, the Eskimos' lawyers had succeeded in temporarily blocking the federal government from issuing its leases and were appealing a state court ruling in the hope of blocking the award of state leases too.

The oil companies saw no reason to delay drilling and every reason to begin. The belief in their own engineering skills led them to think that the Beaufort Sea, like Prudhoe Bay, would prove another in a long list of frontiers the industry had conquered. If drilling in deeper waters beyond the barrier islands posed "a challenge," it was *only* a challenge that would be met and overcome as the companies went along. "Our industry is dynamic," Crosky said. "Our technology moves as fast as the challenge does."

By drilling diagonally, for instance, Crosky said, the oil companies would be able to reach up to two miles beyond the barrier islands to extract oil without ever leaving land. Then beyond two miles, wherever water was still shallow enough, they could build gravel islands. By building berms, or steeply sloped banks, the companies thought they could cause the moving ice to pile up and stop before it reached the drilling sites. And for waters that were too deep for islands, he added, oil companies were considering developing huge, cone-shaped drilling platforms designed to withstand the full force of unhindered pack ice.

"We've been trying to educate the Eskimos on the technology we have available and can develop, so we can give them the best of both worlds," Ed Hillyard of Chevron said. But the Eskimos were convinced more by the ice and by elders' warnings than by oilmen's assurances. Inside the barrier islands, for example, where oil companies said drilling pads would be naturally protected from heavy ice movement, there was the rather discomforting sight of an old DEW-Line building at Bullen Point east of Prudhoe Bay. In November 1978, a sheet of ice crossed a twenty-foot cliff before crushing part of the building's metal structure.

Eskimos and other opponents denied the oil industry's contention that drilling on gravel islands would be the same as drilling onshore. Oil spills onshore could be contained, they said, but offshore there could be no such assurance, especially if the spill occurred while ice was breaking up in springtime.

"The pack ice is a gyre: it spins around the Beaufort Sea in a clockwise motion," explained George Edwardsen, a young Eskimo geologist and oil construction man.* An oil spill, he warned, "will travel with the ice and under the ice, and looking for it would be like discovering oil all over again. If you could find it. But even then, you'd have to look for it from on top of a loose ice surface you and your equipment couldn't travel on, and all the while, it's moving at the rate of the current, around four knots."

According to the chief of sea-ice research for the Canadian government, oil spills off the coast of Alaska and Canada would probably enter the Beaufort Gyre and begin a long, dirty journey entrapped in the ice and drifting through the high Arctic. Seven to ten years would pass before the pollution came back home. And it would come back, he said, with the ice, in the ice, and through the ice, because in cold temperatures, oil hardly decomposed and it didn't evaporate either. So what the clean-up crews hadn't pooled, mopped up, and pumped out the first time would return for a repeat performance.[22]

It was only out beyond the barrier islands in a zone of broken ice that an oil spill would pose "more of a problem," Crosky, the oil spokesman, replied. "But it may not be as severe as we think," he added. When asked if the technology existed that could clean up a spill amid the ice, he replied, "The problem is one I think we can resolve before we do any drilling."

In addition to their fear of big, ivu-caused oil spills, Eskimos worried about the environmental damage that would result from just the normal day-to-day operations of an offshore oil field. Although the probability of a blowout might be small— "insignificant" was the word preferred by oilmen—small spills were a certainty, and so were the by-products of construction,

---

*His official title: Secretary/Treasurer of UIC Construction Inc. UIC was a division of Ukpeagvik Inupiat Corporation, Barrow's village corporation.

dredging, traffic. There might be no bodies floating, no black ice, and no oil bleeding when it happened, but someday, the Eskimos feared, the animals would be gone, victims of cumulative industrial effects.

If destruction by insignificant increments was something abstruse and abstract, the effect of noise was neither. Like the skin of a drum, ice acts as a resonator, and under the water, sound travels far. For a thousand years Eskimos had observed how easily they could scare off the whale. So sensitive was its hearing that the hunters even tapered the ends of their paddles to minimize the noise they made. Today's hunters also knew the effect of high-intensity noise from seismic explosions, planes, and helicopters; some called it "obscene." But what would happen when the volume was turned up and kept up by drilling, dredging, seismic explosions; and the everyday traffic of boats, choppers, trucks, and planes? Eskimos were sure the stress would frighten off migrating whales as well as seals that used the area to bear their pups.

It was tempting to see the debate over oil development as a clash of two cultures with fundamentally different views of man and nature: one in which man was dwarfed by his universe, the other with man at its center; one full of awe, the other full of confidence. Oilmen liked to see the debate over development in the same light because it made the issue seem no more than a crisis of confidence among Eskimos. Then the Natives' opposition to offshore drilling could be compared to their ancestors' resistance to technologies like guns and steel. Believing such resistance would give way before "education" and an appeal to the Eskimos' own pragmatism, the companies set about engineering consensus as if it were a problem no different from engineering another oil well.

It was tempting to see the conflict this way, but, in fact, the interpretation was only partly true. Eskimos shared a faith in the power of technology that, if not as great as the oilmen's, was implicit in their adoption of Western tools and explicit in the calls many of them made for engineering safeguards. And the oil companies' objections had their root less in the confidence that goes with achievement than in simple profit seeking. They made this abundantly clear when it came time to set regulations to mitigate the environmental effects of offshore drilling.

248   BARROW

In the name of economics, for instance, oil companies fought restrictions that limited seismic work and exploratory drilling to winter months, when whales and pupping seals weren't yet present and the ice had not broken up in the sale area. Oil companies also fought a requirement that they build a drilling structure in waters deeper than thirteen meters (42.5 feet, the depth along which the shear zone began) for a two-year evaluation of how structures would hold up amid the moving ice; they said a test was unnecessary.

As diplomatically as the oil companies talked about working together with the Eskimos, they had actually been at war with Eskimo government for a decade, fighting against home rule, refusing to pay taxes until the Supreme Court of Alaska ruled against them, and then pushing the state legislature into drastically limiting how much the borough could tax their property. The oil companies had also challenged the borough's authority to plan and zone for its only industry, claiming that national concerns overrode local ones.

The borough proposed a five-year moratorium on drilling outside the barrier islands so that more could be learned about the movement of ice and whales before development began. The oil companies and the State of Alaska opposed it, and the proposal died.

When push came to shove, the oilmen turned to hard-selling rationalizations geared to white men, for in the end it wasn't Eskimos but white men, the overlords of an Arctic colony, who had to be persuaded, frightened, or lulled into acquiescence. So, at the time, they prophesied brownouts, long lines at gas stations, fewer jobs, dwindling revenues for government. They even conjured up their own doomsday scenario. "Compare the environmental impact of going to war against Russia to protect our Mideast oil supply with the effects of drilling in the Arctic," said one of ARCO's managers at Prudhoe Bay, "and I think you'll see that doing anything other than drilling offshore is ludicrous." The benefits of having a sure, steady supply of fuel always outweighed the costs in this oilmen's parade of horribles. Yet it wasn't white men, but Eskimos and bowheads who would bear the costs.

Like the haze of industrial pollution that blows into Barrow from across the top of the world, oil development in the

Arctic has an international scope. Across the border to the east, Canada has beaten the United States into the offshore frontier, encouraging drilling in the very ocean habitat that is probably the most critical to bowheads, their summer feeding and gathering grounds. As of 1982, Dome Petroleum, one of the big three Canadian oil companies drilling in the Beaufort, was planning to ship prospective oil and gas out of the Arctic by tankers instead of by pipeline, and to this end, it had already announced plans to build a fleet of nearly thirty icebreaking oil tankers.

En route to the Pacific, tankers would travel in the opposite direction, along the same path bowheads swam in springtime: around Point Barrow, down the northwestern coast of Alaska, and through the Bering Strait. To avoid the heavier, congested pack ice, they would have to stay close to shore-fast ice and leads of open water that were traveled by whales. But if the experience of the U.S. Coast Guard was typical, Dome was in for big trouble, and so might be the whales.

On an oil-industry-sponsored mission to test the feasibility of year-round shipping lanes in the Arctic Ocean, the icebreaker *Polar Sea* made history in early 1981 by becoming the first American ship to reach as far north as Point Barrow in wintertime. A few days earlier, the governor of Alaska, who had been helicoptered aboard the specially designed 399-foot-long ship, said the Coast Guard commander told him that the *Polar Sea* "had encountered nothing to suggest that a ship could not tackle the Arctic Ocean at any time of the year." The governor himself said he foresaw "a whole new vista of prospective polar navigation . . . that suggests that future development in those waters might well move by surface vessels following icebreakers rather than by pipeline."

Two days later, the record-breaking ship jammed its rudders in a collision with thick ice while on its way to Prudhoe Bay and the Beaufort lease area. Abandoning its destination, the ship changed direction, heading southwest and back toward the Pacific. Dismissing reports that the *Polar Sea* was dead in the water and stuck in the ice, Coast Guard spokesmen at headquarters said the ship was in no danger, since it had multiple propellers and could steer with its engines. But a few days later, the icebreaker got stuck in the ice nevertheless, and it stayed there four days, despite repeated efforts to dynamite its way out.

Finally, it got free for a day, before ice damaged one of its propeller shafts as well, making the ship unable to back down and ram its way forward. Trapped in ice and uncontestably dead in the water, the *Polar Sea* drifted with the pack ice for three months. Visions of loaded oil tankers drifting just as helplessly made me think the black plague would surely come.

24. Tribal Dreams and Corporate Schemes

The Eskimos' hunting grounds had one thing the outside world wanted and the oil companies were going to drill for it; the Eskimos couldn't stop them. But the drillers and developers weren't all outsiders. In fact, the North Slope's newest oil exploration company belonged to the Eskimos themselves.

Built to make profits for its thirty-eight hundred Inupiat stockholders, the Arctic Slope Regional Corporation (ASRC) had 5 million acres of land, $37 million of net assets, and an Eskimo board of directors that included Lloyd Ahvakana. Eskimos themselves didn't father the corporation; Congress did. In 1971, it created the ASRC and twelve other regional corporations to administer the Alaska Native Claims Settlement Act. Spurred on by the nation's and the oil companies' eagerness to begin drilling at Prudhoe Bay, the act extinguished the Natives' aboriginal rights to lands their people had occupied, used, and hence "owned" for many centuries.

In return for giving up their collective claims to about three-quarters of Alaska, the state's Eskimos, Aleuts, and Indians obtained legal title to 11 percent of it and received nearly a billion dollars.* But instead of distributing the land and cash outright, Congress chose to funnel both into corporately structured, profit-making organizations that would become the Natives' own instrument of economic development. Each Alaskan Native born before the act became law received one hundred shares of stock in one of the regional corporations. Only Natives were eligible to be stockholders until 1991, after which the stocks could be bought and sold on the open market. Further, by making Native-owned lands taxable after 1991, Congress infused the Natives with the drive to make profits.

Just as the federal government had set out to civilize Indians a hundred years ago by introducing them to private ownership of their communal lands, so today the government was attempting to assimilate Alaskan Natives by converting them to capitalism. As a result of earlier attempts to turn Natives into private landowners, Indians in the Lower Forty-Eight had suffered wholesale alienation from their ancestral lands, losing two-thirds of them to white men within fifty years after such government "privatization" policies went into effect.

The president of the Arctic Slope Regional Corporation was Eddie Hopson, the fifty-eight-year-old grandson of an Inupiat woman and a commercial whaleman from Liverpool, and older brother of the borough's mayor. Through such corporations as ASRC, Eddie Hopson and other Alaskan Native leaders hoped to achieve self-determination and to protect their way of life, while at the same time improving their people's economic condition. How capitalism could be used to preserve a communal way of life that revolved around hunting, cooperation, and sharing was a riddle leaders like Eddie Hopson would have to solve. Meanwhile they were being swept along in the rush that followed the Settlement Act. Overnight Hopson had been transformed from a carpenter and social activist into a fast-traveling, high-paid executive charged with creating profits for his stockholders. He was between trips to Hawaii and San Francisco when I caught up

---

*The actual terms of the settlement gave Native Alaskans fee simple title to 40 million acres of land and $962.5 million over a number of years. In return, they relinquished claim to 325 million acres. Those eligible were Alaskans with one-quarter or more of Aleut, Eskimo, or Indian blood.

with him in his office, set against a panorama of shore-fast ice and water-sky, halfway through the whaling season of 1980.

The corporation had plugged into the high-voltage network of oilmen and builders almost as soon as it was created. One of the subsidiaries it had formed, Eskimo Oilfield Services, provided support services at Prudhoe Bay; another sold communications technology. In partnership with one of Alaska's biggest construction companies (now wholly owned by ASRC), a third subsidiary moved drilling rigs; operated heavy machinery; and built roads, airports, and camps in nearby oil fields. The ASRC boomed with the biggest of Alaska boomers. In pursuit of profits, for instance, it became a limited partner in a joint venture to operate a $15 million rig on the North Slope. Since the oil company it was under contract to would be drilling in the Beaufort Sea and beyond the barrier islands, the venture would generate profits for Native stockholders unanimously opposed to such drilling. ASRC's ambitious arms were everywhere. It even owned a distant fleet of buses that drove white kids to school in Fairbanks and other towns in south-central Alaska.

Eddie Hopson was proud of the way his corporation had been managed and of how well his people had adapted to a world of modern business and corporate organization: annual stockholders' meetings, elections, proxies, and financial reports. The corporation had used the best tools it could, he said, putting together a team of white consultants, attorneys, and business managers to back it up and then going into joint ventures with Outside business partners from whom its employees could get know-how and experience. Toward the dream of someday replacing white consultants and administrators with Eskimo professionals, the corporation gave scholarships and grants to Native students going on to higher education. And to ease the transition from subsistence to the corporate business world, it allowed employees to take personal leave to fill their freezers or ice cellars with Native food.

The corporation's primary economic objective was to find oil and gas on Native lands. According to Hopson, the corporation set up its subsidiaries only as insurance against the possibility that it wouldn't. Entitled to choose 4.5 million acres from an area of 15 million, "We made our land selections to find oil and gas. It's the only thing we're looking for." And to expedite the search, ASRC had leased almost 2 million acres of its lands to Chevron, Texaco, Shell, and Union-Amoco for exploration.

The borough hoped the corporation would become its biggest taxpayer and employer in 1991, thereby filling the gap expected when Prudhoe Bay ran dry. Hopson was confident his corporation could come close to doing that. But opposing the interests of the industry it was wired into would not help the ASRC get where it wanted. The pressure was palpable.

In advance of the Beaufort lease sale in December 1979, oil companies embarked on a full-court recruiting rush. Sohio-British Petroleum, for instance, invited ASRC and several other Native corporations to bid jointly with it for drilling rights to offshore tracts; it offered them the most lucrative of terms to do so, no doubt hoping to coopt Eskimo opposition to the sale and to create an image that Eskimos wholeheartedly endorsed what the companies were doing. Had it not been for his shareholders, Hopson said, his corporation would have bid, but instead it resisted the offer "just to keep the family together."

(Three other Native regional corporations, including one, NANA, whose stockholders were Eskimos living in the coastal region south of the North Slope, did team up with Sohio-BP, however, and when the sale occurred, their joint bids won the leasing rights to drill in areas beyond the barrier islands—the very waters the borough had sued to protect. Although other North Slope Eskimos felt betrayed by this breach of erstwhile Native solidarity, Eddie Hopson said he didn't blame the other corporations. "They were just hustling to get a piece of the action, just like everyone else," he explained.)

Though the ASRC's board of directors decided not to bid for offshore drilling rights, it did vote to endorse the lease sale, with the important qualifier that for the time being it opposed offshore development beyond the barrier islands. In a plea that expressed more enthusiasm than reluctance, however, Hopson told the board he believed bowheads could exist with oil production. It was the same line the oil companies were using.

After the vote, angry dissidents sought to oust the board from power. "They've sold out to the oil companies," scoffed Billy Neakok. "In fact, they've become another oil company. But we'll stop them. I'm not about to change my Native diet, but I'll have to if the oil companies drill offshore. We say the food for all our animals starts from inside the barrier islands. And if they destroy that, they'll destroy our animals."

His rage was shared by a group of young, militant activists—those in power called them the Red Guard—who saw both the borough and the ASRC as "tools of the multinationals" and instruments through which white men waged their colonialism. In comparison to the rest of their community, the militants were well educated and acutely distrustful of white men and of the content of the program we brought with us. "Charles Brower," Billy Neakok said of his grandfather, "was the first crook who was up here."

Dedicated to the struggle, Billy and others fought legal battles against the government, corporate battles against management, and political battles against the borough. Billy stayed out on the ice with his whaling crew back in 1978, for instance, after Barrow reached its legal quota and all the other crews came in in order to avoid a confrontation with the feds. He had also run unsuccessfully for borough mayor against Eben Hopson. Long after the election, a large billboard showing him in his hunting outfit remained on the side of his house: BILLY NEAKOK FOR MAYOR OF THE NORTH SLOPE BOROUGH.

Intent on stopping all offshore drilling, the dissidents pressed a legal case claiming Inupiat ownership of the Beaufort Sea and its submerged lands beyond three miles. They said their people held title to it by virture of immemorial use and that the federal government had never extinguished that title; they claimed, in fact, that none of the North Slope had ever been surrendered voluntarily, or even involuntarily, to the United States, and they also stressed that North Slope Eskimos had voted against accepting the Settlement Act (the only Alaskan tribe to do so). They vowed never to give in or to give up their sovereignty as a separate nation. Billy Neakok told me he'd even threatened to shoot Eddie Hopson because of what the ASRC was doing to his people.

If they lost their legal battle to stop the drillers, Neakok said, "We could blow up any section of the pipeline. It'll take them a year and a half to fix it, so we'll stop them a year and a half at a time if it comes to that. I don't give a shit at this stage. I was brought up to think we had sovereignty and title to all this."

Wild-eyed talk like that kept Billy and other militants on

the fringe of power, scaring away support they might otherwise have had, for, belligerence apart, they did give voice to the anxieties ordinary Eskimos shared about what was happening to their way of life.

On the surface, the corporation might seem nothing more than a modern-day version of community-shared ownership, a sort of corporate whaling crew. But, in fact, its accountability to shareholders was limited, as was the shareholders' role in making its decisions. ASRC's board of directors endorsed the lease sale, for instance, without consulting its shareholders ahead of time. According to critics, the corporation's annual meeting was a tightly controlled event with a row of high-priced corporate counsel from Seattle, Anchorage, and Fairbanks riding shotgun (in the wake of the Settlement Act the Arctic became as much a flyway for corporate lawyers as it was for ducks). The proceedings baffled many of the elders. Discussion was stifled, a phenomenon highly uncharacteristic of ordinary meetings among Natives, meetings that might last for hours, until the last Eskimo had had his say. But the corporations after which ASRC was modeled were not designed as democracies or cooperatives.

A people's cultural and economic future was being largely determined by a Western-style capitalist organization that had taken away grass roots, tribal control of decision making, and centralized it in the hands of a Native managerial class that, earning the highest salaries in Barrow ($60,000 to $70,000 year) had become an economic elite as well.

"It's having a profound effect on relations within each village," observed Dale Stotts, one of the borough's and corporation's critics (and another of Charles Brower's grandsons). To look at Lloyd Ahvakana's house, for instance, or to see oil company lobbyists visiting him and his wife with presents for their housewarming party must have filled some townspeople with both jealousy and resentment.

The elite that Stotts was talking about formed an interlocking directorate over the North Slope's two most powerful organizations. Eddie Hopson and several other ASRC board members were also borough assemblymen, for instance, and along with another ASRC administrator they formed a majority. Trying to appeal to two different groups, they used conservation-minded rhetoric in the assembly and prodevelopment rhetoric inside the corporation, where board members were less accountable to shareholders than assemblymen were to voters.

Given the chance to make money, Eskimo corporations would respond as instinctively as a cat to a mouse. Of that the developers were sure, and, indeed, Eskimos had been responding to white men's financial cues for over a hundred years. Whalers and traders and other white developers held that up as a sign of Eskimo approval of our economic and financial systems. In fact, few of them had the slightest awareness of having made anything more than a simple transaction. As far as they were concerned, they'd made a good deal and nothing more.

The ASRC's board members, who were more sophisticated than that, had resisted the temptation of joining the bidding to drill offshore. Yet they continued to believe that the corporation's well-being, and hence the well-being of their people, resided underneath the Arctic permafrost. At the controls of machinery patterned in the image of Exxon and General Motors, they were driven by the fear of what would happen if they did not make profits. For in 1991, their lands would be subject to taxation.

Confronted with the dissidents' charges, Eddie Hopson reacted pointedly: "After I make a land selection in order to find oil and gas, do you want me to sit down and let it rot? We have to find oil and gas . . . or else we're going to lose our lands." Hopson feared that if the corporation didn't make enough money to pay the land taxes due in 1991, the government would take away Inupiat land, "one chunk after another," until nothing was left. For that reason, he said, speaking synonymously of his corporation and his people, the success of ASRC was "our only survival kit."

Was it? Elders, other townspeople, and especially people in other North Slope villages thought that hunting was the key to survival. "In all the stories about Inupiats starving you never hear of the people along the coast starving," said Eddie Hopson's aunt. "It has always been the inland people who starved to death. That's why none of the coastline should be threatened in any way, because even if people are starving inland, they can go to the coast and make it . . . the ocean never runs out of animals. For the Inupiat, it's like a deep-freeze where food is stored."[23]

Of the ASRC's loudest critics, Hopson said, "I'd like to see *them* come up with something that's profitable." Because they controlled the board of UIC, Barrow's village corporation, the dissidents were in fact in a position to offer an alternative program. But when they talked of how they would develop the economy, UIC leaders talked, like ASRC officials, of oil and mineral extraction—though they said they would not drill off-shore and would use safer methods on land. They also *talked* of starting businesses in reindeer herding and freshwater fish-eries—businesses in renewable resources that might sustain employment without destroying their hunting grounds—but to my knowledge they never actually started such enterprises. What they did do was form a construction company; a mining company; the Umealik (Whaling Captain) Insurance Company to serve Bush residents; and, in a sensational move far afield from Barrow, three subsidiary operations headquartered in the Baha-mas.*

Later that year, however, an Anchorage newspaper re-ported that UIC's shareholders had not been informed of or asked to approve the Bahamas operations, and according to the former UIC president (Lloyd Ahvakana), its present officials could not account for $600,000 in funds; there were concerns the money had been misspent and misused. Circulating at the same time were widespread rumors, documented in an Alaskan court case, that linked the UIC and Billy Neakok to trafficking mari-juana through the southwestern United States. On a second front, a South Dakota grand jury was reported to be investigat-ing the UIC's links to two white men arrested and later convicted for carrying twelve tons of marijuana in a DC-7. Billy denied all connections and charges and said that he was being framed. Yet, at the very least, his purchase on behalf of the corporation of a GMC truck, a tanker trailer, and fifty-seven hundred gallons of aviation fuel in New Mexico, all on record in the Alaska court case, raised questions about the corporation's investments and the way it was being run.[24]

Comparing Native-owned corporations to guns and steel, Eskimo leader Willie Hensley called them weapons that would

---

*Ukpeakvik Bank and Trust, the Inner World Insurance Company, and the Barrow Company Ltd., a holding company involved in Caribbean agriculture, aquaculture, and oil development.

help Eskimos survive as a tribe. I came to expect just the opposite. As long as the corporations remained modeled after other American businesses, the goals of cultural and spiritual well-being would remain subordinate to profit-seeking. Indeed, making profits was the only thing corporations like ASRC might succeed at; and whether they succeeded or failed might not matter anyway in the end, because after 1991, those corporations sitting atop energy and mineral resources would become likely targets for unfriendly takeovers by white energy conglomerates. Anxious for the money they could have and impatient to see dividends, Eskimos were already calling the ASRC to find out if they could sell their stock yet. Corporation officials feared that as soon as the stock went public, Natives would lose control of the ASRC—and more importantly, the lands they fought so hard for. The corporations were weapons, all right: pointed straight at the Eskimos themselves.

It was in the middle of May when Jacob Adams came back to Barrow from the edge of shore-fast ice where he and his whaling crew were camped. A man of many hats,* he represented better than anyone else the interlocking directorate of Barrow's leadership. Ten years earlier he had been working in a warehouse, but now, at only thirty-three, he managed 4.5 million acres of land, legislated borough budgets that had climbed past $90 million a year, and lobbied for Eskimo interests throughout the northern hemisphere (in Washington, London, Tokyo, and Greenland, among other places). The high school could not have found a better speaker to deliver the 1980 commencement address.

In some ways, Barrow's graduation that year was no different from what one might find down south. The stands of the gymnasium overflowed, and at the reception afterward, a well-wishing audience merged with the new graduates for a thousand proud, grinning, and tearful scenes bathed in floodlights and flashbulbs under a metallic crepe-paper canopy. The high school band, the Barrow Whalers, was there in snappy blue-and-white uniforms with the high school emblem on the back: a hunting

---

*He was then serving as president of the borough assembly, vice-president of ASRC, chief of the corporation's land department, and chairman of the Eskimo Whaling Commission—all at once.

crew harpooning a whale. Graduating seniors entered the assembly hall not to a band processional, however, but to the beat of whale liver-skin drums and the chant of elder singers. They passed under an archway of long baleen strips held like crossed swords by a student honor guard.

"The life of this community," Jake told them when it came time for his address, "is a life of two worlds. We must . . . get on with the business of determining the best of both worlds."

During the previous week, Jake made several trips back and forth between whaling camp and Barrow, where he had also presided over budget hearings and conducted negotiations with Chevron. Once the commencement ended, he replaced his suit with a fur parka and knee-high mukluks for the journey back onto the ice. Several weeks later, I saw him again just as he was preparing to leave the corporation office to go goose hunting with his family.

Jake had a round, teenage-soft face with a mustache that drooped on the corners; a pair of big glasses sometimes slipped down his thin nose. He wore a sweat shirt emblazoned with a bowhead whale and the motto, KEEP ON WHALING. Surrounding us as we talked were a mixture of multicolored exploration maps; photos of drilling rigs; and romantic prints, oil paintings, and watercolors of bowheads and hunters done by prominent white artists.

Two years earlier, in his capacity as chairman of the Eskimo Whaling Commission, Jake had testified against oil exploration in the Beaufort Sea, claiming that "this one time cultural and biological concerns should outweigh economic considerations." But as ASRC official and borough assemblyman, Jake had changed his mind. Though he conceded the oil companies had not yet come up with technology he considered adequate for dealing with oil spills, he said now that oil leasing between the barrier islands and the mainland would not create "any great impact."

In his commencement address, Jake told the graduating class, "The choices are not clear. They are almost always hidden in some way. In choosing from each world, we almost always find that we have to experiment or try something out for a while to see if it will work for us. Not all the experiments work well. Not all the choices are correct. We often find conflict in the choices we have to make. . . ."

For Jacob Adams, elected borough mayor several months later to fill the vacancy left by Eben Hopson's untimely death, that conflict would sharpen increasingly as time went by. As mayor, he was charged both with promoting oil development and safeguarding wildlife habitat on lands he was managing as ASRC's land chief. His jobs pitted Jake Adams, oil developer, against Jake Adams, conservationist. Jobs versus subsistence. The conflict was not only between Eskimos and whites, or between groups of Eskimos: it was within Eskimos as well.

Inevitably, the business of the North Slope would be in oil. Offshore, oil would be big business too. Not because Eskimos wanted it, but because we did and they couldn't stop us. The borough had drawn a line at the barrier islands and offered it as a compromise to hold us off, but it had not worked. Federal and state courts eventually lifted court-ordered injunctions, and exploration activities began. The only legal barriers that remained were procedural issues, and they were papered over by both the State of Alaska and the federal government to make the process of what they had done seem fair and proper. In 1981, the oil companies began offshore exploration; and by the end of the 1981–1982 season, they had drilled thirteen wells.

Much more was coming. The feds scheduled another sale for late 1982 to auction off an area of the Beaufort that lay north and west of the first sale area and was four times bigger.* They planned to sell drilling rights to Norton Sound, which lay between Nome and Saint Lawrence Island, a few months later; and after that, they'd open up the Chukchi Sea west of Barrow; then, soon after, the waters off Point Hope as well. The scope of what was to come was staggering and frightful; even the State of Alaska came around to calling the leasing schedule reckless and irrational. Yet compared to what the incoming team of Reagan and Watt wanted to do, the Carter administration had been dallying. The new team was blissfully untroubled by concerns for either environment or the social well-being of Eskimos.

*When the sale was held in October 1982, oil companies bid over $2 billion for drilling rights, showing great confidence in the area's potential for a major discovery. In contrast to their optimism, however, a National Marine Fisheries Service report in May 1982 said that an uncontrolled blowout or major spill in that area "when bowhead whales could be affected is likely to jeopardize the continued existence of the species."

25. Long Live the Eskimos!

Mired in the muck of corporations and government, I stayed in Barrow for much of that spring of 1980, wading through muddy pools of thawed-out topsoil and discarded dishwater as dark as my mood. For a thousand feet down the earth was frozen, but up here on the surface, where it was exposed to the sun and to the influence of man, it melted into a standing pool that the earth wouldn't take back. With nowhere to drain, the pools in Barrow's streets got bigger and drearier with each new day I spent trudging to office buildings in pursuit of a story that seemed just as dismal.

Then one morning, after weeks of waiting, I saw a streak of black clouds scudding above the horizon like stallions galloping on a plain. The sea ice had finally opened up—the lead was a mile wide—and the sight of it in the sky sent my spirits aloft. Animated with hope and cheer, I packed my duffel bag and found some of my captain's crew, and soon Barrow lay behind us like a cage opened up. We were flying free to the edge of ice and to an urge as old as the permafrost was deep. As I felt the brisk bite of wind on my face and the rattle of my sled underneath, I thanked God for the opportunity to be there once again.

Cream-colored and smelling like fresh manure from its new skin of bearded seal, the umiak lay perched over water's edge. The rest of the crew was standing alongside it when we arrived. I had an urge to take a picture but held it in check, for I was aware of the others' cool attention. I took up a silent position on their perimeter, waiting, indeed hoping, to be welcomed into their company. From most of my crewmates the response I got was tense, but it was different with Ralph, who was as jovial as he was big and as magnanimous as a king. Because of a broken ankle, he had not been out on the ice with Johnny and the others the year before, when I spent my first season with his crew— indeed, though he had not even met me at the time, he told Johnny I could stay out at camp; this year he took me into his court and decided to make me an apprentice. But first I needed a name, he said. Otherwise, he explained, "People around here won't know you from George Washington or Abraham Lincoln." From the corner of his eye, Ralph watched my reaction with a sly smile. Yes, I needed a name, he continued, reaching into a canvas sack and pulling out a frozen whitefish the size of a small trout. He whittled off a slice with his knife, dipped it into a coffee can full of seal oil, and savored its taste as he licked his lips. "Tipook," he said. "That'll be your name. It's our finest fish. Good, fat fish. Reeeal tasty." And though I would always be a fish out of water here, Tipook was what they called me.

My oral instruction from Ralph proceeded randomly, in spontaneous, intermittent bursts amid the silence we shared while waiting for whales. Out of the blue one day, he rattled off a score of words and made me repeat each one, correcting me as we went along. "It's not *oo-gruk*," he said of the bearded seal. "It's *oo-grook*." Having finished my vocabulary lesson, he told me next what to do if a whale came upon us. "Always be looking. Don't be like those stupid white people who don't hear anything and don't look for anything," he warned.

Though I worked hard to pay my debt to his generosity, I was so clearly nonessential to the expedition that the only reasons I could discern for his bearing with me were his high- mindedness and a certain vanity too—for I was an attentive and appreciative audience, and he loved to perform. Stealing an oblique glance to make sure I was watching, he would launch into extemporaneous song-and-dance routines in the most implausible of settings. While we were scanning the empty icescape one listless afternoon, he burst out singing "Yankee Doodle," flashing a grin, pretending he hadn't seen me, even though I was laughing idiotically. In the midst of white noise, he was just as likely to sing "Dixie," recite grade-school verse, and quote Mother Hubbard as he was to do bits of Eskimo dances while facing the sea, always avoiding eye contact but smiling smugly at the response he received.

He shifted easily into stories I loved to hear. He told me of growing up in a sod house, of herding reindeer with his father, of traveling the tundra by dog team, and of how he had come to Barrow from Wainwright thirty years earlier to find work as a plumber. Far removed from the managing elite and the workings of corporation and borough, a modest man in a humble job, on the ice he was king.

"Eat! Eat! Eat!" he urged like an Italian grandmother. "You're going to get skinny." All that I could eat was put before me, at his expense, in what seemed like the best of Native smorgasbords. There were frozen haunches of raw caribou, burlap sacks of frozen whitefish, a slab of fermented white-skinned muktuk from a beluga whale, and anything the crew could find for the pot: ducks when they flew overhead, seals when their curiosity brought them too close, and occasional polar bears bagged on the ice behind us. Watching the others eat fermented muktuk and meat that tasted like the ripest cheese, I remembered what Irrigoo had told me in Gambell. "White men's food no good," he chortled. "When it gets old it's bad, but when our food gets old it's good." I preferred the frozen fish, sprinkled with salt from a shaker I kept beside me, and boiled polar bear, which tasted like pot roast. One of my crewmates' favorites was caribou. While keeping watch on the sea, they would take turns carving a haunch with their hunting knives, then pass it back and forth along with a can full of strong-smelling seal oil. When they had had enough, they set the haunch beside the tent; the whole outdoors was their refrigerator. At camp they ate well and often, probably eating a more Native diet than they ever did in Barrow.

Sitting atop caribou skins on the sledge outside the tent, dressed in white snow shirts and furs, and scanning the sea ever so intently, the hunters made a grand sight. "The life of Eskimos is not as easy as you think," Ralph would say. "You never sleep on a bed out here. You're just like a cowboy out on the trail, with never a soft spot to rest." Like other Eskimos, Ralph liked to speak of the hunt as a stark struggle against hunger. Yet the obvious joy he and his crew took in being there on the ice showed that their hunt provided more than just food.

In the end it didn't matter to me that the hunt was no longer a life-or-death struggle. When I first came to the Arctic, I had wanted to believe it still was. Then, disenchanted by what I saw, I scoffed at the propaganda put out by the borough and its team of white men. Showing a slick sense of political sophistication, the borough responded to outside antiwhaling actions by producing and distributing such films as *Hunger Knows No Law*. They knew that in the outside world, hunger sold a lot better than arguments of cultural needs and the Eskimos' right to govern themselves.

Hearing the claims made by corporate lawyers and political operatives the borough employed in Washington, DC, I often confused "the cause" with the people defending it. I could not embrace the borough's lobbyists. They were far different from Ralph, Johnny, Oovi, or Silook. They were wheeler-dealers, political soldiers of fortune who pushed the party line, assailing anyone in their way while all the while working backroom deals with the feds. Still and all, I eventually came to think of their propaganda as a necessary counterbalance to that waged by the other side and was no longer as bothered by such claims or tactics.

It doesn't matter nearly as much to me anymore that what Eskimos say they need for food might be as far or farther from reality than what the International Whaling Commission has said they need. What I believe more than ever is that Eskimos should make their own decision about the whale. Not because their decision will prove superior to the ones made by Outside experts, but because it will be *their* decision, as it should be. Then they will have a vested interest in making sure their choice works, or in changing it if it doesn't. And though the bowhead's survival may well be on the line, allowing people the opportunity so often denied them to govern themselves justifies the risk. Indeed, it may be the only way Eskimos and bowheads will ever survive.

"You can shut down NASA because I've already discovered Mars," someone once said to me about Barrow. It seems like a distant vision now as I sit watching traffic move down a tree-lined street in Seattle. Two years have passed since I was last on the ice with Ralph. The photographs from that spring are on the walls around me. Yet the people and scenes seem frozen, suspended in time and out of my reach. I often wish I could be on the ice with them again, to feel the excitement and anticipation I once did. Maybe it's better that I can't, because I wouldn't want to relive the bad times. Still, I wish the triumphs of those days weren't so far from my grasp.

We had moved our camp often that season, forced by rotting ice to pull back from open water. It was late in the spring—the coming of bowheads had been delayed by a massive ice jam in the Bering Strait—and the edge was melting in the sunshine. Soon it would be too late, as it was already for the whalers in Point Hope who had had to return to shore before they could catch Agviq.

Without a whale in range for a couple of hundred miles, we might as well have been waiting for Godot. Waiting. Waiting, with nowhere to go. It was unsafe for me to walk very far from camp, especially alone. I didn't know the ice well enough, and Ralph didn't want me coming across a polar bear. So I was confined to a small circle in a vast space, a circle crowded with crewmates and cultural conflicts that made me feel claustrophobic. Only once, when I was unable to wait for the whales any longer, did I walk away. Hiking five or six miles across the ice and then up the shore toward Barrow, I basked in an exquisite, warm, white-on-white tranquillity. When I got back to town, I heard about polar bears that had been shot near the trail I'd just followed.

While waiting for Agviq, I waited too for Johnny O, wondering when and if he was coming. Like Ralph, Johnny made my life in camp more bearable, but more than that, he elevated the hunt. With him I got a heady sense of being on the winning side. But to Ralph's dismay and mine, Johnny was hanging around town that spring—partying and watching television on a big Panasonic.

I'd gone over to see him after I walked back into Barrow that day. He was watching the *Benny Hill Show*. I stayed through the end of it and through a western that followed. ("I guess they ran out of Indians," he cracked to a crewmate; "it's just a cowboy-and-cowboy movie.") He didn't say much to me. He never did. He wasn't going out onto the ice for just any reason, he told someone else. He was only going if he could get a whale.

Then finally the whales broke through the Bering Strait. Within a few days, they began to appear to all of us: hunters, biologists, enforcement agents, filmmakers, photographers, and reporters. At first they appeared infrequently, then in growing numbers, like an offshore swell coming our way. Soon Johnny showed up too, riding into camp placidly—always placidly. I was thrilled with anticipation. He looked like a man of destiny, and now that he'd come, I felt we were about to get down to some serious whaling.

More and more whales swam through the lead, some far off, their exhaust like distant cannon fire; others in the middle; and some surging up before us in a shock wave that sent us scurrying toward the boat and into the breach. Their number swelled, crested, and was gone again within a week, but in between we were awash in action.

"Oonalit! Oonalit!" yelled Roy inside the tent early Saturday morning, the last day I hunted with Eskimo whalers. Hearing over the CB that another crew had just taken Barrow's first whale of the season, the normally stone-faced crewman greeted the news with one word shouted happily for the benefit of his sleeping crewmates. Curled together on caribou skins as the walls of our tent shook in a cold wind, we awoke to his message that we would soon be eating "Boiled muktuk! Boiled muktuk!"

It was a day of great anticipation. While we awaited the return of a crewmate sent to help butcher the whale and bring a share of it back, we were poised for a recurrence of what had happened the night before.

On Friday evening, we had just struck the tent to move our camp about one-hundred yards away when, in a great silent ascent, a whale emerged half a boat length from the edge in front of us. We dropped to the ice and kept still, for we could do nothing: the umiak had already been moved to the new camp. Only Ralph had a chance. He was positioned in the new location, sitting in the bow as the whale swam toward him. We watched breathlessly, but at the last moment the whale's flukes came up in a long, slow dive, and it was gone.

All of Saturday, I stood watch outside the tent, under

cold, dark gray skies. Along with a couple of other crewmen, Johnny stayed outside too, poised statuesquely, with his empty sleeves dangling and his arms folded across his chest. Having kept watch through the night, Ralph did not emerge from the tent until the afternoon. Joining us in front of the windbreak, he sat on the sledge smoking his pipe and fixing a gaze that had scored crow's-feet deep into his temples over fifty years of hunting. His dead-serious intensity was enough to tell me I shouldn't go to sleep or even go inside the tent that day. When and if a whale came upon us, the action might last no more than a few moments. Cinched into my motor drive, I had two cameras ready for the shot of a lifetime.

Toward evening, I went inside for a few brief minutes to make coffee and get warm. Numbed by a daylong chill, I was tempted to join the sleeping bodies atop the caribou skin beside me. It felt good to be out of the cold, I thought, and my mind wandered to the warm, green southern springtimes I had missed over the last three years. In the middle of my daydreams, I felt an eerie tug from the outside, but the warmth of the camping stove persuaded me to linger a few moments longer.

"Ti-pook! Ti-pook!" Startled by Ralph's yell, I threw open the flap of the tent and dashed outside to answer his call, only to discover the crew in the umiak and the boat in the water. Ralph told me to grab the line he threw me, and as I did, I could hardly believe what I saw. Without my ever hearing them, they'd launched into the lead. It dawned on me next that they'd paddled after a whale, and then, all of a sudden, I saw the agitation in Ralph's face. The harpoon and the bomb were gone. So were the floats, and Johnny was holding no more than the throwing shaft of the darting gun. A detective I'm not, but I knew then that they'd struck a whale, and now they were rushing ashore to mount the engine so they could chase it down.

The four of them, Johnny, Roy, Fred, and Ralph, had first seen it surface no more than a hundred feet from camp, I found out later. Following the shore-fast edge of the lead, it emerged off a point where the relatively straight line of ice was indented by a small bight like a bend in the road. Anticipating that a whale would surface in just such a spot, Ralph had chosen to locate his camp a bit to the north of it the night before. Camouflaged by the row of ice blocks we'd constructed along the edge, the men quickly and quietly climbed into the umiak and pushed off; though I was only a few feet away, I couldn't hear them.

Because the wind was behind them, only a few strokes brought them within reach of the unsuspecting animal. But the whale was going under. Quickly calculating its length and speed so he'd know when best to strike it, Johnny waited a moment or two, then plunged the harpoon into his back as the whale crossed under the bow. Behind him, Fred threw the floats and the heavy line overboard while Roy, the gunner, went for his weapon. He couldn't get a round off in time, which meant that the whale escaped with only one bomb in it, and that one apparently hadn't exploded.

After we pulled the umiak up onto the ice, I ran back to the tent to wake the rest of the crew—they'd slept through everything, so silently had it all transpired. Scrambling into action, they hurried to follow the orders Ralph yelled like a drill sergeant. Five of them climbed into the umiak with Ralph, then kicked in the Johnson outboard and roared off through the lead. Left behind to mind the store, I squirmed impatiently, while ruing those few brief minutes I'd spent inside the tent.

In an hour they came back, cold and discouraged, for they hadn't found the whale. Their parkas were soaked with water and coated with ice from the spray of choppy seas in the wide-open lead. They pulled them off and put on new gear. They gulped down tea and coffee, and they eagerly chewed hot, oily, fresh muktuk brought back to camp and boiled while they were away by the crewman who had been sent to get it that morning. Ralph looked exhausted. He was breathing hard, his mouth hung open, and his face was slack with disappointment. But only minutes later, the CB brought news that the whale had just been seen. So with renewed hope, Ralph told Johnny to take the crew after it again, and, launching the umiak, the men sped off into the lead once more.

Ba-doom! Swiveling to the right, I saw an explosion of water and then a broad, flat tail smash down in front of the next camp, located a hundred yards north of us. Another whale had been struck, this one with a shoulder gun only, and before I knew it, I was running there at Ralph's command to help out. Awhirl in excitement, I put my finger down on the camera's motor drive and triggered a frenzy of shooting. One of the photographs I'm looking at on the wall reminds me of the action.

Scurrying about their camp, the hunters reloaded their guns and got ready to launch an aluminum umiak. The metal boat seemed ill suited for whaling and incongruous, but so did the crewmen who were dressed in pullovers of black plastic trashbags punched through where their arms and heads went. A couple of them hurried back to the edge of the lead with their weapons to await the whale's return, while the others mounted an outboard; I helped them load the boat with gear. But since the whale had escaped with no floats attached, they had no trail to follow, and, as the adrenaline subsided, they gave up the idea of launching. Meanwhile, Ralph lumbered over to monitor the CB for news from Johnny. We all stood about wondering if either whale would ever show up again.

After some time had passed, the radio brought news. We heard that our whale had been found, drifting belly-up three miles from shore, where it had finally run out of life, killed by the one strike made by Johnny. Thrilled by the news, the hunters in the other crew turned to congratulate Ralph with happy one-pump handshakes. The captain's smile broke through his anxiety and exhaustion.

That night and early Sunday morning were a whirl of images and excitement. Some are frozen on my wall, while others still roll in short sequences of moving frames inside my mind. Looking at the wall, I can see a hundred people straining on a heavy manila line to pull Agviq out of the water. A great block and tackle is anchored taut in the ice, and the whale is yielding to the crowd tail-first. In another shot, the whole of it is lying squat on its belly like the land beast that it once was. Here it seems a not too distant, overgrown cousin of a pig, surrounded by Natives wielding cutting spades, flensing knives, and hooks. Beside the thirty-four-foot whale are pools of steaming blood, holes melted in the ice, and strawberry trails running inland to the snowgoes and sledges where the bundles of butchered flesh were loaded.

Ralph is there too, smiling as he stands beside his catch, his outstretched arm leaning against its head, his finger touching a vacant eye. In a more poignant shot, he stands forward of a semicircle of hunters, his head and theirs bowed down as he offers a prayer of thanksgiving for the whale that lies in the water with its tethered flukes draped over the ice before him. I took lots of photos of Ralph, so many that he liked to point out the ones I'd missed. "You didn't get the one of me lapping the whale's blood," he later told me. He cupped his hands to show how he'd done it, but when I voiced my regret he broke up laughing. "I jokes!" I don't regret I took so many, though, because they remind me of things I might otherwise forget. Among those shots is one of Ralph and his wife, Mary, alone in front of the butchering site early Sunday morning. Nothing but bloodstained ice, a jawbone, and a cleaned rib cage remain behind them, so total was the hunters' take.

The images hang from the walls like trophies documenting past experience, but empty of life now. If only my photographs could show the emotions that had welled within me that night, they might not seem as disembodied.

For the people in those images I felt the warmest admiration. Working with marvelous industry, organization, and camaraderie, they dispensed with the whale within three hours of its being brought to shore. I was amazed by the speed with which they hauled it up, then butchered and divided it. In one way or another, everyone was involved—either in cutting the whale up or in pulling chunks of meat and muktuk away from the body, in sharpening the surgeons' knives or in serving boiled muktuk, coffee, and fried dough. There was an exuberance of sharing and cooperation, and it seemed to me that the night celebrated those values as much as it did the hunters' and butchers' success. Immersed in their triumph, I thought back on the sad, agonizing spectacle of the only whale I ever saw Gambell butcher; my heart was glad that I had seen and felt this too.

Of my time in the Arctic, I remember one moment more than any other. It occurred earlier that night while I was standing on shore-fast ice along with Ralph and a crowd of hunters and townspeople. We had all been waiting for his crew and three other crews to arrive with the prize they had captured out at sea. Too slowly for all of us, they motored shoreward, dragging Agviq in their wake.

Finally they were close enough so we could see the fluttering blue flag with a white diagonal, the crest of Ralph's victorious crew. Thirty yards away now, the hunters were as big as life, with one exception: Johnny seemed even bigger. Sitting in the bow and under the flag, his hands folded inside his sleeves like a mandarin's, he wore that serene, winning smile. Unable to contain themselves any longer, the crowd let out a great sustained cheer of hoorays, hollers, claps, and shouts. Even now I feel myself choking up with pride of having been there among them.

The rest of the crew and I carried Ralph's share of the whale and ours into town on sledges early Sunday morning. As I rode homeward atop the jiggling heart of the whale, a heart as big as a thousand fists, I cheered with all the life within me: Long live the Eskimos! Long live the whale!

Afterword

In July 1980, seven weeks after Ralph and Johnny and Barrow's other hunters returned to shore from the ice, I flew across the Arctic to Brighton, England, for the International Whaling Commission's annual meeting. Here, in a summer resort beside the English Channel, the commissioners of twenty-four member countries had convened to set the next year's catch quotas for commercial and subsistence hunters alike.

Outside the Hotel Metropole and under a huge inflated model of a humpback whale, called FLO, a crowd of about 250 demonstrators gathered on the morning the meeting opened to chant antiwhaling slogans and to hold signs that urged the IWC to "Stop the Murder," "Sink the Whalers," and "Save the Whales." They and the environmentalists inside the meetings hoped that this year the IWC would finally pass a worldwide moratorium on commercial whaling. On the steps of the hotel, security men made sure that only commission delegates and accredited observers and members of the press got inside. At its last two meetings in London, there had been large-scale public demonstrations, and in one incident, the meeting chambers had been taken over by a group of radical environmentalists, one of whom poured red paint on the Japanese delegation.

At the first of those London meetings, in July 1978, the commissioners had heard the results of the first bowhead count ever attempted. Responding to U.S. scientists' estimate that the population was twice what the IWC had originally assumed, they increased the Eskimos' quota for the next year by a few whales, to eighteen landings or twenty seven strikes.* In doing this, the commissioners overruled their own scientific advisers who, expressing concern that the counters had seen only a small number of bowhead calves, urged them to set a zero quota. The increased quota still fell far short of what the Eskimos said they needed, however, and the Eskimos' representatives stalked out, later announcing their own quota of forty-two landings for the coming year.

The commissioners heard little new information at their next meeting in London in 1979. Bad ice, wind, and fog in the Alaskan Arctic that spring had kept both the scientists and hunters from getting what they had hoped for: a reliable population estimate or the larger catch that Eskimos had wanted. In a near repeat of the previous year's proceedings, the scientific advisers recommended a zero quota and the commissioners overruled them. The quota remained the same for one more year.

Now, in 1980, federal scientists had submitted the most frightening report yet presented to the IWC about the world's last stock of bowheads.** Their report was based not on data actually collected out on the ice, but on results derived from a computer model they had designed to resemble the population of bowheads. After entering hypothetical data (such as varying birth and death rates) into the model and running the program, scientists had concluded that *if* their assumptions were correct, the population was declining and would probably continue to decline even if the hunt were stopped. Backed by this "best available information," U.S. and international environmentalists,

---

*U.S. federal scientists reported a "range" in the Bering and Beaufort seas herd of between 1,783 and 2,865 bowheads, or 2,264 animals as the best available estimate.

**This report was known as the Braham-Breiwick Report, after its two authors.

including a growing number of IWC commissioners, pressed for an immediate end to the hunt.

Caught between two sides and trying to balance the interests of both was Richard Frank, U.S. commissioner to the IWC. Appointed by President Carter in 1977, Frank inherited a crisis that might not have occurred had his predecessor shown as much initiative, understanding, and skill at negotiations. But because the Ford Administration had done virtually nothing to meet the IWC's concerns or to encourage Eskimos to reduce their catch or loss of whales, the conflict exploded a month before Frank, a Washington attorney, took office. Believing that the Eskimo hunters must be regulated but that they must also be allowed to continue whaling, Frank worked toward winning both the Eskimos' and the IWC's support for a limited hunt. By 1980 the fragile compromise he had forged was falling apart, and the conflict seemed irresolvable. While scientists and environmentalists pointed out one U.S. study as evidence that any quotas at all would put the whale in jeopardy, Eskimos pointed to another that said they needed thirty-two or thirty-three bowheads for nutrition. Furthermore, the Eskimos' own whaling commission had sent a lobbying team to Brighton to pressure Frank against accepting an IWC quota, and into establishing a domestic quota over which the Eskimos would have more influence.

Trying to sell a quota of eighteen whales landed or twenty-six struck, Frank once again had to persuade his fellow commissioners to look beyond the evidence his own scientists had provided them. He said he, too, would favor a zero quota if the Eskimos were commercial whalers, but subsistence whaling should not be subjected to the same conservative scientific approach. And until the United States could confirm the scientists' preliminary evidence and find alternative sources of nutrition, he argued, the Eskimos' needs warranted the quota he was seeking.

Some commissioners supported Frank's quota, but most didn't. The United States–backed proposal failed, and the counterproposals failed on the second day. Deadlocked, the commissioners took the issue with them into the back rooms where they traditionally had done their horse trading.

For the rest of the week, the Eskimos' hunt became the bitter target of American and European environmentalists inside the hotel. Outraged by the meeting's failure to bring about substantial reductions in the slaughter of whales, they blamed the Eskimos, the United States, and Richard Frank in particular. They said that getting a quota for Eskimos had so dominated Frank's efforts that the United States had stopped fighting for the commercial whaling moratorium, which had gone down to defeat along with another United States proposal for a moratorium on the hunt for the beleaguered sperm whales. Many accused Frank of cutting "sleazy deals" with whaling nations in order to win votes for an Eskimo hunt.

None of his accusers had any proof for their charge Frank was trading off hundreds of sperm whales and others for every bowhead he won for the Eskimos—the negotiations were conducted behind closed doors. Yet the pro–United States votes cast by commissioners of commercial whaling nations left Frank open to the environmentalists' charge of guilt by association. And the only way the United States could cleanse itself of the taint, in his accusers' eyes, was to sacrifice the Eskimos' hunt. For, once the United States rid itself of the ideological inconsistency of supporting one kind of whaling while opposing another, there would be no distractions, no need to compromise or hesitate; the United States could then reassume its rightful position as leader of the conservationists' cause.

By mid-week of the meetings, I felt as disheartened as I had on the ice whenever the hunt went bad. I didn't know whether the forecast of the whales' declining to extinction was right or wrong. I felt uncomfortable questioning the scientists' report, for that put me in the company of commercial whalers who always denied the evidence. But I had gone out to the ice camps off Barrow, I knew the researchers who counted bowheads, and I had heard their doubts and caveats about their science. Those doubts and caveats had not made the trip to Brighton; the results of the researchers' work were accepted with greater and greater confidence the farther they traveled from their point of origin: those around me in Brighton were much more convinced than the counters themselves.

Environmental lobbyists and some of the commissioners proclaimed the science advisers' report as the life-or-death justification for stopping the hunt altogether. But factual evidence that the population was declining to extinction did not exist. The observations that led to that prediction did not come from nature;

they came from a computer room and they were generated by a population model that knew less about whales than the scientists who designed it. As a result, the bowheads in the model were no more real than FLO, the inflated humpback floating in the air outside the hotel. They were "Tron whales"; the scientists who generated them cautioned as much. But by the time the Tron whales got to Brighton, people accepted them as if they were genuine breaching and breathing animals.

Whether or not the quota the United States wanted would jeopardize the whale's existence I didn't know, though I worried that it might. But I did know how no hunt at all would affect Silook and Sook, Ralph and Johnny. I thought of them often that week during the wait for the commissioners to take another vote. It troubled me that so many people believed that the sky was falling on bowheads, but it troubled me even more that so few at the meetings showed any understanding or concern for the Eskimos and their hunt and that many took an openly hostile stance.* Comparing Eskimo whaling to headhunting and cannibalism, one lobbyist told me that like the two other aboriginal practices of the past it could no longer be tolerated. "If the Eskimos' culture needs whaling," sneered another, a spokesman for the Flora and Fauna Preservation Society, "let them go out and hunt inflatable models."

At a very late hour on the last night of the meeting, four days after their last vote on bowheads, the commissioners brought the issue back into open session. The United States was offered a three-year quota of forty-five bowheads landed or sixty-five struck, with the proviso that no more than seventeen could be landed in any one year. In the statements preceding the vote, Richard Frank assured his fellow commissioners that the United States would accept the consensus they had reached. Although he said his country would abstain from voting—to show it had wanted a higher quota—he expressed his hope and belief that the quota would allow Eskimo culture to survive, and he promised to reduce the catch progressively, within the figure set by the IWC. The vote sailed through with the support of nonwhaling countries, who had decided that some quota was better than none at all and that removing the issue from the next few meetings would

*With the notable exception of Friends of the Earth, and a few others.

allow the United States to concentrate its efforts on stopping commercial whaling.

Afterward, the Eskimos' team of lobbyists made another angry exit, while environmentalists, badly disappointed by their failures to defeat the whaling bloc, turned on the Eskimos once more, as if Silook, Johnny, Ralph, and their fellow hunters a world away from here had suddenly become the killers of fifteen-thousand sperm whales, humpbacks, minkes and others. In Alaska, Eskimos branded the environmentalists and the IWC as racists, a perception that hardly increased their acceptance of the sincerity or legitimacy of the scientists' concerns. Far from saving bowheads, the environmentalists in Brighton had succeeded in diverting Natives' attention away from the threat within and toward the threat that came from Outside. The scene at the hotel bar in Brighton was ugly, and like the meetings in Barrow that were its counterpart, it was tragic, too. Both Eskimos and environmentalists had lost.

The story got uglier in October 1980, when the Justice Department, reportedly at the urging of conservationists and State Department officials, launched a grand jury investigation to probe reports that Native hunters had exceeded the IWC's quota the previous spring.* Subpoenas, contempt of court citations, and angry rallies followed.

The investigation lasted five bitter months, through the desk-cleaning days of the Carter presidency until March 1981, when the new Reagan Administration suddenly dropped it as part of a new "spirit of cooperation." Reversing its earlier policy, the federal government switched management and enforcement responsibility to the Eskimos themselves.

And now, something truly remarkable did happen. Allowed to manage themselves, the whalers scrupulously abided by the three-year quota that had been set by the IWC at the 1980 meeting. Barrow hunters came off the ice in 1982, for instance, without catching a single whale—they had reached their limit of strikes and stuck with it. When the Reagan Administration cut all funding for bowhead research on the ice, the Eskimos' own Native government took the initiative once more, assuming a

---

*According to federal enforcement agents, Eskimo whalers had struck a total of thirty-one whales that year, five more than the IWC quota had allowed them.

major share of the costs of continuing and even expanding scientific investigation.

Meanwhile, other developments in 1982 strengthened the Eskimos' position. At the 1982 IWC meeting, both the scientific advisers and the designers themselves threw out the population model that had projected the bowhead's decline toward extinction, along with its conclusion, saying the model's assumptions had been faulty and the hypothetical data entered into it had been inaccurate. Their new conclusion: there was not enough data to determine the trend of the population.

As for hard data, 1981 had proved to be the first good year for counting whales since 1978. Favorable conditions allowed the counters more time out on the ice, and after scrutinizing the new field data, researchers got a much better idea of the whale population's actual size. That same year, a reanalysis of earlier years' data, which was submitted at the 1982 IWC meeting, showed that the population estimate scientists made in 1978 had been wrong. According to an expert biostatistician who reviewed the data, federal scientists had used unrefined statistical procedures in arriving at their earlier estimate. Using better statistical methods and improved counting procedures, researchers now come up with a new estimate—reported to and accepted by the IWC in 1982—that was 70 percent higher than the one presented in 1978.* Furthermore, the researchers expressed their belief that a "very significant" number of additional bowheads was passing outside the range of the counters each year. Scientists still did not know whether the population was increasing or decreasing, but "it's clear," said the biostatistician who had reanalyzed the data, "that it's not doing anything fast."

Although the population estimate had climbed with each refinement of the scientists' methods, international conservationists continued to claim that the bowhead was the world's most endangered species of whale. And after winning an IWC moratorium on commercial whaling, leading spokesmen pledged in 1982 to make a total ban on the hunt for bowheads their number one priority at the 1983 meeting, when the issue would come before the IWC once more.

*They now estimated that there were 3,865 whales, plus or minus a hundred, in the Beaufort and Bering seas' herd.

Notes

1. Thomas Abercrombie, "Nomad in Alaska's Outback," *National Geographic* 135, no. 4 (April 1969): 546.

2. Otto von Kotzebue, *A Voyage of Discovery Into the South Sea and Beering's Straits* (London, 1821), vol. 1, pp. 189–193; Henry Collins, *Archaeology of St. Lawrence Island*, Smithsonian Institution, Smithsonian Misc. Collection 96, no. 1 (Washington, D.C.): 19–20.

3. Richard Perry, *World of the Walrus* (London: Cassel, 1967), p. 124.

4. Dorothy Jean Ray, *The Eskimos of Bering Strait, 1650–1898* (Seattle: University of Washington Press, 1975), p. 252.

5. J. Bockstoce and D. Botkin, "The Historical Status and Reduction of the Western Arctic Bowhead Whale *(Balaena mysticetus)* Population by the Pelagic Whaling Industry, 1848–1914" (Final Report to the National Marine Fisheries Service, U.S. Department of Commerce, 1980).

6. Edward Field, "The Earth and the People," *Eskimo Songs and Stories* (New York: Delacorte Press, 1973).

7. Robert J. Flaherty, *Nanook of the North* (U.S.A.: Revillon Freres/ Pathé, 1922).

8. Kaj Birket-Smith, *The Eskimos* (London: Methuen & Co., 1959), p. 61.

9. H. G. Gallagher, *Etok: A Story of Eskimo Power* (New York: G. P. Putnam's Sons, 1974), p. 103.

10. Ashnithlai of the Klikitat Indians as cited in Julia Blackburn, *The White Men* (London: Orbis Publishing Ltd.), p. 157.

11. According to John R. Bockstoce, Curator of Ethnology, The Old Dartmouth Historical Society and Whaling Museum (New Bedford, Mass.).

12. Guy de Maupassant, *A Woman's Life*.

13. Charles J. Keim, *Aghvook, White Eskimo: Otto Geist and Alaskan Archaeology* (College, Alaska: University of Alaska Press, 1969), pp. 176–177.

14. Charles David Brower, "The Northernmost American: An Autobiography," undated typescript, U.S. Naval Arctic Research Laboratory, Point Barrow, Alaska, p. 845.

15. Gallagher, *Etok*, p. 31.

16. Brower, "The Northernmost American: an Autobiography," pp. 328–329.

17. Dorothy Cottle Poole, "Vineyard Whalemen in the Arctic," *Dukes County Intelligencer* 13, no. 1 (August 1971): 6–7, cited by John R. Bockstoce, *Steam Whaling in the Western Arctic* (New Bedford: Old Dartmouth Historical Society, 1977), p. 36.

18. Hartston Bodfish, *Chasing the Bowhead* (Cambridge, Mass., 1936), p. 63.

19. John A. Cook, *Pursuing the Whale: A Quarter Century of Whaling in the Arctic* (Boston: Houghton Mifflin Co., 1926), pp. 336–337.

20. Everett S. Allen, *Children of the Light* (Boston: Little, Brown & Co., 1973), p. 272.

21. Ibid., p. 145.

22. Rene O. Ramseier, "Oil On Ice," *Environment* 16, no. 4 (May 1974): 12.

23. From an interview with Terza Hopson as it appears in *Qiniqtuagakstrat Utuqqanaat Inuuniagninisiqun* (Commission on History and Culture, North Slope Borough, Barrow, Alaska, 1981), p. 144.

24. Bob Shallit and Don Hunter, "Village Corporation May Lose $500,000 in Bahamas Venture" and "Alaska Connections Tied to Drug Bust," *Anchorage Daily News*, 16 September 1980, p. 1.

Glossary

YUPIK

Aghvengukuut!—*"We have struck a whale!"*

Aghvook—*bowhead whale*

Aapghuughaaq (Aap-gho-waaq) —*"one who asks questions"*

angyaq (ang-yuk)—*long, open walrus-skin boat used to hunt whales*

angyalek—*whaling captain*

duvaq—*shore-fast ice*

I-you-me-rooh-lak—*long, long ago*

ii-ghwil-nguq—*drifting ice floes*

kamik (gam-mik)—*sealskin boot*

Laluremka—*white man*

mahngoona (mahn-goo-na)—*walrus hide with attached blubber and meat*

mukluk—*bearded seal*

mungtuk—*whale skin with layer of blubber attached*

ningloo—*the traditional semisubterranean sod house*

nunivak (noo-ni-vahk)—*plants that are eaten as fresh greens in summer and sour greens in winter*

oosik—*walrus penis bone*

Pugleghiinkut (Puw-luh-gen-kut)—*"A whale has come upon us!"*

qenu (gen-you)—*slush ice*

sallek—*new ice*

Seevookak—*original name for the village of Gambell*

siku (see-koo)—*ice*

slokok—*walrus flipper*

snowgo—*snowmobile*

soospuk—*nitwit*

ugli (*pl.* uglit)—*site where walrus haul out onto land*

uluk (oo-luk)—*crescent-shaped knife*

Yupik—*language spoken by Eskimos of western Alaska, the Bering Sea islands, and the tip of Siberia*

INUPIAQ

Agviq (ahg-vik)—*bowhead whale*

Inupiaq—*language spoken by Eskimos in northern Alaska, Canada, and Greenland*

Inupiat—*the name that Inupiaq-speaking Eskimos of northern Alaska call themselves. It means "The People," "Real People," or "The Men Preeminently"*

ivu (e-voo)—*sudden extreme chain-reaction movement of ice riding over ice and land*

maqu—*torn up*

misigaaq—*seal oil*

mikigaq—*whale meat fermented in its own blood and juices*

mukluk—*skin boot*

muktuk—*whale skin with layer of blubber attached*

Nalukatuk—*whaling festival*

nikipiaq—*"our food"*

oogrook—*bearded seal*

oonalit—*boiled muktuk*

tannik (tun-nik)—*white man*

tipook (tee-pook)—*whitefish*

ulu (oo-loo)—*crescent-shaped knife*

umealit (oo-may-lit)—*whaling captain*

umiak (oo-miak)—*skin boat made of bearded seal-skin hides and used to hunt whales*